Walker Irwin
934-7393

TRAINING
YOUR
POINTER
AND
SPANIEL

TRAINING YOUR POINTER AND SPANIEL

MIKE SUTSOS
&
ROBERT LEE BEHME

G. P. PUTNAM'S SONS · NEW YORK

G. P. Putnam's Sons
Publishers Since 1838
200 Madison Avenue
New York, NY 10016

Designed by Helen Granger/Levavi & Levavi

Library of Congress Cataloging-in-Publication Data

Sutsos, Mike.
Training your pointer and spaniel.

1. Bird dogs—Training.   2. Pointers (Dogs)—
Training.   3. Spaniels—Training.   I. Behme,
Robert Lee.   II. Title.
SF428.5.S87   1987   636.7′52   87-13922
ISBN 0-399-13315-1

Typeset by Fisher Composition, Inc.

Printed in the United States of America
1   2   3   4   5   6   7   8   9   10

To Mike Sutsos, Sr.

Acknowledgments

As the authors we naturally assume full responsibility for the concepts, techniques, and comments described on these pages; but no book is the result of the effort of one or two people. We owe a considerable measure of gratitude and thanks to several who have helped make the book as good as it could possibly be: Mr. Mike Sutsos, Sr., for reading and checking the manuscript; Mr. Benny Larsen, retired president, Guide Dogs for the Blind, for comments and help with technical sections; Mr. Al Bohm for use of his dog for portions of photography; Mr. Bernard Matthys, Mr. George Cook, and Ms. Jean Rader for statistical data; and Mr. Roger Scholl, our editor, for his patience while the book was being written and for his skill when it was being edited.

Contents

1. Why a Dog? 11
2. Selecting a Breed 19
3. Finding the Perfect Source 34
4. Picking Your Pup 42
5. A Proper Diet 50
6. Genetic and Health Problems 59
7. Housing Your Dog 71
8. Getting the Right Equipment 78
9. Training Basics 86
10. Training Your Pup 94
11. Testing Natural Pointing Ability 103
12. Learning to "Whoa" 108
13. Introducing the Flushing Dog 118
14. Spaniels: Advanced "Hup" Training 127
15. Moving to Birds: Staunchness and Retrieving 138
16. Advanced Retrieving and Force Training 150
17. Steady to Wing and Shot 163
18. Wrapping It Up 170
19. Correcting and Preventing Problems 175
20. Seventeen Handy Tips 185
21. First Aid and Safety 193
22. Field Trials 198

23. The Greatest Trials 209

24. Electronic Training Aids 214

25. Some Winning Dogs 224

   Glossary 239

   Product and Information Sources 249

CHAPTER ONE

Why a Dog?

Hunting with a well-trained dog has a long and honorable history, a tradition traced to times before the Romans. Early dogs spotted and sprang game for falconers, later combining that skill with an ability to drive small animals into nets. Things improved measurably with gun powder.

Today the sport is growing faster than ever. Each year I see thousands of new hunters bristling across American fields with fancy new guns—over-and-unders, side-by-sides, and singles fresh out of their packing cases. But for these who like to hunt, the question is not which gun to use, or which bird to hunt, but which dog to choose: the right dog makes all birding better. If you're partial to water birds, you'll probably want a retriever. But if you prefer those half dozen or so feathered treasures I call upland game, you'll want to consider pointers and springers. If you like both sports, as many of us do—and if you can afford it, if you have space and if you have a wife or husband willing to put up with it, you should ideally have two dogs. I have a Labrador for ducks and geese and a German Shorthair for upland birds. But if two dogs are out of the question, and that's easy to understand, one will do; and you can't go wrong with a good upland game dog.

THE ADVANTAGES OF A DOG

At Black Point we're used to well-trained dogs and dedicated hunters. Our headquarters, in the heart of some of the best bird country in California, has a wall crowded with fading photos of customers and their favorite canines. The gallery ranges from movie stars to international businessmen. It includes a lot of beautiful birds and some damn stylish dogs. Many were field champions. Some pictures were made more than thirty years ago, and although those dogs have gone to their reward, not much else has changed. We still sport the same faded print curtains and well-sat-on sofas. Black Point remains a relaxed, easy place where muddy boots and wet dogs are perpetually welcome.

Dad, most often called Big Mike, founded Black Point thirty years ago when I was five years old. He saw it as a place to hunt birds and train dogs. A warm, friendly, barrel-chested man, he's let down a little in recent years. I've taken charge of operations, but he still drops by every day to make sure the place remains on track. He says that when he's doing what he likes it's foolish to retire.

"You can hunt without a dog," he says gruffly, talking about upland dogs, "but it's like flying cross-country on a kite. It's cold, lonely, hard work. The fun and pleasure are missing."

I couldn't agree more. There is no greater sport than hunting upland birds—Blue Grouse, Ruffed Grouse, woodcock, all kinds of pheasant, quail, and Partridge—and every bird is best hunted with a dog. In most terrain there is no other way, and even in flat stubble fields the bird hunter who tries shooting without a dog is limping along on damaged cylinders. Every outdoor magazine in the country has listed the many ways a dog conserves game: fewer cripples escape, fewer birds flush wild, shooting is more rewarding, and the whole day goes smoother. There is one other reason, and ever since I was a kid dad drilled it into me. "A good dog is one hell of a companion. He makes every day more fun and in the end puts more meat on your table."

A hunter who insists that meat is not important is either modest or hasn't tasted a slice of fresh-roasted pheasant. In the west where I live, a lone hunter never had much of a chance. When I was a kid, those unfortunate enough to hunt without dogs used to try their luck on rice cheeks—stubble fields dry after the crop had been harvested. They would work the fields in pairs, playing out a long rope tied between them. Empty cans dangled every few feet, and the two would march cross the field rattling them. The noise would drive the birds ahead, and more often than not a panicky few would flush. It was a primitive way to hunt, and I knew even then that a bird dog was a thousand times better.

What kind of bird dog? You have a long list to choose from, and the selection is personal, but for me the decision has always been easy. Many hunting dogs are one-note specialists. They only retrieve. In comparison, a dozen or so upland game dogs—pointers and springers—do it all. They'll find game, hold or flush it, and retrieve as well. These are my kind of dogs, the special ones, dogs with style.

Let me put it up front. Upland game dogs are designed for special sport. Their background includes centuries of unique experience. That sets these breeds apart.

Whether it is better to hunt over a pointer or a flushing dog is a matter of taste. Today, the largest number of hunters go with a good pointing dog, and you're in the majority if you choose one. But many friends insist a man hasn't hunted until he's shot over a flushing dog. They say the surprise and sudden rush of birds makes for spectacular sport. While I like both, I've been un-ashamedly pro-pointer for years.

The special pleasure of hunting over a pointer lies in recognizing the class and style a well-bred, well-trained dog brings to the sport. There is a special joy in watching a stylish animal work a field ahead of you. It is a unique, damn near reverent experience, almost like being in Westminster Abbey. A flushing dog comes close in terms of style, and the English springer spaniel is a superb example.

When I was a kid helping out at Black Point, dad would tell me, "Half the pleasure of watching a dog work is the intensity of its point. The other half is the way it runs and works up game. That's what style is all about."

Many hunters don't see the truth behind those statements because they've never hunted with a finely tuned animal. They think upland game dogs are limited, though they are not. Pheasants love open field and ditches. Bobwhite and Southern Quail hold tight. Mountain Quail are nervous ridge-runners. Valley Quail like heavy cover. Chukar (or Indian) Partridge, elusive, fast-breaking, transplanted birds, like rocky foothills. A well-trained, stylish up-land dog is equal to all of them.

Nit-picking types tell me some dogs cannot handle every bird. They usually mean pointers cannot cope well with pheasants because the birds break, run, and flush wild. Perhaps they're right in theory, but in the real world a well-trained pointer can do a credible job with any bird you pit it against. A dyed-in-the-wool, 100-percent ground bird, the pheasant only flies when a dog doesn't know how to handle it, and that's the trainer's fault. You are not going to have a 100-percent kill with any animal, but an upland bird dog is a sound investment because he can be hunted in so many pleasant ways. If you demand perfection, buy a machine.

CHOOSING A DOG

Choosing between a pointing or flushing dog depends on the way you like to hunt, your temperament, the temperament of the breed you choose, and whether or not you want the animal to be family. The German Wirehair is an extremely popular choice. He's affectionate and intense, a good hunter, a dog with real style. Some say he's the best all-around dog on the list. The English Pointer is as capable and stylish though a little less affectionate. The Brittany is an excellent hunter with a superb nose. He's especially good in close quarters, when there is not a lot of land to work. There are many other choices, and I'll spell them out in the next chapter. If you currently own a pup, I'll teach you how to train him as well.

QUALITY IS BASIC

You could hunt with almost any breed, and over the years I have seen most in action. One customer used to hunt upland game with a Fox Terrier. The little animal, hampered by size and a cranky, nervous disposition, was forever lost in the tall grass and constantly beside itself with frustration. All the while that pooch sputtered, fumed, and crashed through the grass, its owner praised it as if the dog were a national champion. Although unbelievable, the story emphasizes my point: a sportsman should have enough respect for himself and others to hunt with the very best he can muster. That fellow never understood.

It comes down to this: the best purebred hunting dogs have long, solid pedigrees, track records of proven, successful, hunting antecedents. They're backed by a host of uncles, aunts, parents, and grandparents who have demonstrated a marked instinct to point or flush. Those instincts have been passed along and sharpened in each new generation so that a purebred responds to training. It doesn't take a lot of effort to make any one of these a superior field dog.

At Black Point the operational word is *natural*, and our concept excludes mixed breeds for obvious reasons. If a pointer and springer mate, what will the pup's instincts tell him to do? To point or to flush? The situation gets worse as the breeds become more tangled. At some point the important instincts needed for hunting birds may be completely buried.

I realize today's popular dogs are the result of cross breeding, but those steps were well thought out and carefully planned. A backyard accident is just an accident, and as a professional I would contradict myself and everything I believed if I advised anyone to pick a mixed breed over a purebred with proven parents.

Dad has a special way of explaining that to customers. "The best cross-bred mutt will not make a pimple on a purebred's derriere," he says. While his direct manner spotlights the problem, I'll concede this much: you can occasionally find a mixed-breed worth some training. Few things are impossible, yet if I ever had to make that choice at Black Point, I'd pick a scroungy-looking purebred over an appealing Heinz 57 every time.

Choosing between the best purebred pup available and something mediocre is like choosing between steak and hot dogs. Both are meat but only one has style and elegance. I go for steak. Quality is always worth the effort.

The standard at Black Point can be explained in one word, *class*, and my training methods can be explained in six: choose the best, train it naturally. Class comes through breeding. Some dogs have it; some don't. I believe that if you start with the best purebred pup you can find and hone its instincts through proper training, you'll end up with a dog you can be proud of. But if you want results like this, you can't stop part way. Compromise never created a superior anything.

I realize many people do not believe style, class, and high standards are worth the effort. I meet them at Black Point occasionally, and some have become good customers. I love them all, but the truth is, too many hunters are satisfied with less. They have lowered expectations. They are happy if their dog stays within 20 yards. It doesn't matter to them whether the animal points or not as long as it breaks a bird close enough to shoot and drops it within 10 feet. The sad fact is that they are the guys who always insist their mutts are the greatest.

Those unfortunates don't know the joy of hunting over a classy, well-bred, well-trained, stylish dog, but by the time you finish this book I hope to convince you. At the very least I'll prove two things. First, an upland game dog has to be staunch. Second, staunchness—the ability to hold firm on point—is an important element of style. Style makes a dog superior, and a superior dog is the entire point of this book. It's what the Black Point method is all about.

MAKING OF A BIRD DOG

A superior dog will always have a pedigree, but whether or not everything on that official-looking paper is important depends on a number of factors. A pedigree is not always the bottom line: when you're talking upland game dogs, the title *champion* may be of questionable value. There are two types, those winning their titles at bench shows and those winning them in the field. Too often the instincts so important to training have been bred out of bench dogs. Turn one loose on a hunt, and nine times out of ten it's lost. Pups whose

parents have been field trial champions, sometimes noted as FLD.CH., are
much better; and offspring from parents who are not champions but have
years of successful hunting experience are often just as good. Experience is
more important than titles.

Dad and I have been training field dogs for three decades and in that span
have developed a seven-point philosophy that is at the heart of our method.

1. Any decent purebred pup can become a reliable field dog.
2. No complicated training should be given the first year; a pup is too
   young for it.
3. Despite a pup's youth, you can teach obedience. These essentials
   lay the groundwork for all training that follows.
4. You can begin field training when the dog is twelve months old.
   Spaniels start younger.
5. You can't train a field dog without a field.
6. Once you begin training, and that includes first-year obedience, the
   process never stops.
7. Almost everyone spoils his first dog. Without experience, you generally make wrong moves and overdo everything. I did.

Whether this is your first or your tenth dog, you'll be learning—just as we
are after thirty years. The dog that is the toughest to train can teach you
important things. If nothing else, he'll prove no technique works every time.
He'll prove that dogs, not breeds, are trained. He'll prove that each animal is
an individual, and he'll prove that each is a challenge. A trick successful on
one may not click with ten others. But take heart, of all the dogs dad and I
have handled in thirty years, those we've had to return as "untrainable" can
be counted on the fingers of one hand. You can make a difficult dog a reliable
hunter if you are willing to be patient. That's why I will often suggest several
ways of solving a problem. If one solution doesn't work, try another.

UNDERSTANDING THE BLACK POINT METHOD

The Black Point program differs from other training systems in several
ways. Sometimes the difference lies in our emphasis on style and sometimes
in our approach to basics. As an example, some trainers insist a pup is ready
for rigorous field training at six months of age. With the exception of spaniels,
I do not agree. Pups under one year are not accepted at Black Point. I advise a
prospective customer to take his animal home, socialize it, and give it a
double dose of love and security. A young dog is like a kid. It has a short
attention span and is emotionally immature. If it learns a few basic com-

mands, that's all you should expect. At the end of the first year, it is truly ready for the pressures of field training.

I know everyone is eager to begin training, and a year-long wait seems like spinning your wheels, but the first twelve months are far from wasted. They should be a learning experience for you and your pup. You've got twelve months to teach your dog to trust you, to build confidence, and to establish a rapport that has to last a lifetime. These are months when you measure the range and intensity of your dog's instincts, when you discover whether they are full-blown or need to be reinforced. The pup plays and chases birds, building confidence and sharpening instincts and hunting skills. Between two and four months, he can be taught a carefully chosen obedience drill that lays the groundwork for the field commands he will learn the following year.

While there is not much you can discover about conformation, personality, or heredity from a quick look at a litter, you can test for intelligence and instincts. I'll outline a few simple tests. For example, you can determine intelligence, in a general way, by the time it takes an animal to learn simple first-year commands.

I'd been without my own hunting dog for some time and a couple of weeks ago decided to pick one from a new litter in our kennel. Five beautiful German wirehair pups had been born to a bitch who is one of our best hunters. She has all the instincts and intensity anyone could want plus an easy, cooperative disposition. A few months ago she was mated to a champion sire that belonged to a customer. I knew the pups would be as good as their parents and before they were weaned selected one using a system I've trusted for years. First, I compared all of the pups in the litter, focusing on the boldest ones. Next, I noted the way each carried its tail. A high tail is a sign of soundness. Then I evaluated the way each pup responded to its litter mates. A pup doesn't have to be at the head of the pack to interest me, but if it hangs back or refuses to fight for some attention, I'm not interested. By the time I had gone through the process, a bold, happy, eager little female caught my eye. I knew I had to have her.

At eight weeks I took her home and introduced her to a portable aluminum kennel that was to be her new home. The importance of this will be explained later, but in the first few weeks the crate serves a basic function. While the pup often has the run of the house—this is an important period of socialization—I taught her to return to her kennel. I put her there at night, whenever she becomes too active or is underfoot. Now, a pup that learns the kennel command quickly is bright—and fresh out of the litter that little girl learned what to do in four tries. She's quick. I expect a lot from her.

You can also tell much from the way a pup responds to stress, a scolding for example. If it accepts a reprimand without cowering, understands what you want and bounces back, that's great. And you can learn from the way a pup reacts to strangers. Is she bold, frightened, or uninterested? Boldness is important. And curiosity is important, too. A pup should be interested in the world around her. An animal with these traits is one you can train, hunt over, and be proud of. My little pup takes correction in her stride and bounces back, eager, friendly, and ready to learn. She will be learning her "p's and q's" as I write my book and I'll tell you how she progresses.

At Black Point we emphasize style and staunchness because that's where the real satisfaction of owning a dog lies. Anybody can field a half-trained dog, but it will ruin the day and maybe the hunter. Life is too short for that kind of frustration. If you are going to have a bird dog, you might as well own a superior animal, one that delivers a full measure of pleasure every time you hunt. I'll show you how to create that, from the first step to the last.

Is a dog like that worth the effort? Certainly. By the end of the book you'll have trained your own field dog, and if you follow my system, he'll be superior, a stylish, classy dog. You can be proud of him. Don't you deserve that?

CHAPTER TWO

Selecting a Breed

Four kinds of dogs interest the bird hunter: flushing dogs, pointers, retrievers, and setters. The upland game hunter focuses on three of them. Retrievers, essentially bred for water birds, are covered in an excellent companion volume, *Training Your Retriever*, by James Lamb Free.

Despite their names, pointers and setters are similar, bred to locate game, point it, and hold it for the hunter as well as to retrieve. The flushing dog alone is unique. He is bred to find game, send it airborne, and retrieve. Aside from herding and guarding, he represents one of the oldest forms of cooperation between man and canine. More popular in the past, the flushing dog is sometimes said to be past his prime. Not so! Pointing dogs are the common choice today, but the flushing dog is still appreciated by a small, enthusiastic coterie who toil diligently to keep his art alive. In the end, the choice between pointer and flusher should be based on several factors—canine temperament, conformation (the way a dog looks), and the way a person likes to hunt. Both types of dogs are equally good, quality born, as purebred as any canine can get.

From at least one point of view, the term *purebred*, Holy Writ to a nation of dog fanciers, is puzzling, both paradox and hapless balderdash. Most experts will readily admit that today's popular breeds are the result of numerous mixes and crosses. If so, one may ask, how can the results be pure?

There is no easy answer. From antiquity, spaniels have been bred to hounds, setters have been crossed with Cockers, and by now half the field dogs in America are linked by ancient bloodlines. It must be obvious that *pure* cannot possibly relate to one historical animal.

It doesn't. If there is honesty to the term (and there is), the answer leads in another direction. To the faithful it is this: from pointer and setter to flushing dog, the characteristics accepted as standards today were established years ago, sometimes by plan, occasionally by accident. With a few exceptions, such as the late-blooming Boykin Spaniel, they were proven and in place by the mid-1800s. *Pure* refers not to the beginning, but to the end, to an animal superior to anything before, to the fact that progeny generations later conform to standards set a century ago. Today's English Springer, German Shorthair, or you-name-it, has the same spirit, the same instincts, the same intensity as its great, great, great grandparents. Like family recipes, standards are formulations carefully preserved, controlled, and repeated with great care and caution. When changes come, they are small, generally introduced to polish and perfect the breed.

Where did the "purity" begin? I don't know, but during the first Crusades, dogs and horses traveled the length of the known world with their masters. Before 1096 English, Spanish, French, and Arab animals interbred, and these accidental matings created historic root-stock. Two early bird dogs with long and short hair surfaced about that time. Both were called *Oysel* after the French word for bird. They were among the earliest pointers, and their instincts have been focused, sharpened, and honed in the intervening centuries. Even today that historic trail of breeding is interesting. Fascinating facts still surface in the strangest places. For example, pointers with a hound cross someplace in their past seem to me more temperamental than those without, but *vive la difference*. Let's take a closer look at the possible choices:

POINTERS

ENGLISH POINTER. (See Illustration 3.)

While all pointers probably can be traced to the Oysel, the breed was refined in England. Most of its history can be credited to a British breeder, William Arkwright, who, sometime around 1890, gave pointer fanciers their first definitive (and still sound) breeder's bible.

Ranked as America's 88th most popular dog by the American Kennel Club (AKC), today's standard is surprisingly close to that of Arkwright's time. A good Pointer is adaptable, easy to manage, obedient, and eager to please. With an aristocratic head, he ranks among the royalty of gundogs. He has a good bird sense and is able to locate game quickly and accurately. On point he is characterized by a rigid body and accurate orientation to game—which I call "intensity of point." You see this best when the dog is quartering (working the field in a particular pattern). His head is his hallmark: a dished face with a raised brow, a well-defined stop, and bright, friendly eyes that look straight forward. The soft nostrils are wide-set. He holds his head higher than other breeds and focuses on airborne scent.

Pointers in England and America, though from the same stock, are different. The English dogs are larger, probably because they are bred for bench shows, and the American-bred dogs are often wider-ranging. To the experienced upland hunter there are "horse-handling" and "foot-handling" pointers, and the terms indicate not only the manner in which the animals are commonly handled, but also the distance they cover and the way they work. Horse-handling pointers are big-running animals who cover tremendous distances, working far from their handlers. Many American-bred pointers, especially those from the south, are in this group. They are trained on large farms by hunters on horseback. Some, destined for championship trials, are given special training in the Canadian prairies where they run on miles of unfenced land. These dogs are uncomfortable working restricted areas. I wouldn't recommend them for a hunter limited to hunting the smaller fields common in many states.

Foot-handling dogs do not range as far from their hunter, and several eastern kennels breed them. Perhaps the most famous is Elhew Kennels (the name of which is derived from the backwards spelling of owner Bob Wehle's name). These are high-tailed, lightly marked, aggressive bird dogs, highly regarded by most hunters. Elhew is based in Henderson, New York. Other names for foot-handling include "walking dogs" and "gundogs", both indicating pointers bred to hunt smaller areas. If you hunt in any number of states where preserves and public lands are restricted and want a pointer, a foot-handling version is your best bet.

The difference between foot- and horse-handling dogs, if you've never heard the term before, can be seen most clearly in field trials competition. Dogs in all-age stakes competition are always big-running dogs. The popular choice is the English Pointer, and it is usually handled from a horse. A good one will range one-third to one-half mile ahead of its hunter. In comparison, a foot-handling dog, such as a Brittany, works 200 yards out, seldom cutting in much.

If there is a drawback to the breed, I'd have to say it is this: pointers have a one-track mind—day in and day out focusing on birds, birds, birds. Consequently, most are neither as personable nor as friendly as one might hope— not because they distrust people, but because they are continually ready to hunt. Neither is the breed noted for a willingness to retrieve. Yet despite these slight and very minor disadvantages, the pointer comes highly recommended.

I'd like to emphasize that a number of breeds, the pointer is only one example, are now being bred more wide-ranging than they once were. This is both good and bad. In some areas the man who wants to leisurely hunt alder thickets for woodcock or lightly wooded areas for grouse may have a difficult time finding the right dog.

FRENCH POINTER. Though not common in the U.S., the French Pointer is one of the world's oldest pointing breeds, probably originating in the Pyrenees. It supplied stock for the British Shorthair Setter and the French name, *Braque Français*, helps explain the history of pointing breeds. *Braque* is derived from an Old French word that means "to aim," probably indicating the dog rigidly pointed its body in the direction of game. There are two varieties, a large *Braque Français* and a smaller *Braque Français de petit Taille*. The larger strain is nearly extinct: the smaller is still popular in Europe.

GERMAN SHORTHAIR POINTER. (See Illustration 4.)

The Kurzhaar, or Shorthair, the result of a cross between the Spanish Pointer and Bloodhound lines, is an extremely popular dog, ranking 28th on the AKC list. The breed was well established in Germany by the end of the eighteenth century and not only points but tracks scent as well. A noble, stylish dog, the German Shorthair has amazing power, endurance, and speed. It is alert, calm, of medium size, and more tractable and well-tempered than some. The clean outline of its head is especially important, along with its powerful body, long shoulders, deep chest, short back, and muscular hindquarters. A high, well-carried tail is an important part of its style and, according to custom, is always docked (shortened). The skin should be tight, without folds, and the coat short, flat, and hard to the touch, slightly longer beneath the tail. English and American standards require colors of solid liver or liver variations, that is, ticked with white. In the U.S. colors other than liver and gray-white are not accepted. Tri-colors cannot be registered with the AKC. The breed would be my personal choice for a biddable dog capable of learning under pressure and working a field well.

GERMAN LONGHAIR. Though not recognized by the AKC and seldom seen in America, the German Longhair has an interesting history. One hundred years ago German sportsmen preferred hunting over Gordon Setters because the breed's temperament suited them as precisely as its coloring suited local forests. A philosophical problem developed when it became difficult for local breeders to meet rigid Gordon color standards and continue to produce a dog local hunters wanted. The solution was the German Langhaar.

GERMAN WIREHAIR. (See Illustration 5.)

The Drahthaar, or rough-coated German Pointer, is a relatively new dog, quite popular in the U.S. It ranks 71st on the AKC list and a number of kennels specialize in the breed. Hunters from New York to California swear by it.

The dog is high-spirited and bold and takes well to training. The fact that it was developed from temperamentally calmer stock only emphasizes the many outcrosses, some to the English Pointer. Even a few touches of Airedale have been noted by some experts.

The accepted colorings are similar to those of the German Shorthair except that white fronts are not highly regarded in Germany or the U.S. The muzzle should be long, wide, and powerful, the eyes small and bright, and a Roman nose is ideal. The ears should be short and carried forward. The hocks should be bent and the tail docked. With its tremendous power, the breed is not often equaled for field work. As with the Shorthair, it has excellent ground-tracking abilities, makes an excellent retriever, a near-perfect pointer—and a great family dog. If there is a drawback, it could be this: from puppy on, German Wirehairs tend to be obstinate. Temperamentally I'd say they are a sound but sometimes stubborn dog.

STICHELHAAL or German Roughhaired Pointer. The breed was extremely popular half a century ago. It has gradually given way to the wirehair and is rarely seen today.

GRIFFON POINTER. The Wirehaired Pointing Griffon dates to 1880 when it was first bred in Holland by Edward Korthals, a brilliant fancier of the period. It was developed from French Griffon Pointers and crosses with two other French field dogs, the Braque and Barbet. Today it is more popular with show fanciers than with hunters but can be a good field dog when you find one bred of sound working stock. It can also be a good water dog, and since the Griffon has no hound blood, it is not as temperamental as some breeds. In appearance it reminds one of a German Wirehair, though less stubborn and more tractable. It is a close-hunting dog and, according to the AKC, is America's 122nd most popular breed. A number of people feel this is a dog that has yet to arrive, perhaps even the upland hunting dog of tomorrow. "Griffons," one man said, "are people dogs."

HUNGARIAN VIZSLA. (See Illustration 6)

Established long before 1800, the Vizsla was literally conceived as the "unisex" upland game dog, developed to appeal to women and men and to be an all-purpose hunting dog. That's a lot of press to live up to, but in many ways the Vizsla succeeds. It is extremely popular in the U.S. and Europe and is ranked 57th by the AKC. The dog has a bold, high-strung nature and must be handled gently. It can be difficult to train, and in the field many handlers consider the dog "always on the brink of disaster." It is a good tracker, likes ground game, and can be a very good field dog indeed. Like the Griffon, the Vizsla does not range far and is recommended for preserves and similar restricted hunting areas.

WEIMARANER. (See Illustration 7.)

Nicknamed the "gray ghosts," early Weimaraners were used to hunt larger game, boars and deer. The breed became a bird dog later. A Weimaraner is fearless, generally friendly and obedient—to a handler who controls it with a firm hand—though the dog is not always highly regarded for field work.

In my view there are problems. The dog is often stubborn, is consequently hard to train and handle, and often has a hard mouth. It is not gentle as a retriever should be and tends to "crunch" the birds it retrieves. The Weimaraner is ranked 43rd on the AKC list. The greatest number of registered dogs are either companion animals or bred for big game hunting. Few are used for birds.

OTHER POSSIBILITIES

The *Bracco Italiano* is wirehaired, reminiscent of the German Shorthair, and a good pointer. It reminds some of the Spinone, also Italian-bred and an excellent pointer. The Bracco is the only Italian Pointer with short hair, seen mostly in colors of white, white and orange, and white and brown. Occasional variants are speckled. It is not common in America.

The *Drentse Partrijshond*, an excellent all-around bird dog, was developed in Holland. It rarely seen in the U.S., and it is not recognized by the AKC.

The *Barbet*, a French gundog, is one of the earliest building blocks dating to the time of the Oysel. It looks more like an English Sheepdog than a pointer and was cross-bred with early stock to create the Griffon, German Wirehair, Pudelpointer, and others. Pure Barbet stock can still be seen in Europe. It has changed little since the 1500s.

There are a number of *Poodle- or Pudelpointers* (See Illustration 8) in the U.S., though they are more popular in Europe. Not a cross between an English pointer and the French poodle, as the name might imply, the breed can be traced to the Barbet, and more recently, via a planned cross, to an English Pointer and Pudel. The early German Pudel was an excellent waterfowl dog. Today's version is a good field dog, though rare.

The *St. Germain Pointer* dates to the nineteenth century, is light colored, and is rarely found outside of Europe. It is the result of a cross between a French Pointer and the Porcelaine hound.

A *Spanish pointer*, the Perdiguero de Burgos, noted for strength, a keen nose, and an easy disposition, is one of the oldest of all Spanish gundogs. Today it is a large dog, just under 30 inches high. Though slow, it can be taught to retrieve and point. The *Old Danish Pointer* was a heavy-bodied, large-headed dog imported into Spain about three hundred years ago. Little is known of it today.

The result of a cross between a Pyrenean Braque and the Gascony Pointer, the *Auvergne Pointer* is a large dog, distinguished in body and head, weighing up to 70 pounds. Seldom seen outside of Europe, it is a slow dog with a deep, square muzzle and a short, white coat with ticking and black spots.

Named for the Portuguese word for cartridge, the *Portuguese Predigeiro* is a powerful and popular breed of uncertain origin. It is not recognized by the AKC and is rarely seen in the U.S. It shows considerable Mastiff influence, has a broad head, a short muzzle, and a pronounced stop.

DEVELOPMENT OF STYLES

Over the centuries man has developed a neat distinction between dogs that point and those that flush. Pointers are hunted in open areas, wheat fields, rice checks, and on large farms where they can run. Flushing dogs are more often used in smaller areas. They are especially good at hunting ditches, brambles, and small areas a man couldn't work any other way.

It is no more sensible to compare them than it is to compare apples and oranges. They have been bred to different work. A variety of canine temperaments are available in both categories, and your choice should depend on at least two things—the kind of dogs you enjoy and the way you like to hunt. The sensible hunter matches his dog to the birds it handles best. As an example, I don't think I'd match a flushing dog to pheasants because the birds prefer to run rather than flush. There are other birds the flusher can handle better.

FLUSHING AND NONFLUSHING SPANIELS

The point I am leading to is this: a novice might reasonably think that pointers point, setters sit, and flushing dogs flush. Nothing could be simpler, and it sounds as if the theory should hold water; but in reality pointers and setters point, and in America only three dogs flush game. Let me emphasize the fact that there are only three flushing dogs common to the U.S. All are spaniels, and though all flushers are spaniels, not all spaniels are flushing dogs.

To add to the confusion, you might think "spaniel" implies a dog of Spanish origin. It doesn't. The term has been traced to an Old French word, "s'espanir," which means "to flatten oneself" or "to lie down." It is probably the most direct indication of what the early bird dog was bred to do—to flush game and then drop so the animal could be netted or bagged by falcon or greyhound. Today's spaniel category includes flushing and pointing dogs. The springer and Brittany spaniel illustrate my point. The English springer spaniel is a flushing dog, one of the best. The Brittany spaniel is a pointer, one of America's most popular. There is a move underway now to not even call it a spaniel.

THE BRITTANY SPANIEL (See Illustration 9.)

The compact *Brittany Spaniel*, with an almost endless reserve of stamina, has to be considered one of America's most popular field dogs. It is ranked 24th by the AKC, just behind Labradors and German Shorthairs. It was developed from a Breton with a touch of Welsh Springer. The objective? To create a dog of "maximum quality in a minimum size," according to early records. That is a good description of the Brittany, which is small, courageous, reckless, strong, fleet, and fearless. The breed has a deep-bred instinct for pointing and is the ideal dog for small, restricted hunting areas. It is friendly, affectionate, and gentle; and if there are flaws, you'd be hard-pressed to list more than this: a Brittany is the most sensitive of all breeds. Most can be "voice-beaten" and are said to sometimes lack intensity on point (as compared with a pointer or shorthair). Many owners consider the long coat a disadvantage in the field and at home. On the plus side: once a Brittany learns something, the concept sticks for life. It is a "close-knit" dog; that is, it bonds well to people and makes an excellent family companion. A hobby trainer in suburbia will have better luck working with a Brittany than with many breeds I might name.

The dog has a short, choppy run, especially in high grass, and is very popular with hunters because it is small, not far-ranging and perfect for restricted areas such as hunting preserves and clubs.

I like the breed. They are stylish in the field, and I have only one complaint. The standards call for a short tail. In my view that detracts from its stylishness.

COCKER. More often than not, the American Cocker is called a Cocker Spaniel and is considered a distinct breed, apart from the generally smaller English Cocker. A true flushing dog, it has been tracked further into history than most breeds since drawings resembling Cockers have been found in Egyptian tombs. Chaucer wrote of the Cocker in 1340, and in those early times "Springer," "Springing Spaniel," "Cocking Spaniel," "Cocker," and "Cock Flusher" were used indiscriminately for a variety of spaniels. The smallest were called "Cockers" because they were used to hunt woodcock. Today, Cockers are America's most popular dog, long ranked number one by the AKC. Most of the dogs are companion or bench show animals. Few are used for hunting and that's a shame.

The original Cocker was both a land and water spaniel and has been used extensively in breeding. Even the English Setter was derived from it. The English Cocker, which can lay claim to be one of the oldest and most popular of all spaniel varieties, is generally smaller than its American counterpart, though size can be misleading. The dog is snappy, fast, and an excellent hunting companion. A cocker from a kennel specializing in field dogs is to be recommended. The English Cocker is ranked 64th on the AKC list. The *Field Spaniel* is closely related. It resulted from a separation of Cocker lineage in 1892 and is not common in the U.S.

THE ENGLISH SPRINGER SPANIEL. (See Illustration 10.)

The English Springer Spaniel is as important historically as it is popular, ranking 17th on the AKC list. In the U.S. it is the most popular of all flushing dogs and the oldest of sporting spaniels and is considered root stock for most land spaniels. The breed was well known before 1570 when its name was first recorded. Popular in the U.S., springers have won many national field trial championships. The dog is easy to train, makes an excellent family animal, and is a superb gundog. If there is a problem, it is that Springers love hunting so much it is difficult for even the most avid hunter to keep a good one busy and properly exercised.

The best Springers have a compact, upright body with the highest legs and raciest build of any field dog. The head is of medium length, broad yet rounded, with a definite stop or division between the eyes. The ears are lobed, set in line with the eyes, and feathered. The tail is low and is never carried above the back. The coat is close, straight, and resists weather. As a result, Springers are better suited to cold-weather sport than many shorthaired breeds. Spaniels are often high-strung, extremely fast; they make excellent retrievers and are highly recommended.

The *French Spaniel* is similar though stockier, heavier, and not as fast. It is rarely seen here and is not often bred in the U.S. The *Wachtelhund*, or

German Spaniel, reminds one of a Springer but has shiny, slightly wavy fur. It is an excellent retriever and superb gundog, though it is not often seen in the U.S.

OTHER SPANIELS

The *Clumber Spaniel,* the heaviest of spaniels, is of French origin and is probably the result of a cross with a Basset Hound. Its coat is generally white with few markings. The AKC ranks it 120th in terms of popularity. The *Pont Audener Spaniel* is also of French origin and was first bred in Normandy. It had a large European following at the turn of the century but has since virtually disappeared.

Even after a century *Sussex Spaniels* remain best known in southern England where the breed apparently began. They are a small-boned, sturdy dog weighting less than 50 pounds. Their rarity is indicated by the fact that the AKC ranks them 124th out of a possible 129 recognized breeds. The German *Munsterlander,* related to the Breton, is not popular outside Germany and is actually two dogs, a large version and a smaller one. Both resemble a Brittany but have a longer muzzle. The larger breed is disappearing, though the smaller dog remains popular. The *Welsh Springer Spaniel,* bred and hunted before 1300, shares a history with the Brittany. It is popular in England and ranks 101st in the U.S.

The *Boykin Spaniel,* only now building a following, has a most interesting history. Some time in the early 1900s a Methodist parishioner in Spartanburg, South Carolina, spotted a small, brown dog outside his church. He took it home and quickly realized the dog possessed unusual hunting traits—an aptitude for pointing and an amazing instinct for flushing. A companion, L. Whitaker Boykin, took the dog and through a series of breedings and crosses created the Boykin Spaniel, an American original. By 1986, 3,508 purebred dogs and 677 foundation stock have been registered in the U.S. Can AKC recognition be far behind? Perhaps the Boykin story illustrates the way many older breeds developed.

ENGLISH SETTERS. (See Illustration 11.)

Some people think of setters as flushing dogs. They are not. The setter is a pointer and ranks as one of the oldest of hunting breeds, used even before guns. The English Setter has a written history that dates to the fourteenth century. For six hundred years many of England's noblest families have kept kennels of them just for sport. Late in the 1800s breeding split in two directions. On one side was Edward Laverack who founded the prestigious Kennel Club in 1860. He bred dogs for show. On the other side was R. Purcell

Llewellin, who bred Setters for show and field. For our purposes, the important difference is that Laverack believed in in-breeding while Llewellin relied on various outside strains and mixes. Today, dogs that can trace lineage to the Llewellin side are unquestionably the better sporting animals.

English Setters are affectionate and gregarious and make excellent companions. They prefer not to be left alone much and are easy to train. More tractable than pointers, they make excellent retrievers and have a superb nose, hunting with their head held higher than most breeds. Their long fur is the one drawback. In stubble and fields with burrs it requires frequent brushing. On the AKC's list, the English Setter ranks 70th and is one of the most gorgeous dogs you can see in the field. Its tail is fabulous, especially when the dog is onto a bird.

THE GORDON SETTER. The *Gordon Setter*, the 67th most popular dog in America, is the only gundog native to Scotland and is probably related to sixteenth-century black-and-tan setters. Their name, shortened from Gordon Castle Setters, comes from the Duke of Gordon who kept large kennels of the animals. Though a fairly heavy dog, Gordons are fast and more docile than the English Setter. They are hard-running but do not range as far as English Setters and, on average, do not make good retrievers. The colors, black and tan, have been long established, and a little white is permissible only if it is limited to the feet and chest. White on the head or collar is considered a serious fault. They are very popular with hunters.

IRISH SETTER. (See Illustration 12.)
While the history of the *Irish Setter* is closely linked to that of the spaniel, much early data has been lost. We know the breed has some Bloodhound mix and that by the end of the sixteenth century it was a superb shooting dog. All that has changed. Today, the Irish Setter is predominantly a show dog, though those few animals bred to field work still display a spark of their renowned sixteenth-century intensity. From the right stock they can make excellent hunting dogs. A number of American kennels have contributed to their development, St. Cloud, Lismore and Clencho in New York State, Culbertson in Illinois, and Shagstone in California are examples. Most of the dogs have been bred for show. The breed ranks 44th on the AKC's list.

A large, deep-chested, bulky dog, the Irish Setter has an aristocratic, distinctive look, with a long molded head and an almost chiseled look to its face. It has a well-defined muzzle and low-set ears, a long neck, sloping shoulders, and a shiny coat. The tail is normally carried low and slopes when pointing. An offshoot, not really a separate breed, has a more reddish color, from chestnut through mahogany, which is the source of its name, the "Red Irish

Setter." The Red Setter has a slightly higher tail. On AKC registrations it is regarded as an Irish Setter. In both forms the breed hit a low watermark of popularity in the '20s but has since regained some standing. Though not highly regarded as a field dog today, it should be. The Irish Setter has an excellent nose, is fast and hard-driving, and makes an excellent retriever. The breed is more popular in the east than in the west.

CHOOSING A BREED

Selecting a pup can be compared to buying an automobile. Not every model is designed for the same use, dealers offer a variety of choices from the sedate to the racy, and some unscrupulous salesmen try to peddle models completely unsuited to your needs. With pupflesh as with motorcars, the rule is caveat emptor. You're expected to know what you want, and my point is this: the possibilities are greater than anyone need consider.

While every dog on my list has been bred for birding, the rare and exotic have obvious drawbacks. Some are difficult to find, and in the case of exotic dogs bred abroad, are difficult to import. The hard-to-get breeds are generally not worth the effort. As a rule, you are wiser to select an American-bred pup and wiser still to choose one that is popular and readily available. Owners, trainers, and veterinarians have more experience with these, and when problems crop up, whether in terms of health or training, there is usually a ready solution. As a clincher, when and if you wish to try your own breeding, you'll have a wider selection of possible mates, and a choice of bloodlines is important. There are instances in which those with rare breeds have been forced to breed their dogs outside the country, and the expense, paperwork, and problems involved are overwhelming. Finally, a number of breeds are not recognized by the American Kennel Club and cannot be registered—which means that, on this side of the Atlantic at least, an exotic pup may have no passport and little recognition. And as you shop around, remember one thing: breeds are generalities, pups are individuals.

At Black Point I'm often asked, "What breed would you recommend to an owner who is impatient and strict?" I have a pat answer: I don't recommend that anyone short on patience try training a dog. But if the question is reversed to, "Which dogs are more forgiving?" I'd have to say an English Pointer can overlook trainer errors better than most breeds. My second nominee would be a German Shorthair.

Bird hunters are also concerned with a dog's mouth, the way it handles a bird on retrieve. Though some breeds have a softer mouth than others, the question is difficult to answer. My best response is this: pointers are not known to be good retrievers. The Brittany, while not much better, has a softer mouth. Perhaps the upland dog with the nicest mouth is the German Wirehair. That's one reason I like hunting with them.

Sometimes a first-time dog owner wants a breed that can also be a good family dog. I say, "Let's turn that question around, too. You are not likely to choose a Weimaraner. Pointers are not often affectionate, but only because their mind's always on hunting. Shorthairs are good and Wirehairs and Brittanys are better."

The most common question concerns an "all-around dog." Even old-timers sometimes ask if there is such a thing. For waterfowlers the Lab comes close and for upland game the German Wirehair is number one. It is the most popular breed in Germany, can be trained for water, tracks well, and with its tight fur can tolerate extreme cold.

One afternoon when Dad and I were relaxing in the clubhouse we got around to considering what dog we'd own if we could choose only one breed. After an hour or so we each completed our list. First place ended in a tie between the German Shorthair and German Wirehair. Second place went to the Brittany because most new hunters will have better luck training it than an English Pointer. Third place went hands down to the Pointer. The English Setter and the Vizsla rounded out our list.

After all is said and done, the breed is not as important as the pup. A good pup of any breed on my list can make a hell of a field dog. He'll give you everything you want—intensity, obedience, and a touch of style.

PAPERS AND REGISTRATION

Several kennel clubs offer national registration of purebred pups. The two largest, the United Kennel Club and the American Kennel Club, do not always recognize the same breeds and seldom cooperate. A third, the American Field Club, offers registration of some breeds that neither of the others include. Their emphasis is on pointers and setters, and they are especially popular in the south and southwest. The AFC also sponsors field trials.

While the UKC is possibly older, the AKC has an obvious edge in popularity. It is the nation's premier clearing house for purebred dogs. Records of 129 breeds are carefully maintained at AKC headquarters in New York, and a dog bred from stock registered with the AKC is certified purebred, a claim recognized around the world. An AKC certificate for a dog is like a passport or insurance: you know what you've got and you feel a hell of a lot safer for it. It is equally important to buy pups from AKC-registered kennels, or from owners who have registered sires and dams, as it is to register your pup as soon as you buy it. A "papered" dog is worth more as a pup and is more valuable if it is ever sold or bred. Animals recognized or accepted as special breeds in

Europe or Asia may not be considered so in the U.S., and it is where you are that counts. The AKC will recognize and accept a new breed only when there are a certain number of owners and animals and when bloodlines, paperwork, and other criteria meet their standards.

There are other listings, registers, purebred studbooks, and lists of field champions, which can affect your choice. I'll explain those as I progress.

The chart below lists the AKC registrations of bird and retrieving dogs in order of popularity. Registrations are not categorized by show or field use, but do indicate the overall popularity of breeds. In most cases breeds not listed are not recognized by the AKC and cannot be registered. For specific information, contact the AKC directly. Their address is listed in the section called "Product and Information Sources."

Several interesting facts can be gleaned from the list. The Cocker, which has ranked first for years, is increasing its numbers, though most of those registered are not hunting dogs. English Cocker registrations have dropped slightly. Brittanys are holding their own, neither increasing nor decreasing. German Pointers, Wire- and Shorthairs, are losing ground, while pointers, a grouping which includes English Pointers, are on the rise.

AKC registrations: January 1–December 31, 1984 and 1985 (out of 1,071,299 total registrations for 1984 and 1,089,149 total registrations for 1985)

Ranking	Breed	1984	1985
1.	Cocker Spaniel	94,803	96,396
3.	Labrador Retrv.	71,235	74,271
5.	Golden Retrv.	54,490	56,131
17.	English Springer Spaniel	21,660	20,628
24.	Brittany	17,046	15,058
28.	German Shorthaired Pointer	9,018	8,351
43.	Weimaraner	4,107	3,938
44.	Irish Setter	4,553	3,804
57.	Vizsla	1,730	1,683
64.	English Cocker Spaniel	1,371	1,215
67.	Gordon Setter	1,008	1,096
70.	English Setter	1,066	1,045
71.	German Wirehaired Pointer	1,037	988
88.	Pointer	439	463
101.	Welsh Springer Spaniel	239	237
120.	Clumber Spaniel	102	93
122.	Wirehaired Pointing Griffon	84	77
124.	Sussex Spaniel	23	54

Dogs registered by group	1984	1985
Sporting breeds	289,299	290,850
Hound breeds	108,350	109,800
Working breeds	149,850	145,350
Terrier breeds	74,950	75,100
Toy breeds	135,150	145,650
Nonsporting breeds	187,450	196,799
Herding Breeds	126,250	125,600
Totals	1,071,299	1,089,149

Litters Registered January 1–December 31, 1984 and 1985

Ranking	Breed	1984	1985
2.	Cocker Spaniel	35,243	36,869
25.	English Springer Spaniel	5,778	5,664
26.	Brittany	4,977	4,466
36.	German Shorthair Pointer	2,377	2,136
46.	Weimaraner	1,066	1,079
51.	Irish Setter	1,069	887
60.	English Cocker Spaniel	435	430
74.	German Wirehaired Pointer	268	258
77.	English Setter	286	252
78.	Gordon Setter	229	251
93.	Pointer	113	106
109.	Welsh Springer Spaniel	56	52
121.	Wirehaired Pointing Griffon	25	18
125.	Clumber Spaniel	27	14
126.	Sussex Spaniel	7	8

Litters Registered by Group	1984	1985
Sporting breeds	81,700	84,000
Hound breeds	44,549	45,650
Working breeds	46,949	46,450
Terrier breeds	30,750	31,650
Toy breeds	80,750	88,149
Nonsporting breeds	95,050	101,049
Herding breeds	42,350	42,600
Totals	422,098	439,548

CHAPTER THREE

Finding the Perfect Source

If one factor is obvious, it is this: you must decide on a breed before you can find a place to buy your new pup. The imperious Sherlock Holmes might say, "That's elementary, Watson!" but basic or not, finding the best place to buy a pup can be a slow and difficult process. In addition to sifting through a lot of advertising you may have to sort through a lot of soft fur and gentle eyes. If this is your first dog and you really can't decide on a breed, watch various dogs in action. See them under field conditions. Discover how they relate to hunters. Learn how their temperament compares with yours. Talk with owners. A little investigation can speed your decision.

If there is a bird club or preserve in your area, drop in. Field trials are equally good. And breed clubs, which hold meetings, get-togethers, and trials are another possibility. You'll be welcome at all three. Dog-owning friends and neighbors also offer opportunities for questions, and the list goes on.

DISCOVERING SOURCES

The pup you want comes from sound parents with proven hunting abilities; and from Bangor, Maine, to San Diego, California, kennels specializing in quality field dogs can be difficult to find. They're never located in the heart of a city and seldom in the suburbs. If you find them at all, they are most often isolated, in rural settings. Like Black Point, they are probably surrounded by fields where a kennel master can train his charges.

Professional facilities are a prime source. Other possibilities include thousands of amateur kennels, backyard facilities operated by dog lovers and hunters. Since amateurs need less land, their facilities are closer to town. You *can* find their kennels in the suburbs, and occasionally you may hear of a lone purebread available in the heart of town. Nine times out of ten it will be a half-trained dog reluctantly sold because the owner cannot keep it.

If you enjoy playing detective, you can follow leads like these. Occasionally you'll discover a gem, but if time is important, zero in on places with the greatest potential. I'd recommend tested professional kennels and dedicated amateurs with proven records. You can find these by attending field trials and by reading advertisements in local newspapers, field-trial magazines, and other specialty magazines. It is impossible to say one group is better. Both breed superb dogs. I know amateurs who are surprisingly successful, many producing some of the country's finest dogs. I'd visit both sources.

PROFESSIONAL KENNELS

You'll find two types of professional breeding facilities, those specializing in bench-show dogs and those breeding for the field. In a hunter's view not every dog is equal. The problem with a bench-show champion is that it is bred for appearance and conformation, and more often than not it is short on the instincts essential for a field dog. In almost every case, the pup with a proven potential for finding game will come from a kennel where the emphasis is on field dogs and where the owner is interested in just one thing: breeding the best possible working dogs. He'll be a dedicated hunter or a professional trainer-breeder.

Bird clubs like Black Point were rare until a few years ago, and there are still areas of the nation as devoid of clubs as a desert is of grass. But today the idea is growing faster than a well-fed teenager. At last count, bird clubs were common in the west and especially numerous in California.

If you can find a facility like Black Point, visit it before buying any dog. A shooting club offers multiple advantages for anyone wanting to learn about field dogs. Many members bring their own dogs, and others rely on a pool of animals bred and trained by the club. One day at a good club can give you an opportunity to see a number of breeds in action. You can even shoot over some. Most clubs have a reservoir of popular breeds, Brittanys, German Wirehairs, and others. You can rent them for about $5 an hour or $20 for a normal hunting day, and in a few outings you'll have experience with a variety of breeds. It can help make up your mind.

And there is another advantage. Club dogs are generally bred annually and the pups sold. Regular customers have first call, and if you find a dog you like, you may be able to reserve a pup from the next litter. You'll probably have to act fast, though. Club dogs usually come from enviable bloodlines, and the pups are spoken for before they are born. The last litter at Black Point was a litter of five German Wirehairs, the very one from which I got my pup. The dam had been mated to a sire with proven bloodlines and considerable trials experience. Customers had seen both dogs in action. Pups were reserved before they were whelped.

FIELD TRIALS

Field trials are an excellent place to see well-trained dogs in action; they let you evaluate contestants as they are put through their paces, judged, and rated. Held across the country, trials are competitive events where field champion titles are decided. Publications such as *American Field* (American Field Publishing Co., 222 West Adams St., Chicago, Il 60606) list all national and most local events. Any event sponsored by the National Shoot-to-Retrieve-Association (110 W. Main St., Plainfield, IN 46168) is especially worth while. The AKC also sponsors similar events. Dogs entered in All-Age, Gundog, Derby, and Puppy classes are proven champions. Many trials are sponsored by local breed clubs.

You'll be welcome at trials, and you'll meet people from all walks of life. Women are as active as men, sharing an enthusiasm for the field and a love of dogs. Most trainers will answer questions and once started may even talk your arm off. You'll be able to see a number of breeds and should find that certain dogs and trainers dominate. These are the kennels you should visit first. You may even find a few pups for sale at the event and may be able to pick up a trained or partially trained older dog on the spot.

The most common opportunity, though, is the chance to sign up for a pup from a coming litter. The best of these are booked in advance, but it never hurts to ask questions. A dog currently running at the top of its class in competition was trained at Black Point. Though not yet bred, hunters are lining up to buy her pups. There have been so many applications that the owner can pick and choose. If you can sign up for a pup like this, consider yourself lucky.

ANIMAL SHELTER

Your local animal shelter is a necessary service in a pet-loving society, and the animals detained there make good companions; but it should not be considered a source for hunting dogs. Even if you find the exact breed you're looking for, don't buy it unless you plan to make the animal a house pet. You can never be sure of the pedigree; you know nothing of the dog's background and may never discover the reason it is in the shelter. The same argument holds for a stray. Its background is uncertain and even if the mutt looks like a purebred, it can never be registered with the AKC. If a pooch like this appeals to you and seems tractable, and if the idea of passing it by breaks your heart, buy it—but only as a pet. Whether or not you can make a hunter of it depends on fate.

A purebred dog usually ends up in a shelter because it's a chronic runaway or because a heartless owner has dropped it off as gun-shy. More pedigreed dogs end up in the pound because they are gun-shy than for any other reason. The unfortunate owner doesn't know how to handle the problem and doesn't want to take time to work it out. His solution is to separate himself from his dog in the quickest way possible.

It's a sad situation, certainly regrettable for the pup, but believe me, there is one basic rule: you get what you pay for. You can spend months trying to break a gun-shy dog and may never succeed. You're better off avoiding the problem. Purchase a reliable pup from a reliable kennel, one that's never heard a gun, one you can break in yourself.

PET STORES

Pet stores sell purebred dogs, but the majority come from bench stock and the odds against any having much hunting experience in their background are astronomical. Store-bought pups are not supposed to be hunters. They are companion animals. They run true to breed in terms of conformation, and a good store will back its pups against all common problems, but the store is not selling hunters. Don't expect to find a field champion there.

NEWSPAPERS

In major cities Sunday papers carry a considerable amount of advertising for purebred pups. Sporting dogs are sometimes segregated from bench-show stock, but most often purebreds are grouped together. You have to do the detective work; you must segregate kennels breeding for bench competition from those breeding hunting stock. And, undoubtedly, if you shop by paper you'll absolutely have to weed out unscrupulous "back-yard" breeders. You'll be inundated by them. You can usually eliminate the bench-show kennels with a phone call, but the unscrupulous breeder generally requires a visit—a total waste of time.

The term "back-yard breeder" as a derisive put-down is well known to dog enthusiasts. It is a cut implying that the man or woman involved has no interest in hunting, very little interest in dogs, does not understand blood-lines, and cares nothing about scientific breeding. In its most demeaning definition, a "back-yard breeder" does not know how to breed animals for any of their desirable qualities and does not care to learn. Most have never seen a field trial. Their stock comes from the least expensive animals available. The pups have not been properly socialized and may not even have been ade-quately fed. Back-yard breeders seldom care about anything except the fact that the parents have an AKC registration they can pass along to an unwary buyer. These people talk a good game, but if you buy you'll be taken.

CHECKING KENNELS

There are ways to protect yourself and to guarantee the quality of the animal you buy. The first is to check the kennel. Has it been in business for some time? Or is it new? If it is new, ask questions. Then check general conditions. Look first for cleanliness, then at the pups. If it has a dirt run, if the kennel is filthy and messy, leave immediately. Don't waste time discuss-ing dogs. You don't want the ones sold there. The pups probably have worms and a host of other problems. The kindest thing you can say about such a breeder is that he doesn't understand canines, and the most critical, that you've stumbled into the den of a back-yard breeder. If the run has a gravel or concrete base, check further. No matter how old, if the kennel is neat and clean, you may be in the right place. A reputable kennel breeds reputable pups.

Check the parents. Do they have a hunting background? What about the grandparents? Are the pups healthy, uncrowded, and happy? Skinny? Fat? Bold or timid? When you go into the kennel, do they snarl and snap? Even at eight weeks pups instinctively protect their little piece of the environment, and while a little hostility is o.k., the owner should be able to take you inside with no more reaction than a backward glance from one or two pups.

The pups should be free of infections and deformities; and if they seem bold and curious, trotting eagerly to the front in welcome, these may be dogs worth considering. Check the dam, and if the sire is available, see him, too. Then check the pedigree. If that seems sound, if there is some hunting background, then one of the pups may well be the right one for you.

BUYING AN OLDER DOG

New customers often ask me, "If I visit a kennel long after whelping season and find a single pup available, a four-, five- or six-month-old unsold remnant of a litter from which all the other dogs have been sold, should I buy him?"

The decision depends on the reason the animal is there and the way it has been handled. There may be a legitimate answer. Sometimes a guy buys a dog and in a month or so discovers he can't keep it. Perhaps it's not the pup for him. Perhaps his landlord complained. Perhaps his wife put her foot down. These are legitimate explanations. If an animal has been well socialized, age doesn't matter. A reputable kennel will guarantee every pup.

Occasionally a not-so-reputable kennel is stuck with a second-rate pup, and that's a different story. Often that animal has been given minimum food, no attention, and less love. It remains confined until someone buys it. Avoid that pup. The instincts you hope to develop are probably buried in a badly mixed-up psyche.

You can tell the amount of attention a kennel has given a pup by the way the dog responds when released from his run. If it bolts out boldly, bounding toward you with obvious happiness, it's probably a sound animal. If it acts as if it's been out before and knows its way around, that's a good sign, too. But if the dog comes out as if walking on eggs, glassy-eyed, uncertain, and slinking up to you with tail between legs, be wary. The animal has not been as thoroughly socialized as the owner would like you to believe. That pup will require a lot of special attention, and most dog owners are not willing to spend the time, even when the pooch is bargain priced.

Other dogs, equally old, are better buys, and you can find them advertised in newspapers. Consider the owner who buys a sound, well-pedigreed pup from a reliable kennel and six months later discovers he must sell it. His company is moving him to another city, he is getting a divorce and the dog is part of the settlement, or for reasons of health the owner can no longer hunt. The animal has probably been thoroughly socialized and could be the best buy you'll find. Check the animal as closely as you would any young pup, and if it seems healthy and sound of body and has good bloodlines and a pedigree that indicates a real hunting background, buy it. The only difference between a half-grown dog like this and a pup purchased from a kennel is the right of return. At a kennel you can bring a dog back. You can't when you buy from a private owner.

Bargains like this are surprisingly common. I've seen many good dogs come from similar situations. Even though the animal is one or two years old, if its pedigree indicates a sound background, it is worth considering. And if it has no obvious faults—even if it's never been out of the house—you can still turn it into a sound hunter. If its instincts are strong enough, you can sharpen them with training. I have a friend who bought a two-year-old that had been nothing more than a house pet. In just eighteen months he created a tremendous game dog.

When you buy an older dog there are advantages. An eight-week-old pup is an uncertain commodity, cuddly, sloppy, and unformed. It is difficult to see exactly how it will grow, but with an older pup conformation is obvious. Hard-to-spot birth defects may have developed enough to see. You can also discover more about the animal's character and habits. Test the instincts. Be sure there is an interest in birds and a desire to point, since these indicate a reservoir deep enough to train. If the dog is tractable, friendly, and biddable, chances are good you can mold the animal.

PROBLEM PUPS

Perhaps someone has to buy problem pups—animals not properly socialized, strays with no place else to go, the gun-shy and the ones with problem personalities. All need homes. But need that home be yours? The problem pup—and I am not discussing deformities—will take longer to train. You may have to erase bad habits, and if there are personality problems, you may have to spend time building confidence, changing a timid dog into a bold one or eliminating aggression.

Buying the best pup from the best kennel is no guarantee an animal will develop into a good hunter, but the odds are in your favor. If I could translate the differences into percentages, I'd say you'd be lucky to have a 25% to 30% chance of success with a problem pup. With a good one your chances jump to 85% or more.

To put it another way, you could turn the best possible pup into a great hunter in less than two years. A problem animal might require twice the time and never be as good.

READY-TRAINED DOGS

You can often find advertisements for partially trained and fully trained dogs in local papers and gundog magazines. In the "Trading Post" section of *Gun Dog* magazine (416 Green St., Adel, IA 50003), in *American Field*, and in other publications, ads such as these can be seen almost every month. Prices range from $600 to $700 for a partially trained yearling and up to $2,500 for a fully trained animal two years or older.

"Partially trained" can mean almost anything from an animal that has barely learned basic obedience to one that has been hunting. Both have yet to be fine-tuned, though one has further to go than the other. Terms such as "green-broke" and "started dog" usually identify these animals.

You'll pay most for a fully trained animal and should expect more, but the term also has a broad range of meanings. A dog ready for the field should be staunch on point; willing to retrieve; trained to obey voice, whistle, and hand commands; it should understand "whoa" or "hup," honor the point of another dog, and be accustomed to guns. Whether it is steady to shot and wing, understands backing, and is force-broke depends on the trainer. "Force-broke" means the dog will bring a downed bird to the hand of his owner every time and will not release it until told to "give." Such terms will be explained in coming chapters. The only way to evaluate such a dog is to hunt with it, and a reliable owner should be willing to provide time for this test.

I know it is difficult to remember everything when you're at a kennel, peering into the eyes of a sweet little animal, his wagging tail signaling he's ready to go home with you; but that's when you need the information most. That's when you must think straight and be as unemotional as possible. Don't jump for the first animal you see. Don't buy the cutest pup, or the one with the prettiest markings. Choose the animal with tallest tail, soundest walk, best parents, and most experienced grandparents. That animal may cost a little more, but it'll earn its keep.

One afternoon Dad opened one of the runs, swooped up a pup, and waved it under the nose of a new hunter who was protesting price. "Think like an accountant," Dad said. "You'll pay about $300 for this eight-week old pup—not a lot of money. Yet for that sum you get a purebred dog that will deliver twelve of the most pleasurable years of hunting you'll ever have. That's just $25 a year. There isn't a hunter worth his salt who doesn't spend four times that on beer and soft drinks."

He held the pup gently in two large hands and continued, "How much could you save cutting corners? Ten bucks a year? Isn't it stupid to risk a few bucks on something you might regret? Only the best pup you can lay your hands on can guarantee happy days and pleasant memories. Twelve years is a sizable slice out of your life."

CHAPTER FOUR

Picking Your Pup

In summer California lives up to its nickname. From the Oregon border to San Diego the flatland and foothills are a brilliant golden-brown. In the spring you see the other side of the coin. Then Black Point, looking toward San Francisco 40 miles to the south, is as bright as Ireland, its runs surrounded by fields of green, knee-high grass.

And in spring there is a special sense of excitement. In our kennels a new generation of pups is coming into a world they cannot yet see. The first litters of the season whimper and nuzzle their mothers. This could be the perfect time to find the pup you've been looking for.

If you've decided on a breed and narrowed the sources to two or three kennels, you've come a long way. The difficult part is nearly over. You need only inspect the breeding facilities, sample a few litters, make a choice, and wait for the pup you want to become old enough to come home. It is a federal regulation—and often a city or county ordinance as well—that a pup cannot be separated from its littermates until it is eight weeks old. That is not an arbitrary age. Not until the eighth week is a pup old enough to sample life on its own.

All pups are cuddly and cute, and appearance is not much help when you're making a final choice; but there are other ways to sort through a litter. In a good kennel every pup will have been socialized and most will be bold enough for training purposes. How do you select one pup and one kennel over another? For me, one deciding factor is genealogy. The sire and dam with the best field-dog background generally produce the best pups.

THE PEDIGREE

Although a pedigree is nothing more than a genealogical report, it can tell you a lot if you take time to examine it. The much-cherished paper is supposed to indicate the amount of class and instinct an animal offers, and in a way it does. More mercenary breeders believe that any canine with a "champion" or two in the background is superior to a dog lacking high-blown antecedents, and this revelation is expected to lull you into parting with a few extra bucks. This is not always a sound move. Sometimes parents and grandparents are the wrong kind of champions. Sometimes a pedigree warns the hunter, "Don't buy me!"

A pedigree simply lists the names of the pup's sire and dam, their parents, grandparents, and so on. It also includes the name of the kennel or breeder. It implies nothing more, although unscrupulous breeders may try to tell you that if one or two ancestors were champions the pup will automatically inherit their finest qualities. A pedigree does not guarantee that any ancestor had qualities worth passing on—and, indeed, that they actually were passed along. The scroungiest mutt might have a similar paper if someone cared to uncover its history.

CHAMPIONS

I've mentioned that a purebred dog can earn sufficient points to be ranked as a champion through active participation in AKC and other events. A champion that has won its points in AKC bench shows is indicated by "CH." "OTCH" indicates that the Kennel Club has awarded the animal the title "Obedience Trial Champion," generally an indoor competition. Neither involves the tracking of game, and both normally indicate a bench-show dog.

I'll be the first to admit these are important honors. To earn them a dog has to be better trained than the average and must exhibit superior conformation, patience, and endurance. I would not imply that either type of champion is not worth its salt. But neither bench shows nor obedience trials have anything to do with field work. On the show circuit the emphasis is on an animal's physical appearance, not its hunting instincts. The events are seldom held out of doors and do not test either a dog's ability or desire to find game.

Certainly, appearance is important—the animal should conform to breed, have no physical defects, and look good enough for a man to be proud of—

but a dog's reservoir of hunting instincts is far more essential in field work. If a pup does not have an adequate measure of the will to hunt, no amount of training can help him find his first pheasant.

A background of field championships can be extremely important. A field champion is indicated by "F.C." or "FLD.CH.", and the title can be earned in only one way: in active outdoor competition locating and retrieving live birds under hunting conditions. There are a number of other championships that can also be important. You'll find them as shorthand notations on the pedigree. "AM.C" means "Amateur Field Champion," which means the dog could have been professionally or owner trained but was handled by its owner or another amateur during competition. "NC." means "National Champion. "CFC." stands for "Canadian Field Champion." "DC." means a dual champion, a dog that was both field and bench champ. "DRC". means "dual regional champion." Any of these titles means the dog has better than average hunting training and experience.

If you consider "instincts" to be the result of genetic input, then the closer these ratings come to the pup's generation, the more bearing they will have. If the sire and dam were field champions, there is a good chance a pup will inherit a full measure of those qualities. But if a lone FLD.Ch. is as remote as the great-grandparents, its impact is greatly diminished. In general the sire and dam have the greatest genetic impact (experts say about 50% of the total input). The four grandparents contribute about 25%, and by the fifth generation (which includes the input of sixteen dogs), antecedents contribute no more than 6%. If you think one or two champion ratings among eight (fourth generation) or sixteen pups (fifth generation) does much for the bloodlines, you are an optimist.

If you opt for a background of field championships, they should either be numerous or come as close to your pup's generation as possible. There can be a sprinkling of bench champions as well without detracting from the animal's hunting abilities, but championships of any kind are not essential. I'd choose a pup with a nonchampionship background as readily as one with field championship heritage if the nonchampion parents were proven hunters. In every case I'd avoid a dog with a straight bench-show background.

FOCUS ON THE LITTER

You should be able to tell many things by inspecting the litter, although you'll never find support for the myths old-time hunters cherish. A good kennel master will never let a litter develop its own hierarchy—which is the way "pecking orders," "Alpha pups," and other communities of wild animals based on "survival of the fittest" develop. From the moment hunting pups are whelped it is their future to interact with humans, and a conscientious breeder begins handling his pups early. These are the first stages of socialization. They are important.

When I sell a litter, I want my pups to be as equal as possible. I want each to have a chance to become a bold bird dog. If there are psychological problems—and I've learned to spot many of them at three or four weeks—I'll give the insecure and regressive pups extra attention.

Consider the litter of German Wirehairs I've mentioned before. One male was noticeably more cautious and shy than the others. For two weeks I removed the pup from its littermates each day and played with him for a few minutes. Before the litter was sold it was impossible to tell which had been the shy pup. As I write, that animal is six months old and its owner insists the dog is a "tiger." If you find a litter with marked character differences, the trainer has probably not spent sufficient time with them.

And this underlines an important truth. Although no pup is a clone, although intelligence varies, and although some personality traits are inherited, you should be able to select any pup in a litter with confidence. If previous choices have reduced the selection, relax: the fact that only two or three pups remain shouldn't matter. Similarly, if the kennel owner suggests one or two pups over the others you should trust his judgment.

MALE OR FEMALE?

Since the Garden of Eden, the question of sexual superiority has been with us, and there is no quick, easy answer. There should be no difference in intensity or hunting abilities between male and female dogs, though some hunters are prejudiced toward one sex. There are some who insist that the female has more intuition, that she can "sense" your moods and thus has an edge; but this has never been proven. For every hunter who agrees, there is another who doesn't. Male pups are "macho," which does give them a special character; but by the time field training is completed, most males will become as tractable and easy to handle as females. Even so, the argument continues and the decision remains a personal one.

Even Dad has an opinion—almost. He says, "Personally, I like females. In the wild females do most of the hunting. I like 'em for that reason, but I'll admit, the final choice depends on the individual dog."

In the final analysis there is only one important issue in relation to sex—procreation—and that may or may not be important. A female comes into her estrous cycle twice a year. Whether you breed or not, the season is a difficult one unless the bitch is spayed. During the estrous cycle the unspayed huntress must be kept in a stout run—one that she cannot escape from and that no male can break into. You should not take a bitch in heat hunting. She can disrupt a shoot faster than a bottle-happy drunk, and in many clubs (though not at Black Point) females in season are "verboten." If a female is bred, a step not to be considered lightly, you face a host of problems. Never breed a female because you think it might be fun. It can be a fascinating, exciting hobby, but it is also exacting, demanding, and damn hard work. You begin with the problem of finding the right male, continue with the necessity for whelping facilities and prenatal care, and end with the difficulty of disposing of the pups. Not every sportsman may see your little ones as possessing the same great future you predict. The final ignominy is to be forced to give them away. "Priceless" but free purebreds are never appreciated as much as those one has to pay for.

WHAT TO LOOK FOR

(See Illustration 14.)

Barring obvious deformities, there is no way to predict, at eight weeks, conformation or such genetic problems as hip dysplasia, but in other ways a young pup is like a crystal ball. If there is a marked difference in the character of pups in a litter, choose the boldest animal, the one with the active tail and curious character. He should make a stout, sound hunter. Disposition is also important, and the better the disposition, the easier the dog is to handle. But you must remember that at eight weeks evidence of boldness, intelligence, and disposition are fleeting at best. Young pups sleep a lot, and one curled up in a corner now may become a pack leader in a couple of hours. Pups with obvious deformities should have been removed before the litter was offered for sale.

Be sure the animal's eyes are clear and bright, that its bite is even, that the teeth meet properly. Slight discrepancies can be acceptable, but excesses should be avoided. The coat should be clear and soft. The size of the chest cavity is important. Some dogs, such as Irish Setters, are naturally large-chested—and in all breeds a deep chest is best. Overall size is not as important as some breeders insist. Assuming hunting instincts of equal intensity, a small dog can develop into a sound hunter as rapidly as a larger one.

Many trainers place importance on the legs, and in broad terms I agree. As with an athlete, good legs are basic and straight; long front legs that reach out to pull in the ground, along with powerful back legs to push off, add up to a swift runner. Other breeders believe that a dog with slightly bowed or cow-hocked legs makes the best hunter because its legs have a "natural" spring. They say it gives the dog greater speed and a beautiful gait. I do not agree. Hunting upland game is not a footrace. Speed is of secondary importance.

Stamina is also important, although there is no way you can spot it in a pup. It is an inherited trait. If the mother and father conform to breed and are of sound, hard-running stock, the pup probably has it too. Stamina, another word for hard-hunting characteristics, comes from heart, guts, and intensity. If a pup lacks stamina he tires long before a day of hunting ends.

There is as much argument over color as there is over any factor. In general, a dark-colored dog reacts to intense sun faster than a light-colored one because its coat absorbs more heat. If hunters could select any color, most would pick light tan (because it camouflages best in dry fields) or white (because it reflects the sun); but specific patterns and color combinations are part of every accepted breed standard, and unless you have some strong reason for opposing it, choose a pup with coloring common to its breed. The animal will be worth more and can be used for breeding. An off-color dog cannot. Finally, though color has no effect on instincts or ability, a strangely colored animal is bound to be the butt of numerous jokes.

EARLY TESTING

(See Illustration 15.)

If you are interested in testing a young pup, you can try a few simple, easy tests before you buy. Separate a pup from the litter and place it in a quiet place. Clap your hands. Does the pup come quickly, its tail up? Does it lick your hand? Gently roll the pup onto its back. Restrain it gently with one hand on its chest. Does the pup struggle to right itself? Does it submit? Does it relax? Try petting the dog for 20 to 30 seconds. Does the pup growl? Or does it lick your hand and squirm? Finally, with two hands beneath the belly, raise the pup above the ground for a few seconds. Does it resist? Growl? Or does it relax and submit? Pups that continually struggle and bite are probably aggressive, dominant animals. They may not like people and could be hard-headed and difficult to train. Those that submit too readily are often shy, regressive pups. They will require an extra effort to build confidence and may have inherited traits you'll never eliminate. Those in the middle are probably the better adjusted, confident with people and eager to learn.

GUARANTEE

Many reputable kennels offer long- and short-term guarantees. In the short-term, normally a period of one or two weeks, you'll be able to return a pup for a full refund or replacement—if the animal is not as advertised, if it doesn't fit into your life, or if a member of your family cannot tolerate it. The kennel should also guarantee that the animal is free of congenital diseases. Since neither you nor the kennel master can predict these, that guarantee should be good for a year or more. Hip dysplasia is an example. If you spot it two years down the line, the kennel should willingly replace the pup.

On the other hand, if the animal is healthy when you buy it, the kennel is not responsible for diseases, injuries, or health problems contracted when it reaches your home. If the pup has been properly wormed and later develops worms, becomes ill, dies, or is injured, you are responsible for the animal and all related veterinary bills. A kennel may ask you to sign a memorandum or agreement to be certain you understand the way in which these responsibilities are divided.

COMING HOME

Before you accept delivery of your pup, make an appointment with your veterinarian. If you don't have one, ask a friend for a referral or call your local American Veterinary Medical Association headquarters. Take your pup for an immediate checkup including heart and lungs and order any shots that may be Required. I prefer a doctor who specializes in hunting dogs, though most general practitioners should be competent.

Young pups have an immunity to disease that comes from their mother's milk. It begins at birth and lasts ten to fourteen weeks, gradually losing strength. At six to eight weeks most kennels begin a series of procedures to supplement the weakening natural immunity and to protect the pup. These include vaccinations and worming.

Temporary and permanent vaccines are used. As their name implies, temporary vaccinations last a short time, generally a matter of weeks. "Permanent" shots are good for one, two, or three years. Young pups are given temporary shots as their natural immunity weakens. These are later replaced by permanent shots. As a rule, the first permanent shots are given in the third month.

Be sure to ask the kennel owner to list all vaccinations and medication the pup has received. Write the name of each shot, the date it was given, and the manufacturer's name on a piece of paper. Don't trust your memory. Several shots have names that sound alike, and not all manufacturers' formulas are indentical. Next, add the date when the pup was wormed. Such information helps your veterinarian protect your pup. It is also a good idea to collect a sample of the pup's stool and have your vet check it for signs of worms. Reputable kennels worm all pups as a matter of routine, but many back-yard breeders do not. It pays to be certain.

Be sure to ask your vet about heartworms, especially if there are mosquitoes in your area. The worms have become a serious problem in many parts of the U.S. Protective medication is available in pill and liquid form. Pills are usually easier to administer. Also, ask your doctor about supplemental vitamins and calcium. Some feel a good diet is all a pup needs, and others insist supplements add a measure of security.

SPAYING AND NEUTERING

The decision to leave your pup as nature intended or to have the organs of procreation altered is not an easy one, but unless you have a strong motive for breeding, I suggest that you consider spaying (for a female) and neutering (for a male). Neither procedure affects an animal's ability to hunt, and there are many reasons sufficiently compelling to consider it. The procedure is much less expensive than caring for unwanted or unexpected litters. Those who insist that a young female will "settle down better" after one litter are wrong. Neutering a male will diminish neither his ability to hunt nor to protect a home, and the procedure does not make an animal lazy or fat. Over-feeding alone is responsible for that. In addition, many localities offer cut-rate licenses for altered animals.

A female has her season twice a year, though a male dog is continually ready. An active one can easily sire 750 litters during his lifetime, and most will be unplanned neighborhood escapades that have nothing to do with advancing the breed. The serious sportsman should be willing to avoid these pregnancies. Neutering does. Macho men who wonder, "Sexual fulfillment is essential to my life, so how can I deny my dog?" are confusing apples with oranges. The human sexual response is based as much on emotional chemistry as on anything else. In a dog it is strictly hormonal, and an altered animal will not notice the change.

THE FIRST DAY

Timing is important when you bring your pup home. Try to arrive when the household is quiet. Avoid an afternoon when your wife hosts her bridge club or an evening when a party is scheduled. Even the soundest pup needs quiet time to adjust to the sudden changes in its world.

If you have young children, pick up all toys small enough for the pup to chew, swallow, or destroy. Remove your own shoes and clothing. Your pup can be taught to obey and not chew wearing apparel, but not on the first day. If you remove temptation, you'll have less to correct. And if you have a baby, be sure to keep pup and child separated. In time each will grow to appreciate the other, but again, not at eight weeks.

And remember, a number of house plants are dangerous. Philodendrons can make a puppy sick. Crown of thorns, *Euphorbia splendens*, is extremely poisonous, and *Dieffenbachia*, or dumb cane, causes intense pain. These plants should be placed out of reach of your pup. Christmas trees, ornaments, and lights are also dangerous.

CHAPTER FIVE

A Proper Diet

At this tender age some things about your pup may seem uncertain—his conformation, the depth of his intensity, and whether or not he has a good "bird nose"—but there is one thing you can count on: the minute the little fellow arrives he will be hungry. Adequate nourishment keeps your pup happy, healthy, and growing; and veterinarians say day in and day out he'll need 43 nutrients, each in its proper proportion.

Wild canines get most of what they need from their kill. The vitamin-rich intestines are consumed first because the nutrients there are vital. Next they devour muscles for protein and bones for calcium, and if they've caught a bird, the feathers add important trace minerals. Missing nutrients are found in grasses, fruits, and berries. When salt is required, wild canines find it in the earth.

Obviously, a man-made dog food has a lot to live up to, but most of today's popular brands do a good job. If there's a problem, it lies with the outrageous advertising with which manufacturers bombard us. Each spends an enormous sum trying to get you to buy their food. But disregard the bizarre statements and forget foods that smell like Irish stew or look like a New York strip, and you'll discover most reputable kibbled foods are good for your dog.

ALL-MEAT DIET

Some dog lovers insist that since canines are carnivores, a one hundred-percent meat diet is perfect. Not so. Meat lacks important essentials, including calcium, and a bird dog needs about 50 mg of calcium per pound of muscle, about 6,000 mg for an average animal. To get that amount from meat, your dog would have to consume more than 100 pounds each day. Young dogs can utilize more of the available protein, calories, and fat found in meat than can adults, but even for them an exclusive meat diet is dangerous. It can cause severe nutritional and digestive problems.

Commerical dog foods are commonly made of grains or combinations of grains and meats. Either is acceptable. Although a pup is descended from a tribe of notorious carnivores, the "meat instinct" is long gone; and as far as today's canine body is concerned, the important point is whether or not the food contains essential nutrients in the proper proportions. For example, soy beans, which originated in China, have been an important source of protein for humans for centuries. They are equally good for pups. Other grains supply important carbohydrates and are also acceptable. The problem with canine diets is not the source but the balance. If an ingredient is available in the wrong quantity, too little or too much, it may inhibit the assimilation of other components.

Let's take a quick look at today's dog food. It is available in four styles.

SEMIMOIST FOODS. These foods were probably devised to appeal to humans. The group includes stuff that looks like beef cubes, bones, burgers, and hash. Dogs don't care what food looks like. They are concerned with the way it smells and tastes. Read the labels. Most of these foods are loaded with sugar and chemical additives. While manufacturers insist nothing harmful is included, I avoid the entire group.

CANNED FOODS. Canned foods run the gamut from one hundred-percent meat to combinations of meat by-products and grains. The best are nutritionally balanced: the worst are as bad as bargain kibbles. Many are seriously lacking in essentials. Some contain 50% to 75% water. Pound for pound they are more expensive than most choices, and aside from a questionable convenience, have little to recommend them. I avoid these, too.

BISCUITS AND TREATS. Cookies, biscuits, and similar products are often shaped like bones and paw prints. Even so, they make excellent snacks. The large, hard biscuits are perfect for dental hygiene. I give them to a pup when it is teething and to an adult dog to help keep its gums healthy. Some snacks are fortified with vitamin and mineral supplements and are doubly recommended. To discover a product's composition, check the box. Treats should never be fed in place of a good dog food.

KIBBLED. The category includes any dry food—chunks, cubes, meal, and such unlikely extruded forms as stars, circles, and squares. Brands such as ANF, Carnation, Gaines, Iams, Ralston-Purina, Science Diet, and Waynes' can be considered nutritionally balanced. Special "puppy-chow" kibbles provide higher protein levels than adult mixes and should be given during the first ten to twelve months of a puppy's life. I recommend adult-formula dry foods thereafter. Some kennel masters switch products from time to time just to keep a dog from being bored, but at Black Point, I've discovered that if the food is tasty the dog will down it happily no matter how many times it's served. If you have any doubts about nutrition, compare ingredients. These are always listed on the bags.

Popular brands are available in a range of sizes from two-pound boxes to fifty-pound bags. As a rule the larger the size, the more economical the cost per pound. Keeping a large bag in a dry place, away from insects and mice, is the recommended approach. Protected, a bag should remain fresh for months. I keep ours in a covered plastic container. You can find good kibbled foods in supermarkets, feed stores and pet shops.

I avoid generic and bargain brands because the quality can vary. Many are not as nutritious as their labels indicate. A study conducted by Dr. Thomas Huber at the University of Georgia proved that puppies fed a diet of low-priced dog foods suffered from numerous health problems including stunted growth. Test puppies fed national brands gained an average of 21 pounds during a ten-week trial, while pups eating low-priced food gained no more than 16. And more to the point, puppies fed nationally advertised brands required just 4.45 pounds of food for each pound gained, while pups fed low-priced mixes needed nearly 6 pounds of food for the same increase. Obviously, I avoid these foods.

Dozens of low-priced generic dog foods have cropped up in grocery stores across the nation, some at half the price of major brands. Many advertise that they are "100-percent nutritionally complete," and this claim plus low prices make them appealing. But according to Dr. Huber many have not been tested on animals and the quality varies from bag to bag.

FEEDING SCHEDULE. Dog owners who work at night often prefer to keep dry food and water continually available, but others like to feed on a schedule. If you are a "feed-all-day" person, a self-feeder is a good idea, but a regular schedule makes more sense for several reasons. A dog's life runs best on routine, and when it is fed on schedule you know exactly how much your animal eats. If the pup is losing its appetite, you can tell instantly, and if it does not consume its portion in fifteen minutes or so, you may assume you are overfeeding. Scheduled feeding also means that the pup's elimination will be as regular as its food, a helpful point when housebreaking a young animal. When you take a dog for a romp immediately after eating, it's ready to eliminate. Believe me, that beats cleaning—and recleaning—a run.

You should always serve portions according to an animal's size, but the charts in books and on bags of dog food are only suggestions. Eating habits vary. Some pups dine fast, some take their food slowly. Some inhale a dish, virtually swallowing their food whole; others carefully chew every bite. These characteristics are an expression of the canine personality and probably reflect early litter conditions. A small, nondominant pup surrounded by greedy brothers and sisters has to eat fast to get its share, and this habit can be carried into later life. Metabolism also plays a part. Some pups burn calories quickly, some do not. The only way you'll discover the proper quantity is by watching your dog and the way it eats. If, after fifteen or twenty minutes, food remains, reduce the portion. Be sure your pup seems satisfied. If it wolfs its food and wants more, feed larger portions. If the pup seems ill or lethargic, it may need supplemental vitamins and minerals or even special high-protein foods. Check with your veterinarian. Then check your dog. Your final judgment should be based on the way it looks. Is it fat or thin? If it seems chubby, reduce portions. If it seems thin, increase the feedings.

A good kennel master keeps water continually available once the pup is weaned, and you should do the same. If at first the little fellow makes a mess, stepping in the dish, splashing and playing, either substitute a heavy ceramic dish that cannot be tipped, or place the water dish in a small cardboard box. The box will confine spills and should keep the dog from making drinking a game. You can also try light discipline. Each time you see the pup playing in its water say "no" or "don't" (whichever word you are using) and remove the animal from the dish.

FEEDING A PUP

An eight-week-old pup has a very small stomach and cannot stock up as an adult dog can. It needs to be fed several times a day. Some breeders like a four-times schedule—breakfast, lunch, supper, and a late-night snack—but I prefer to feed slightly larger portions three times a day. The schedule is easier on me and satisfactory for the pup.

When a pup arrives, use the brand of food (or formula) then fed at the kennel and, after a week or so, wean the animal to the formula below. Do this by combining portions of my formula with the kennel's food until the pup is eating my formula exclusively. An abrupt change generally causes diarrhea.

In the early months (at Black Point it is from weaning through the tenth or twelfth month) I feed young pups a special combination of commercial meat loaf, kibbled puppy food, yogurt, and cottage cheese. Young pups need a high-protein diet, and the meat loaf and kibble supply protein, the cottage cheese has calcium and more protein, and the yogurt adds lactobacillus, an enzyme which improves digestion. I realize many veterinarians feel the addition of lactobacillus is not required since it is found naturally in the puppy's stomach, but I believe a little extra is not out of line. I use chicken loaf, generally available canned or frozen. Years ago I switched to chicken because it readily digests and produces better stools than beef. Chicken loaves are usually made of ground necks and are rich in protein and vitamins. In the west, Breeder's Choice produces a good chicken mix in five-pound frozen loaves. It can be thawed, cut into serving portions, and served cooked or raw. Tyrell (made in Seattle) has a canned loaf that is also good. You'll find other fine regional products around the country.

Straight kibble is never enough. Whether a pup or an adult, a dog needs meat as well. If you don't like chicken you can buy special ground beef at many supermarkets. Some call them "puppy-burgers," pet meat made from the ends of beef. This, too, can be served cooked or raw. If you prefer beef use the same proportions as those given for chicken.

At Black Point I cook the loaves, then combine kibble, yogurt, and cottage cheese in the portions below. I divide the cooked meat into single serving portions and freeze any not used the first day. You can do the same thing. Baggies are just right for a single feeding.

For an average pup, say a German Wirehair, I'd combine two tablespoons of meat loaf, one cup of puppy kibble, one tablespoon of yogurt, the same amount of cottage cheese, and water. At Black Point pups are fed this three times a day. If your pup is larger or smaller, like a Brittany or Cocker, vary the portions accordingly. In ratio form, that translates to ¾ puppy kibble, ¼ cheese, yogurt, and meat mix, and water. Check with your veterinarian on the advisability of adding supplements. Some doctors feel vitamins and minerals should be added and others do not. I rarely use them.

I feed this mix to my pups three times a day until they are five months old. At that time the pup will probably be nibbling at one of its meals, perhaps not even finishing it. This is the signal to convert to two feedings a day. The two portions should provide a little more food than the three did, and one meal should be smaller than the other. I feed one cup in the morning and two at night.

If your dog is a fussy eater, you can only blame yourself. Occasionally a canine boarding at Black Point will stage a hunger strike to see if it can force me to provide some special food. I refuse to pamper it, and if your dog tries, do not give in. Relent and your pup will end up demanding New York strip. Instead, feed it its regular meal. Keep the food in the dish for fifteen minutes then remove it. Offer nothing until the next scheduled feeding. If it refuses to eat again, withdraw the food after fifteen minutes and when the third meal comes repeat the offer. Provide fresh food each time. The most stubborn dog will usually be willing to eat the third time around. Before attempting such drastic measures, however, be certain your dog is not refusing food because it is ill.

Continue the two-a-day feeding schedule until the pup is at least ten months old. Remember, your pup still needs more food than it will as an adult and complete nutrition is important because it is still growing. At this age field dogs need a lot of calcium since bones are maturing and permanent teeth are developing. Check with your vet to see if supplements can help.

From the tenth to twelfth month the pup is approaching maturity, but the operative word is "approaching." Some breeds may not be fully mature until they are sixteen to eighteen months old, though growth slows after a dog reaches its first birthday. At twelve months I reduce feedings to one a day.

A dog on a single feeding schedule can be fed morning, noon, or night but, unless you work a night shift, I suggest the evening. It is not wise to feed in the morning, and then leave your dog alone for eight or nine hours. It receives no exercise and the stool remains in the run a full day. It is better to feed your dog in the evening. Stool can be removed before you go to bed or, better, walk your pup after feeding and it will have an opportunity to eliminate as it exercises.

Do not change from two meals to one abruptly. Reduce the morning portions gradually, and when the first feeding is virtually eliminated, substitute a milk-bone treat in the morning if you think the animal cannot face a day on an empty stomach. I cannot do this at the kennel, there are too many dogs; but many of those I board receive a morning biscuit at home.

At the same time, I wean the pup from its puppy formula to adult foods. At Black Point this means a shift to adult formula kibbled food with cooked chicken added. You can buy chicken necks and cook and grind them yourself, or you can use prepared chicken loaves, the same suggested for the puppy formula. Substitute one-quarter cooked chicken for kibbled food.

Again, this is a ratio designed for most, not all, dogs. You may want to vary it for your dog in relation to size and season. In summer, when a hunting dog is not working, it does not need as much meat. In the winter, when temperatures drops and the dog is hunting, increase the amount of meat. A dog needs more body fat then.

Make any change gradual so it will not upset the animal's digestive system. If you have been feeding vitamin supplements, you can probably stop these as well. Some vets suggest the addition of cod liver or vegetable oil. Oil is especially useful in the winter when a heated house or run may cause dry skin. Cod liver oil is my first choice because it is highest in vitamins A and D.

A LITTLE BACKGROUND

The origins of commercial pet food in the United States can be traced to 1860 when a traveling lightning-rod salesman, James Spratt of Cincinnati, invented "dog cakes" for his pet Cocker. A combination of white meal, vegetables, beet root, and meat, the cakes were sold successfully across the country. Canned pet food was introduced in 1922 but remained unpopular for nearly four decades. It came into its own in the late '50s when three major cereal manufacturers, General Foods, Quaker Oats, and Ralston-Purina; two soup companies, Campbell and Lipton; one candy company, Mars; and one dairy, Carnation, gambled on the market. Today the seven dominate.

Americans spend more than $4 billion annually on pet foods, about four times the amount earmarked for international aid, five times the amount spent on cancer research, and nine times more than the American Heart Association has had in its 35-year history. Some industry analysts say the boom is due to the size of the market, and according to statistics, there are a lot of hungry mouths—42 million dogs and 25 million cats.

There was a time when pet foods were not as reliable as they are now. Initially, they were made to please owners and provided very little nutrition, but in recent decades serious research has brought major changes and, most vets agree, a general improvement in quality. Experts recommend that a diet for a medium-sized dog contain 16%–22% protein, and research has helped eliminate such mistakes as Alpo's "all-meat" food, a product widely advertised twenty years ago. That vintage Alpo had almost twice the recommended amount of protein. After protests by numerous veterinarians, it was removed from the market and reintroduced in a new formula.

While most veterinarians insist current products are safe and nutritionally balanced, not every expert agrees. Dr. Larry Chaulk, a well-known veterinarian in San Bruno, California, is a vocal opponent. For some time he has appeared on West Coast radio charging that many pet foods are inadequate.

Dr. Chaulk claims that about the time pet foods began adding sodium chloride to semimoist foods, the incidence of feline hyperthyroid disease increased. He adds that meatlike canned and semimoist foods could be considered dangerous because they include parts of the lung, spleen, kidney, brain, stomach, and intestines, organs Chaulk insists are heavy with concentrations of toxic wastes and pesticide residues accumulated while the animals graze.

Dr. Glen Brown, a professor of nutrition and food sciences at the University of Massachusetts, disagrees. He says animal parts found in pet foods are not known accumulators of hormones and pesticides. He insists commercial dog foods do not contain more than the required maintenance amounts of protein. But Dr. Chaulk counters by saying, "There is no definitive way to be sure."

Part of the problem appears to stem from a lack of clear pet food labeling regulations. The AAFCO (Association of American Feed Control Officers) was established in 1909 to provide uniformity. To one degree or another it governs pet food labeling, and some say it is controlled by pet food manufacturers. True or not, its regulations are often vague and seem to favor the manufacturer. Certainly AAFCO-approved labels can be misleading. The beef in a "beef dinner" or the chicken in a "chicken buffet" is often less than 25% of the content. It is the imprecise terms "dinner" and "buffet" that allow that. Without them the manufacturers would be forced to use at least 95% of the ingredient named.

A FEW DO'S AND DON'TS

Here are few diet tips I've learned from experience:

1. Do not feed table scraps. Your dog will not be heartbroken if it cannot share your food. Scraps can cause gastric problems, and if a dog eats highly spiced foods long enough, it can be difficult to convert it to dog foods—which are blander but better for your pup.

2. Avoid *raw* eggs. They prevent the dog's body from absorbing an essential B vitamin, biotin, and several important minerals. They do not make the coat shiny or soft and do not improve the skin.

3. Fat is not a sign of health in pups. A sleek dog with a thin layer of fat is the goal. Slim down the butterballs!

4. It has been centuries since dogs were wild carnivores, and they do *not* need all- or mostly-meat diets. Excess protein robs a dog of other nutritionally important elements.

5. A dog, if it is healthy, will not intentionally starve. A pup may suffer a temporary loss of appetite for a number of reasons, but if a dog refuses to eat for more than 48 hours, take it to a vet. If the refusal is coupled with other symptoms, vomiting or diarrhea, for example, do not wait. See a vet immediately.

6. Worms and related parasites are not caused by sugar, though candy is

bad for dogs because it causes tooth decay and an imbalance in blood sugar. Some hunters will share a candy bar with an adult dog in the field, and that may not be a bad idea. The sugar can provide a quick burst of energy on those summer days when the combination of heat and humidity drains a dog's energy quickest. This is the only time one might feed some candy to his dog, although I do not do this with my pups.

7. Not every bone is safe for a dog since domestic canines have lost much of the ability to digest bone particles. Though bones promote chewing and offer little more than temporary solace, they can be helpful for a teething dog and diverting for a chronic chewer. If you insist on giving your dog a bone, the only safe type I know is a leg bone of beef. I've discussed that in another chapter.

CHAPTER SIX

Genetic and Health Problems

Your pup is an unfortunate heir to a host of problems: a lengthy list of viral and bacterial illnesses and a number of internal and external parasites. Happily, the dog can be protected against most.

Before leaving the litter the little fellow should have been wormed and given vaccinations that protect it from a number of dangers including distemper. If this hasn't been done you should either refuse to accept the animal or take it immediately to a veterinarian. I would be suspicious of a kennel that did not provide this protection routinely.

If an eight-week-old pup can be readily protected from the world's viral and bacterial dangers, it sadly has less chance against problems its parents may have passed along. Defects that could keep a dog from becoming the hunter you expect—deformed bones, over or undersized organs, and deformed features—are not as easy to deal with. There is no gold-plated natal warranty, and the most common genetic defects cannot be diagnosed while a pup is young.

CONFORMATION

A breed standard is only an ideal, a description of what the perfect dog *might* be. Few canines, even champions, do more than come reasonably close, and genetic defects can be defined as any marked deviation from an accepted norm, in a word, deformities. As long as a dog is bred for hunting rather than show, does it really matter? I believe it does. A man likes to have a pup that looks good, one other hunters can admire; and proper conformation is certainly an important part. Genetic defects can affect the way a pup looks, runs, and hunts. Slight deviations may not be important, major changes are.

Pups are not made from molds. A stylish, good-looking dog is the sum of his parts. No piece should be out of scale. The front and back legs, chest, body, and head should seem designed for that particular animal. Legs that look right on one dog may appear out of place on another. For most upland breeds the body should be neither compact nor elongated. The coat should be full and glossy (and wiry if that is called for). Though standards may require feathers along the legs, I prefer a pup that is lightly feathered. Excessive feathering can cause problems in a field heavy with burrs and cover.

The pup should also have a good, deep chest, one that allows plenty of room for the heart, lungs, and other organs. A full chest lets a dog run farther without tiring.

Field dogs are runners and should have straight legs. The length depends on standards. The front leg must not bend out at the elbow and should not be splayed, a condition called "fiddle feet." With either, the dog will probably be a slower runner. Be sure to check the toes. They should be close together. Dogs with close-set toes have fewer problems with pebbles and thorns. Toes that are splayed or widely separated are called "paper feet." They are easily snagged and broken. Then watch the rear legs in action. If the legs are so close they strike together as a pup runs, the knocking will affect speed, endurance, and appearance. Dogs with legs and feet that splay outward are "cow-hocked."

The head should be full-sized with a shape proper for the breed. A Brittany head, for example, should never be apple-shaped or rounded, or with an indented stop. For some, and German Pointers are one, a Roman nose is perfect. On others, and the Brittany is again an example, this shape should be avoided. The nostrils should open wide for easy breathing and sharp scenting. Tight nostrils should be avoided. The eyes should be wide and alert. A "pop-eye" should be especially avoided in dogs that face briars. The skull should be well chiseled so that the lower lid is not pulled back, creating a pocket that can catch seeds and dust.

Eyelid defects can affect a number of breeds. The lid's function is to protect the eye, to spread a film of moisture over it, and to facilitate drainage. In some cases the lid is malformed, causing problems. *Ectropion* is an outward rolling or drooping of the lid. It can sometimes be controlled by flushing the eye. Serious conditions must be repaired with surgery. *Entropion* is a reverse condition, an inward rolling of the lid. The eyelash rubs against the eyeball, irritating the pupil. Symptoms include a rubbing of the eyes with the paw. The problem may be congenital or acquired and is found in Labs, German Pointers, Irish Setters and Goldens. It is most often corrected with surgery.

Then check the bite. The teeth should be straight with well-joined incisors that match, giving the pup a true scissor bite. While you can accept a minor misalignment, a substantial over- or undershot jaw should be avoided. For most breeds the ears should be firm, not floppy. Short, "leafy" ears are also to be avoided. The lips should be tight to the muzzle, the upper one slightly overlapping the lower.

GENETIC PROBLEMS

The worse genetic problem is hip dysplasia, a defect normally found in breeds weighing more than twenty-five pounds. Some animals are more likely to be affected than others, and experts say that in certain upland breeds as many as 50% of all pups have it. One veterinarian suggests that 75% of all Labs may develop it and perhaps 86% of all Goldens.

Though dysplasia is common, it is not readily understood. Basically, it is a defect that develops with age and affects the way the hip and leg bones interact. Medically it can be described as an abnormal development of the hip joint.

"In a dysplastic hip the socket is generally less concave and more shallow than normal," one expert told me. "When the ball-and-socket is abnormally formed, the working efficiency of the joint is lowered. Related ailments such as arthritis develop, reducing the usefulness of the animal."

The problem is most widespread among working and sporting breeds and becomes evident with age. Doctors do not know the cause: they think it may be partially caused by trauma—a bruise, subsequent inflammation, and increased fluid in the joints. They also feel some genetic predisposition is involved. Some feel it is not a congenital abnormality since dogs who develop it are born with apparently normal hips. It cannot be seen in very young pups, even with X ray, though clinical signs may appear as early as two to four months. The condition generally worsens during the first year. (See Illustration 17). Dogs affected by it may sway when walking or may run in a "bunny hop" with the hind legs working together. On the other hand, many dogs seem to get along without discomfort even when X rays reveal severely affected joints.

If your pup develops dysplasia, you may want to replace it, though if you've become emotionally involved you may not. I cannot give you an answer; but if you hunt, I feel you should use the best dog possible. A field dog with dysplasia is usually handicapped. It will only be able to hunt at speed for a few minutes and will probably be laid up for two or three days after. On the plus side, a dog with slow-developing dysplasia can often lead a long, useful life—as a pet. While there are no cures, there are practical measures that can ease an animal's pain, though seldom enough to allow it to continue hunting. Mild physical activity, walking, slow running, and even swimming are sometimes beneficial, and medication can bring temporary relief. A simple surgical procedure is often used. The muscle on the inner thigh (the pectineal muscle) is partially severed. This neither cures dysplasia nor repairs the damage, but often relieves the pain. A veterinarian can suggest the best procedure.

Though you cannot expect a breeder to predict whether a pup will or will not be affected, there is a substantial measure of protection available when you buy a pup. Since there is some kind of genetic link, you should be sure the sire and dam are free of the problem. To be absolutely certain, both parents should be OFA certified. A breeder can do this by sending an X ray of the bitch's and stud's hip to the Orthopedic Foundation for Animals, University of Missouri—Columbia, Columbia, MO 65211. For $15 foundation experts will certify the absence or presence of hip dysplasia, and before you buy a pup you should see that certification. Only dogs 24 months of age or older can qualify for an OFA breed registry number. Younger dogs will be evaluated by the foundation, but a "consultation report" only will be issued. Finally, the breeder should provide a written guarantee to replace the animal if dysplasia develops later.

There are a number of other possible defects you may wish to discuss with your veterinarian before purchasing a pup. Among them are these:

Idiopathic megasophagus—This is an inherited problem that affects a pup's ability to successfully swallow food. The throat or esophagus moves food along its length by contractions, and at the end a sphincter muscle relaxes enough to allow the food to enter the stomach. In some dogs this process does not occur. Eventually the dog vomits its food. The condition can be treated with medication, and while it affects a number of dogs it is most common in Cockers.

Glaucoma—Caused by an increase in pressure in the eye, the problem can be treated, sometimes with surgery and sometimes through medication. A number of breeds including the Cocker have reported a high incidence.

Other retinal problems—Some 48 breeds including the Irish Setter have progressive retinal problems that can affect vision later in life.

Testicles—Male pups occasionally have problems with testicles. In rare cases neither will drop, but more commonly, if there is a problem one testicle drops and the other does not. A check by a veterinarian can uncover this.

GENERAL HEALTH

Internal parasites common to canines are worms that live and often reproduce inside the canine body. They can be especially dangerous for a young pup since they absorb nutrition needed for growing tissue, teeth, and bones. Some directly siphon off blood, causing anemia.

Most worms are transferred via the stool of an infected dog, and just one egg can trigger an infestation. In formative stages parasites are extremely hardy. An egg can remain dormant long after all signs of the stool have vanished. A pup may become infected through its foot, as it walks over an area laden with dormant eggs. Worms can also be transmitted when a pup sniffs the stool of another dog. A pet owner may carry eggs from one kennel to another on his shoes. Some dogs eat the stools of other animals, and the source of infection in that case is obvious.

Other worms—tapeworms are an example—are transmitted by fleas. If a pup nibbles at its flea-infested fur and ingests one containing a tapeworm egg, it becomes infected.

Worms are not inevitable, though myths perpetuate the idea that they are. Dogs can be infected anyplace. Worms are as common in city dogs as in those raised in rural areas. Garlic is not the great worm-killer it is cracked up to be. It may kill a few roundworms but does nothing to de-worm an infected dog. Only medicated pills can do that. Pups should be wormed before they are sold, and stool samples should be rechecked two weeks after worming. Stools should also be rechecked every three or four months until a pup is fully grown, and then, once or twice a year for life.

Stools should always be checked by a veterinarian since a nonexpert can rarely spot worms. Do not try to treat a pup with home remedies. Each species of worm responds best to specific medication, and a veterinarian should examine the stool to make the diagnosis.

While diagnosis of specific infestations requires a specialist, general symptoms may offer an early warning.

1. Persistent diarrhea or a thin bowel movement. You may or may not see blood.
2. Excessive thirst.
3. The animal may be weak and listless.
4. The coat may be dry, rough, and coarse.
5. There may be drowsiness or loss of sleep.
6. There may also be a loss of vitality.
7. The dog may appear bloated with a fat, protruding stomach. The sign may be especially noted in puppies.

8. A pup may vomit, often with signs of worms in the vomitus.
9. A pup may also faint after vomiting or coughing.
10. There may be a loss of appetite or a lack of interest in food.
11. Or you may see the opposite, an increased interest in food without a sign of weight gain.
12. A loss of weight and dehydration.
13. A pup may chase its tail and bite its anus.
14. A pup may rub its body and hindquarters against the run.

If you suspect your pup has worms, take a fresh sample of its stool to your veterinarian. Fresh in this case means stool collected on the day of the visit, and a spoonfull or so in a plastic bag is plenty. The vet will verify the existence or lack of worms and, if found, will give you the proper medication. The medication will make the dog diarrheic and affect the worms so they release their hold. The purge literally flushes them out. If your dog has been constipated, be sure to tell the vet since most do not like to worm dogs in this condition. Be sure to get all instructions in writing. Follow them precisely.

Your pup can be wormed at home or by a veterinarian, and if you have open space there is little reason why you cannot do it yourself. Give the pills as recommended and leave the dog in a place where you can clean up the stool after it has been passed. If you have other dogs, isolate the pup. Clean the area thoroughly after all stool has been eliminated.

In most cases a veterinarian will ask for a follow-up sample in about two weeks. He may or may not give you additional medication. The life cycle of some worms requires a second worming.

Below are the most common worms and symptoms of their infestations:

COCCIDIA   Microscopic parasites or internal protozoa that cause an intestinal disease. Infestation can lead to substantial fluid loss and dehydration. Severe infestations can cause death.

FLUKES   These are not currently common since their primary host is fish. To prevent flukes, avoid feeding raw fish. Either cook all fish your pup consumes or avoid fish altogether; the latter is easy since pups are not natural fish eaters. When your dog is at a beach, keep him away from all catches, and especially from dead fish washed up on the shore.

HOOKWORM   The small worms are named for the hooks or anchors that are a part of their mouths. These are used to attach themselves to the intestines, both anchoring the worm to a territory and providing a way for it to absorb nutrition directly from the blood. Hookworms cause anemia, lowering a pup's resistance to other diseases. They can be transmitted by the mother before birth. The problem is commonly attributed to unsanitary kennel and breeding conditions.

TAPEWORMS   With long, pinkish, segmented bodies, tapeworms also attach themselves to the walls of the intestines where they absorb nourishment before a dog can utilize it. They weaken an adult, can be fatal to pups, and are difficult to cure since they bury their heads in the intestinal wall. A new worm can develop from any head even though its body has been removed. Tapeworms can be transmitted by fleas, the raw meat of wild game (especially rabbits), and fish. If your pup has fleas when you bring him home, ask your vet to check for tapeworms. Though difficult to detect, they can often be seen as tiny grainlike segments around the anus. Generally a pup must be left at the vet's for a full day of treatment.

WHIPWORM   A small, round, tapered worm that is found in the colon and cecus (similar to the human appendix), the whipworm is considered more serious, though not as persistent as tapeworm. It causes diarrhea and a consequent loss of blood and fluids. If not treated promptly, it can cause permanent intestinal injury.

EXTERNAL PARASITES

External parasites are defined as bugs that bite, and the list includes fleas, lice, mites, and ticks. All can transmit disease and are an annoyance your pup can do without. Though each is difficult to eradicate, a clean kennel, a clean house, and a clean dog go a long way toward that end.

FLEAS   Almost everyone knows about fleas. They can be transmitted from dog to dog and from dog to humans. A house dog with fleas will inevitably leave traces in the carpet and furniture. Fleas may be found anyplace on a dog's body but prefer the more hirsute areas—the tail, chest, and neck. They can be controlled with dips, soaps, sprays, and powders. When using the latter two, protect the dog's eyes. And protect yourself with rubber gloves.

Begin at the face, ears, and neck and apply the powder or spray slowly from head to tail. A good dip, such as HiLo's Original Dip, contains safe organic pesticides and is recommended. A professional groomer or your veterinarian can also treat your pup.

Once your dog has been treated, be certain to de-flea your house. Launder all canine bedding with a strong disinfectant or replace it with fresh material. Spray rugs and other areas a dog may have used, and finally, use a room fogger. The necessary materials are available from pet stores and veterinarians.

MITES   Mange is a skin disease caused by three species of mites, those that cause demodetic or follicular mange, those that cause sarcoptic mange, and the last, an ear mite that causes otodetic mange. All are very contagious. Scabs, bald spots, bloody pimples, and inflammations are certain signs. Medications are available from pet shops, and a veterinarian can offer a quick cure. Of the three, ear mange is the more dangerous since it can cause permanent damage. If you see a discharge coming from your dog's ear, or if the animal carries its head at an angle, have your vet take a look. He will take a scraping from the skin and examine it under a microscope. Mites can be removed with medication.

LICE   Lice are difficult to see. They are smaller than a pinhead, burrow into the skin, and extract blood. They can kill hair at the follicles, and an extreme attack can cause anemia. Canine lice can be transmitted to humans and may cause irritation, though they will not remain on a person.

Skin problems and hair loss can be signals, but since lice are small, the diagnosis will probably have to made by a veterinarian. They can be removed by a dip, spray, or powder.

TICKS   In comparison, ticks are the largest of all external parasites and can be readily seen. They pass through three stages, the first two growing and breeding, and the third on a host dog. In the first two they can be found in tall grasses, bushes, and cracks and crevices around a home. When ready to find a host, ticks move to high places where they can drop onto a passing animal. Once on their host they burrow their small heads into the skin and gorge on blood. When fully gorged, they can be red in color. Most ticks cause irritation, and a serious infestation can cause anemia. Some ticks carry dangerous Rocky Mountain Fever.

Commonly, only one or two ticks are found on a dog. They must be removed by hand, not with sprays or powders. Despite folklore that insists you can remove a tick by unscrewing it, twisting only separates the body from the head, causing infection. There is an easier way. Ticks breathe through their body. Soak a piece of cotton in alcohol and hold it against the tick. The tick will back up to move to another spot, and once you see its head, grasp the insect with tissue, cotton, or tweezers. Flush the creature down the drain or burn it, but never squeeze it for by doing so you run the risk of infection if its fluid should enter your blood system through a cut, scrape or sore.

Flea collars are effective against fleas and ticks and sprays, powders, and dips are excellent against fleas, ticks, lice and mites. It is a good idea to brush your dog after a day's romp since brushing dislodges fleas and ticks before they settle on the fur. In seasons of heaviest infestation, you may want to add a good powder. Incidentally, if you use a flea collar, keep it loose (with room for two fingers) since a tight collar can cause irritation. The collars should never be worn in a closed car. Chemical fumes created by the heat can build up enough to injure a dog.

VACCINATIONS AND DISEASE

Every field dog needs regular check-ups by a veterinarian and periodic inoculations as protection against the more common diseases. There are several kinds of protection. The first is a temporary immunity given to a pup by its mother. It comes through the milk and normally protects a pup during its first weeks of life. Older pups are protected by inoculations given by a veterinarian.

A temporary vaccination is sometimes given adult dogs as part of a treatment or to pups to provide short-term carry-over immunity. When you bring your pup home from the kennel, he will probably have received a series of temporary shots. Take him to your vet for immediate follow-up protection.

Permanent vaccine is made from living and/or dead disease-causing virus. The concept and procedures are similar to those used for vaccines for humans. They generally require follow-up shots every one, two, or three years. Many permanent shots can be given to a pup after it is three months old. Only a healthy pup should be vaccinated.

Below are a list of common diseases that can be controlled or prevented by vaccinations.

CANINE HEPATITIS A viral disease, hepatitis attacks the liver, gastrointestinal tract, and occasionally, the kidneys and brain. It requires a one-week incubation period and attacks dogs of all ages. Puppies are especially susceptible. Hepatitis can be transmitted through urine, stool, and saliva. A recently cured dog may also transmit the disease.

The signals surface rapidly. A dog may be well and active one day and extremely ill the next. Symptoms include dehydration, extreme thirst, listlessness, diarrhea, and vomiting. A pup may rub its belly on the floor, or hump its back to relieve internal discomfort. Take the dog to a vet immediately. To prevent the disease be sure the pup has its first permanent shot early in life. Follow-up boosters are required once a year.

CORONAVIRUS   (Canine Viral Enteritis)–A relatively new virus, coronavirus was at first considered a form of parvovirus. Though it has probably been around longer, it was first noted in 1971 in the feces of military dogs and is considered a new disease. Luckily, it is less virulent than parvo.

Symptoms include vomiting, diarrhea, lethargy, and a loss of appetite. An infected dog is depressed and dehydrated with an elevated temperature. Puppies are especially susceptible, and in advanced cases the heart can be affected. Corona can be treated and the survival rate is excellent. Vaccines, which can be given at eight to twelve weeks, help control the disease.

DISTEMPER   A virus, distemper first attacks the body tissues and eventually the brain. The incubation period is one week. Puppies are extremely susceptible. It is transmitted through urine, saliva, the stool, and nasal discharge and can also be transmitted through the air when an infected dog sneezes. An owner can carry it on his shoes, clothing, and hands.

Symptoms include a running nose, flat, hacking cough, loss of appetite, a foul-smelling stool, discharge at the eyes, and even depression. The dog may exhibit a sensitivity to light and may have a temperature two or three degrees above normal. As the symptoms progress, you may see fits and convulsions. Antibiotics can help in early stages but a cure is rare. An infected dog should be taken to a vet immediately.

A pup should receive temporary shots at weaning, repeated regularly until the animal is ready for its permanent shot. A booster is normally given at six months and once a year thereafter.

KENNEL COUGH   (canine adenovirus, canine parainfluenza)–A disease that affects the respiratory system, kennel cough can be caused by a number of viruses. It affects the respiratory tract and especially the windpipe. Symptoms can include a hollow, hacking cough, lethargy, and a loss of appetite. Normally an infected dog appears healthy except for its cough.

The disease can be cured. Most veterinarians suggest MLV-CPV vaccinations when a pup is eight to twelve weeks of age.

LEPTOSPIROSIS   A spiral-shaped bacteria (hence its name), the virus attacks the kidneys and liver. It is transmitted through the urine of infected dogs and rats. A dog can become infected merely by licking its paw after stepping in infected urine. The disease attacks dogs of all ages, and while it can be cured, a recently cured dog may remain a carrier.

Symptoms include a change in the color and odor of the urine. A dog may vomit shortly after eating and may have abdominal pain. There may be blood in the stool. The skin, eyes, gums, and palate may become yellowish. The hindquarters can become stiff and sore and the gums may bleed. The animal's temperature will rise rapidly, then drop.

The disease can be prevented with a permanent vaccination at an early age, generally about twelve weeks. DHL, a combination vaccine, will protect against distemper, hepatitis, and leptospirosis. Booster shots are required annually.

PARVOVIRUS   A relatively new disease, Parvo has become a problem of national concern. Caused by a virus, it attacks the gastrointestinal tract and affects all dogs. Puppies are especially vulnerable. Highly infectious, it is transmitted through an infected stool. The virus can survive for more than six months outside a dog's body.

Symptoms include depression, vomiting, and diarrhea, often with blood. High fevers accompany the disease, especially in pups. Mature dogs can generally survive if treated quickly. Small pups have a reduced chance of survival. The spread of parvo can be prevented by separating your dogs and cleaning each run with chlorine. Recently a new vaccine has been introduced. Most veterinarians have it.

RABIES   The disease attacks the brain and nervous system. It is transmitted through the bite of a rabid animal or from contact with infected saliva against an open wound. Unfortunately, an animal can transmit rabies several days before symptoms appear. If a dog in the field is bitten by any wild animal, the wound should be examined immediately by a veterinarian.

There are two types or rabies, Dumb and Furious. With Dumb Rabies the lower jaw hangs limply open, the tongue drips saliva, and the dog is motionless. With Furious Rabies the dog is irritated by anything that moves. He will appear alert and anxious with dilated pupils. When young pups are infected they may come close for companionship, then bite a friendly hand. A dog may also run in circles chasing his tail, biting anyone who approaches. The disease paralyzes throat and jaw muscles and an animal may have difficulty swallowing. Such a dog will refuse to drink. You may see the traditional frothing at the mouth though this alone is not always a symptom. Frothing may also occur because a dog is thirsty.

Rabies is a terminal disease without cure. Cases must be reported to your veterinarian, local health department, and in some areas, to police. It can also be fatal for humans.

While rabies can be controlled with vaccinations, it is still a dangerous disease because wildlife—skunks and bats for example—may be carriers. Whether your state requires a vaccination or not, I highly recommend that every field dog be protected. A pup should be vaccinated at five or six months and given boosters every two years.

TAKING TEMPERATURES

The new-fangled temperature strips aside, the best way of taking a canine temperature is with a rectal thermometer. Insert the thermometer an inch or so into the anus and keep it there for a minute or more. If you have any doubt about the technique, ask your vet for a demonstration. An average healthy temperature for a dog is 100°F though it varies with breed and size. Any temperature above 102°F demands action.

GIVING MEDICATION

Somewhere along the line your pup will require medication. The dog commonly will need worming pills and preventive medication. There is no easy way to give it. Some pups will swallow a pill if it is wrapped in meat or a favorite treat. Others will have no part of the procedure and must be forced to accept one.

Try stroking the animal's Adam's apple. Often this make a pup open its mouth, stick out its tongue, and swallow. Put the pill as far back in the throat as possible, close the mouth, hold it closed, and stroke the throat again. The animal should swallow.

If that does not work, put one hand on the dog's upper muzzle and gently press the lips inward toward the teeth. At this point almost every dog will open its mouth. Fold the lips under to prevent the dog from biting (if he clamps his mouth he'll bite himself) and place the pill as far back on the tongue as possible. Hold the mouth closed and stroke the throat. Nine times out of ten this will force the dog to swallow. The tenth? He's the dog who can fake it and the minute you relax will spit out the pill. If all else fails, your vet may need to do the job.

Liquid medication is more difficult to administer. The procedure requires practice. If the same medication comes in pill form, order it. If not, try to sneak it into the dog's food. If that fails, force the mouth open as above and create a pocket by pulling the lower lip out near the back teeth. Tilt the dog's head up and pour the medicine into the pocket. Close the mouth immediately. If you hesitate even an instant, you could get a shower of medicine in the face.

CHAPTER SEVEN

Housing Your Dog

First impressions are important, and for a young pup fresh out of the litter, homecoming can be frightening. Your pup has just severed family ties, the only bond he has known, and his immediate problem is one of adjustment. An eight-week-old pup, set adrift in a world he has never seen, needs all the security, reassurance, and love he can get. Initially, keep the animal close. Let him sleep in your bedroom the first nights, and when he whimpers, as he will, comfort him. He may need to go outside, he may be cold, he may be lonely: you can't solve these problems by ignoring them. A little love, attention, and understanding can go a long way.

Your pup will become acclimated in two or three days, and when he is, you can establish a permanent sleeping place. While small he should remain in the house. A partially enclosed cove or a basket with a warm blanket are acceptable, but the best is a portable box. Made of aluminum or plastic, pros call them crates or kennels. They are designed for transporting grown dogs, and you can buy them at sporting shops, pet stores, and by mail. Choices include plastic versions from Doskocil, Nez Perce Plastics, Old Timers, and others, and aluminum models from such firms as Creative Sports Supply and McKee Industries. Although your pup is young, he's not too young for his own crate. A portable kennel is a long-term investment. Most hunters use the same one for years to transport their dog to and from home. In the first year alone a few trips to the park will more than cover your cost.

A transportable kennel offers a number of advantages. A good one is nearly indestructible and has enclosed sides and a solid top to protect your animal from wind and rain. It provides a significant measure of security; later, when as an adult your dog returns from its first hunt soaked to the skin and covered with mud, you'll praise the crate even more. If you put your dog in its kennel instead of hooking it to a tether when you leave a hunting camp, you'll both feel more secure. Your eight-week old pup is not too young to become accustomed to a kennel that it will use the rest of its life.

Knock-down wire cages are also good. I'd buy one if I carried my dog in a station wagon, but not if it was to be transported in the back of a pickup. In an open truck a dog is exposed to the vagaries of weather. An open cage will have to be protected by a tarp.

Remember, the crate you buy now should be sized for your dog as an adult. It should be tall enough for the dog to stand comfortably and wide enough for it to turn, though this does not mean you must buy the largest size. Mild, temporary cramping is not inhumane. If you watch a dog when it's traveling, it is usually curled into a ball. The dog doesn't use all the room, and if it's in a kennel it's had since it was a pup, it will be secure and comfortable.

I recommend starting a young pup in a crate for many reasons. Place it in any out-of-the-way corner and you can teach the command to "kennel." Whenever the pup is under foot, when you want peace or a night's rest, send it to its crate. Close the door and you will know it is safe. You can also use the crate to help bathroom train the animal. A pup will not foul its sleeping area if it can help it; so if you put it there—and are sensitive to its needs—you're training it not to go in the house. But you must realize a small pup does not have the control of an older dog. For the first weeks set your alarm to let it out one or two times each night.

CHOOSING YOUR DOG'S HOME

In a few weeks your pup will be old enough to have a permanent home, and the common choice is a box in the house or garage. The decision is often clouded by the question of whether or not a hunting dog should be a family pet. I think a good dog can be both, and the best choice of housing for a young pup is neither of the above. A dog does not have to be a live-in guest to become your buddy.

If you live in a condo or apartment, you may prefer to board your dog, though I do not recommend it. If you want to train a pup to love, obey, and hunt birds, absentee ownership is a difficult approach. A basic assumption of this book is that you are able to keep a dog at home. If you prefer, you can keep your dog in the house as a family pet, letting it eat and sleep there, without ruining it for hunting. One of Black Point's oldest and best friends keeps his German Wirehair exactly this way. During the week the dog has the run of the sofas and chairs, and on weekends it is a consistent trials winner. Still, if you can swing it, the best housing is a back-yard kennel.

With even a small yard you have a number of possibilities. If the yard is fenced you *could* let your dog run free—but don't. Given the run of the yard, any dog is trouble waiting to happen. You'll have to train the animal not to dig, not to scratch at the screen door, not to raid the garbage can, not to—you get the drift. Sooner or later, and probably sooner, romance will beckon, and even if you think your yard is as escape-proof as Stalag 17, a dog in the mood for romance will find a way out. You may never see the animal again.

A second possibility is to build a free-standing doghouse and then chain your dog to it. This is not an ideal solution, but it can work. The best I've seen was made from a metal drum with one end open. It was mounted two feet above ground, welded to a metal pipe at the center. The pipe was buried in the ground. The elevation eliminated rust and corrosion, and when the dog was chained to the pipe the ground clearance gave the animal a full, un-tangled circle in which to roam. It was a good idea, one you can copy if a run is impossible. The drum is weatherproof, and the elevation makes the animal exercise as it jumps in and out. A wooden barrel, providing it is clean and free of odors, would work as well. A baffle should be placed on the bottom half of the open end, providing protection against wind. On the debit side, mobility is severely restricted by this plan: if you do copy it, remember: your dog's world is limited by the length of the chain.

A combined kennel and run is better. Potential problems such as digging, theft, and vandalism are eliminated; the dog has more scope and more free-dom; and the run itself is sanitary, safe, and humane. You can let your pup out to spend time with you and your family, yet when you put him into the run you know he is safe.

FINDING A PLACE

A good run must meet two requirements: it should have a warm, weatherproof doghouse and an open area enclosed by sturdy fencing (see Illustration 18). A run like this can be constructed in a number of places. The shelter segment can be part of an existing building, a garage, a tool shed, or an outbuilding or it can be freestanding. The advantages of using a ready-made building are obvious: you have less to construct, and the dog house will be normally warmer in winter and cooler in summer. You need only cut a doorway in the existing structure, adding three walls inside for the doghouse. The roof is ready-made. The run itself can also be attached to the building. A site like this should meet three requirements. It should have some sun but not too much, there should be good drainage, and it should be protected from prevailing winds. If a site can't meet these demands, consider erecting a free-standing kennel.

The perimeter of the run should be fenced, and upright supports, to which the wire is attached, can be of lumber or metal. While wood is less permanent—a dog will chew and scratch it—it can be used if the posts are 2 x 4s or larger. Avoid redwood and cedar since resins found in them can make a dog ill. Any portion of wood buried in the ground should be treated with a termite repellent.

Professionals prefer metal. It lasts longer, looks better, and requires less maintenance. Three-quarter or one-inch galvanized pipe uprights are ideal. Welding is not necessary since the ends can be threaded and joined as you would any pipe. Ready-made runs are also available. Most are made of metal and are sold in prefabricated sections (see Illustration 19). The best can be assembled in about one hour with sections combined to create a kennel of almost any dimension. Many are advertised in hunting and dog magazines.

DIMENSIONS

A dog generally drops feces in one area and trails around it so that, in a narrow run, it is not unusual for him to rub against the fencing. Frequent rubbing can wear thin his fur or bare the tip of his tail. With this in mind, the basic rule is the wider the run the better. At Black Point ours are 4 feet wide and 12 feet long. That's not as wide as we'd like, but the number of dogs on hand limits the size. If you're building just one run, you may have more freedom. Make the run as wide and long as space and budget permit. Bigger is better.

You may have heard that the bottom of the run can be of bare earth, pea gravel, or concrete. Bare earth is out. Rains will turn that kennel into a mudhole, and earth is impossible to keep clean. It harbors worms, parasites, larvae, and their eggs. Pea gravel is better. Some trainers swear by it, claiming gravel is best for a dog's feet. They say it "naturally" builds the lower leg muscles. Perhaps, but gravel has some of the problems of earth. It is difficult to clean and retains odors. Every kennel has to be cleaned once or twice daily, which means the gravel has to be raked, rinsed, and screened twice a day. That alone is a job, and you'll throw away a lot of good gravel in the process. And forget sand. The only way sand can be made safe is with the addition of lime. Unless it is worked in properly, lime creates more problems than it solves.

I prefer concrete. Some experts, mostly those breeding dogs for show, feel concrete affects a dog's feet, makes the toes turn out and weakens the animal. Others say it relaxes dogs too much, making them "sloppy." I do not agree.

Concrete can be cleaned in a matter of minutes. It is better for your dog and is certainly better for your yard. A shovel and a hose keep a concrete run clean, and chlorine, water, and sunlight control diseases and parasites.

The concrete floor should be sloped, from a high point at the dog house to the gate. The slope carries rain away from the kennel and lets you flush debris to a single collection point. The amount of drop is open to judgment, though too much is as bad as too little. With too little, water will puddle, and with too much, even a thin sheeting of rain can ice over, sending you and your dog spinning. One-quarter inch per linear foot is minimal, and three-quarters to one inch is probably better. If your property has a natural slope, utilize it. The concrete should be three to five inches deep, deep enough to withstand frost. The ends and sides should be two or three inches wider than the run.

There are two ways to handle the edges. First, they can be level with the floor, allowing water to run where it will. The second possibility is to build a low wall on the two long sides, two to eight inches above the floor, to control the flow of liquids. I prefer the second approach, especially if you add a drain at one end. Certainly it is the preferred solution if you keep two or more dogs. The wall keeps urine and other debris from shifting from one run to another. It allows you to wash each kennel to its own pick-up point and is much more sanitary. Without it you run the danger of spreading disease. The wall can be made of poured cement or concrete blocks. The upright fence supports should be embedded in the cement (see Illustration 20). Metal uprights are best. Wood will eventually rot and is difficult to replace.

Commercial runs include a drain to carry water and feces. Some trainers place it inside the run and others outside (see Illustration 21). The position is a matter of choice, and whether or not a drain is necessary in a one-dog kennel is open to discussion. Local laws may not allow you to drain to a city sewer. You may have to build a sump. If you use a drain, make it wide enough to accept a flat-faced shovel, which makes cleaning easier. A full-width concrete pad at the front is another wise investment. It keeps you from standing in mud and contamination as you open and close the gate.

FENCING THE RUN

The best fencing is diamond-shaped cyclone fencing, commonly available in rolls six-foot wide and fifty-feet long. Six feet is a good height for most runs, and with a low cement wall the finished height is generally greater than that. If you use wood uprights, the wire can be attached with staples; and if you use pipe, special clips are generally available. The wire should always be as tight as you can get it; and the uprights, especially those on the corners, should be braced.

The gate is commonly placed at the end farthest from the dog house, and while I do not suggest any other arrangement, it does have drawbacks. A dog will stool as far from its house as the run allows, which inevitably puts the mess near the gate. The only other solutions are to enter at one side or from the end closest to the doghouse. If the door is at the doghouse you've got instant congestion. Some commercial breeding kennels use this approach, but few trainers like packing clean-up tools and hoses along narrow corridors congested with squirming dogs.

Wherever you place the entry, make it as wide as possible. If your run is four feet wide, the gate should be at least three feet wide and the full six feet high. Be sure to install an easy-to-use, foolproof latch, and if you have children, add a hasp and padlock. Mount the latch and lock at least waist high. Five feet is better. The added height keeps you well above any splashing by happy pups. Many commercial kennels use double fencing so that if a valuable boarder manages to escape from its run, it can get no farther than the perimeter. It is doubtful that you need anything as elaborate.

Even with six-foot cyclone fencing you can loose your dog if the top of the run is uncovered. Most dogs can climb, and I've seen some who could get over cyclone fencing faster than a man. A covered top is just good, sensible insurance. If the run is sunny, add lattice so the animal has a shady area in which to rest.

THE DOGHOUSE

Whether your doghouse is built-in or freestanding, it must be draftproof in winter and well ventilated in summer. Most breeds can handle cold weather if they have a dry, draftproof place in which to sleep. Excess heat is more of a problem.

Some breeders insist that the ideal doghouse is made of concrete block and tile because it is cool, permanent, and easy to clean, but for most of us, wood is the best we can do. If you are building an independent doghouse, use exterior-grade plywood over a framework of 2 x 4s. The house should be at least three feet wide and four feet long. The front can be open if you add an L-shaped baffle inset a foot or so. Your dog can sleep comfortably behind it, safely out of the wind and rain. The sleeping area should be raised for warmth and protection against moisture. If your dog is a chewer, cover the open edges with metal sheeting (see Illustration 22).

I do not use "bedding" but instead cover the floor with removable carpeting. It is better than a wood floor since it can be cleaned and can also be burned if disease becomes a problem. The roof should be sloped to shed water and snow. Cover the plywood top with any good waterproof roofing material and add a good overhang, at least a foot all around if you can. An overhang keeps the house cooler in summer. To provide access for cleaning, to check on a dog, or to remove one that is ill, hinge one of the walls. Place hinges at the top and a clip or bolt to lock it at the bottom. On hot days you can open the entire side to provide maximum ventilation. When you're finished, paint the house white since white reflects the sun. If for any reason you can't cover the entire run, be sure to cover the portion above the doghouse. Even the dullest-witted animal will quickly realize that if it jumps on the roof, escape is easy. Some trainers place the house on legs, one or two feet above the ground, not only to protect against moisture but to make the dog jump as it enters and leaves. That's a good idea. Exercise never hurt any pup.

Most kennels will not require heating, though in a handful of super-cold areas they may. There are a number of possibilities, from radiant heating in the concrete floor to a portable blower brought in on the coldest nights. What ever you use, be sure it is out of reach of the dog and completely safe, with no chance of either fire or electrocuting your animal. If you can't guarantee that, bring your dog into your house on cold nights.

It is essential that you have a water outlet with adequate pressure at the run. You must wash the run daily and must supply your animal with fresh, clean drinking water as well. Most yards have standpipes for gardening, and it is easy to add an extension. Be sure to bury the pipe—to keep it safe from lawn and garden maintenance, accidental digging, and freezing. The colder the temperature, the deeper the pipe. In most parts of the nation six inches is adequate. Place the outlet outside but close to the run so you can attach the clean-up hose without the interference of a wiggling dog. If you carry a second pipe into the run, you can install a self-watering nozzle, providing drinking water on demand. Dogs easily learn to use the device.

If you use a water dish, be sure to place it above ground, high enough so a male cannot micturate in it. The action is related to the territorial urge, and given the chance, most males do it. Electrically heated water dishes are available for use in extremely cold areas. They prevent freezing and have other advantages. You may also need to use plastic wrap and duct tape on exposed pipes to prevent freezing. Automatic feeders are also available.

In most areas a private citizen can keep one or two dogs without special permits, but local ordinances vary. Be sure to check regulations in your area.

CHAPTER EIGHT

Getting the Right Equipment

If you lack the equipment necessary to set up housekeeping for your pup, make a list of essentials before it arrives. It's an easy job. My list is divided into items required now and those needed later, when your pup is ready for training. Since cost is not a factor (believe me, the best costs just pennies more than second-rate), buy the finest. Good equipment will outlast junk every time. Supplies are available from local pet stores and supermarkets, though items such as rope can be found in hardware stores. If you have or previously had a dog, you may have some items. A new dog can use hand-me-downs, a food dish or water dish or training lead that belonged to another, as long as it is clean and sanitary.

WHEN THE PUP COMES HOME

Begin with two bowls. One should be continually full of fresh water. The other is used for food. Though your pup is small, buy bowls that will accommodate the animal when it's full-grown. Most stores offer a choice of stainless steel, ceramic, and plastic. The three materials should be equally serviceable if the bowls are well made. The best have weighted bottoms so a dog cannot move them, and I recommend them. If you live in the suburbs, you may have nocturnal visitors such as raccoons. Inveterate robbers, raccoons will steal lightweight bowls. They can't lift weighted ones. Whatever your choice, be sure the interior is smooth. I prefer stainless steel. It is sanitary, easy to clean, and unbreakable.

Toys are tolerated in some quarters, but in most kennels they are controversial. At Black Point they do not exist. I don't like them. I'll admit that as their teeth develop, pups need things for teething, but chew toys are not the answer. Bones are okay in moderation. Pups allowed to chew for pleasure often grow into dogs who mouth birds. When my pups are teething I give them a Milk Bone. Older dogs receive one bone a month because it's good for their teeth. Let them chew it for half an hour or so, then remove it.

A leg bone of beef is the only one to ask for. It cannot chip or splinter. Have your butcher remove the knuckle joints and give them to your dog. Some people cook these first. I do not. Bones are more apt to splinter if they are cooked. Do not use veal, pork, or lamb and avoid steak bones like the plague. Everyone knows the dangers of chicken bones—they can splinter in a dog's mouth and cause serious internal injury.

There's no reason to consider a litter box. Your pup can be taught to use the great outdoors in a few days. Most pups are familiar with newspapers because they are commonly used to line the whelping box, and in a pinch you can break a pup to newspapers first; but I prefer a more direct approach. I try to recognize the moment a pup needs to go and to act before it can do anything in the house. If you take the animal outside just before it needs to relieve itself, you should be able to establish a routine in three or four days. When I put the pup out, I make a big fuss when it goes, clapping my hands and praising it. Believe it or not, a dog trained this way will often go to the bathroom on command. Just put the animal out, clap your hands, and *voila*! If your pup seems uneasy, wanders aimlessly looking into corners, he's sending a message. Act! When you let the dog out, keep it on a leash and remain with it. Given freedom, it will escape.

If a pup goes in the house, the act may require punishment. You'll have to decide; but if the animal has diarrhea, and a lot of young pups do, punishment is cruelty. The first rule with a pup is to be fair. I rarely discipline a young, newly arrived pup for going in the house, concentrating instead on getting it to do its duty outside.

BEDDING/HOUSING

I've discussed bedding and sleeping facilities in another section, and there is no need to repeat it. In that section I strongly suggested using a transportable crate as your pup's first sleeping place; but if that is impossible, a dog bed, box, or corner in the house will work. Whatever your choice and wherever the place, the spot should be warm and free of drafts. The bedding can be an old blanket, old clothes (with the buttons removed), or anything else that is soft and comfortable. When the pup has his own run, I use a piece of carpeting because it is removable, sanitary, and easy to clean.

COLLARS

A pup should learn to wear a collar as soon as possible, and you'll have to buy two or three before he reaches full size. Never skimp. Never buy one that is obviously too big and never make an animal wear one that is too tight. While you can buy a collar with some room for your pup to grow into, it should not be so large that a long section of strap hangs limp beyond the buckle. A three- or four-hole surplus is the most you should accept. A collar fits properly when you can place two fingers, one on top of the other, between the collar and the pup's neck.

You can choose between nylon and leather. Leather is good-looking and the standard by which quality is judged, but it weakens with age, sunlight, and weather. Nylon is a better buy, costing less and lasting longer. Better collars have both a metal buckle and a sturdy D-ring. The ring is the place to attach the leash, tie-out cord, and check line. It should be sturdy and ruggedly attached. Most pet stores stock several lines of quality collars. Coastal, Mustang, Nylorite and Whitey's are among the leading manufacturers.

Avoid chain-link slip or "choke" collars. While some obedience trainers require these, I do not recommend them and will not allow them at Black Point. Pulled too tight, they can harm the windpipe, and even in normal conditions the links twist and pull against the fur. If the slip end catches on a bush, fence, or anything else, an animal can choke to death. Classic Products in Malibu, California, imports a "humane" chain collar that is better. Its design features a second chain that limits the amount the collar can close. Even so, there is much less danger with a buckle collar and I prefer them. If an animal stubbornly refuses to cooperate, you may need to buy one of the special "emergency" training collars I'll describe later.

Flea collars are popular and well advertised but I rarely recommend them. The base chemicals can produce dangerous vapors in a warm, closed room, and collars are not as effective as dips and other preventative measures. A flea collar should never be used on a young pup.

LEADS

Just as you want your pup to become used to a collar early, you also want him to quickly discover the feel of a lead. I recommend beginning with a light-weight six-foot lead. It should be purchased when you buy your collar. Like collars, leads can be made of leather, chain, or nylon, and for the reasons above I suggest nylon. It should have a comfortable loop on one end, smooth-edged and large enough for your hand, with a good bolt or spring-action snap on the other. At first, attach the lead and let the pup drag it around the house. Since a tiny pup has a short attention span, do not do this for more than five or ten minutes at a time and never more than two or three times a day. If the pup takes the lead in its mouth and plays with it or chews on it, don't interrupt. I'll explain the sequence in detail later.

EQUIPMENT NEEDED LATER

Almost immediately, you will begin teaching your pup basic obedience and confidence. Each step is important, and you should add equipment as it is required. The first item is a check line. It allows the pup more freedom than the short lead and gives it an illusion of freedom though you retain control. Used properly, a check line teaches your pup that you can monitor its actions far beyond the length of your arm. It is the first step toward the day when your pup will be so well trained that it will respond instinctively to hand and voice commands no matter how far away.

The check line used now is neither thick nor long. A length of light-weight rope of ten or twelve feet is adequate. While ready-mades are available (they are called long leads or training lines), I prefer to make my own. Some trainers use snaps on one end, but I don't. I don't trust them. Most snaps are made of pot metal and can break. If the dog is going one way and you're heading the other, the snap can part with an explosive "bang," the line whipping back, possibly striking you. A tied check line will not do that. In place of a snap I tie the rope to a conventional nylon collar, using the D-ring as the attaching point (see Illustration 23). The end can be braided back on itself or can be tied in a square knot (no "granny" please). The end of the knot should be melted with a match, open flame, or cigarette. Treated this way, it will never open. Later, you'll want to add a heavy-duty check line for field training. I use thirty feet of yellow "ski rope" and tie the ends just as with the shorter line. This means that instead of attachable checklines, you have two combination checkline-and-collars, a short one of twelve to fifteen feet and the longer thirty-foot version.

WHISTLE

Though some type of attention-getting noisemaker is essential (two short blasts send the dog off, one long one calls him back), no one says you have to use a whistle. You can train your dog to respond to anything from a kazoo to a trumpet, but most trainers prefer a whistle because it is convenient. A number of versions are available and can be purchased at pet and sporting goods stores as well as by mail. I prefer the Roy Gonia Special. It has a high, loud, penetrating sound. Since most hunters I know also use whistles, I remove the pea from those at Black Point. This gives ours a distinctive sound like a bosun's pipe. I recommend a plastic whistle, especially if you live in the midwest. Winters there can be mean and cold. Putting your lips to a cold metal whistle on a freezing morning is an experience you'll never forget, if you have lips left to talk with. Both pointers and spaniels are taught to respond to the whistle.

BLANK GUN

(See Illustration 24.)

There are several ways to prepare your dog for hunting over guns—by banging pots and pans and by walking him in heavy traffic, for instance—but at some point a gun is essential. The timing varies with your schedule and your pup but usually comes prior to field training. Whether or not you need the blank starter's pistol professional trainers use depends on several factors. If you have a conventional 22 handgun, you may load it with blanks. Some hunters use small bore shotguns with special loads, but lacking either, a blank pistol is recommended. Harrington-Richardson makes a good version. Various hunter's catalogs list them. Be especially careful using blank loads. Many contain black powder, and it is possible to start a fire shooting hot wadding and black powder into dry grass.

OTHER COLLARS

The need for special training collars depends on the response of your dog to regular procedures. The compliant dog, easy to manage and train (I call them "biddable"), will not require tougher, special measures. But one that is stubborn, and that resists training, may need one of three devices.

1. If a headstrong dog will not respond to "heel" or "whoa" commands using ordinary training methods, you may have to try a bent-fingered pinch collar. Those who do not understand the collar, the way it is made, and the way it works swear at it, but professionals swear by it. It is made like a choke collar but with blunt metal fingers inside (see Illustration 25). The fingers are bent so that the ends cannot puncture the skin. What would be considered the knuckles press against the animal's neck only when the chain is tightened. These pinch the flesh (that's the point of it), but they are not inhumane. Pressure is applied only for a second or two, and the collar is just traumatic

enough to shake a really stubborn dog into compliance. Many trainers call it the "R.C." or "religious collar" for obvious reasons. It makes a believer out of a difficult dog. It is a last resort, used only once or twice in a dog's life when nothing else works. An animal that minutes before refused to listen to its trainer becomes instantly attentive. Some trainers use leather collars with pointed nails inside. I do not.

2. Every dog eventually progresses to a point at which it is free of restraint. Suddenly there are no leads or check lines and the exhilarating sense of freedom is so overwhelming that the dog becomes carried away. The animal refuses to obey commands it followed well on a check line. At this point the dog is normally returned to the check line to repeat previous training. It may run with the check line dragging, so you may want to substitute a remote-controlled electronic collar here. This beats running down the line to pull the animal up short each time it ignores commands. Press a button on the portable sending unit and a radio wave triggers a low-level, uncomfortable jolt of electricity. It's a better solution for a dog that refuses to learn because there is no delay between disobedience and punishment. The result is instantaneous. The punishment comes so swiftly that the animal associates it with disobedience. More importantly, the dog learns a basic lesson: no matter where it runs you're in control. Two or three sessions with an electric collar is all it takes. The collar is both humane and useful. For more information on the electronic collar, see Chapter 24.

Since 1979 several brands of high-quality remote-controlled electronic stimulators have been marketed. Early units relied on high-intensity shock and were considered negative training devices. New low-voltage units are more humane and more effective. A number of firms make such devices. One of the best, and the one I use, is made by Tri-Tronics (7060 East 21st Street, P.O. Box 17660, Tucson, AZ 85731). Not all collars are the same, and comparisons should consider the ranges at which they work. To be effective in field training, a collar should be able to be triggered at a range of one-quarter mile or more.

3. If you kennel your dog, constant barking can be a serious problem for you and your neighbors. If you have two dogs, a calm one can pick up the habit from an excitable kennelmate. Nonstop barking is more than just an annoying habit. Veterinarians now believe it can create stresses that affect a dog's immune system. Surgical debarking or chemical tranquilizers are not the answer, and a muzzle does not solve the problem, but a special automatic electronic collar usually stops the most difficult dog in a matter of days. Tri-Tronics' MBL Bark Limiter straps to the neck and is activated automatically when a dog barks (see Illustration 26). Other models, some imported, are also available.

CANTEEN

Heat is the number-one killer of dogs, and in the field water is important first aid, especially on hot, sunny days. A canteen can prevent problems and provide comfort. A surplus army model, the traditional aluminum shell in a canvas carrier, is best (see Illustration 27). It may already be a part of your hunting kit. If not, you can find it at surplus stores. The contents, about one pint, provide enough water to comfort a dehydrated dog or, in an emergency, to wet the head of an overheated one.

FIRST AID KIT

A dog in the field is susceptible to any number of accidents, from scratches to broken bones and accidental gun wounds. A first aid kit can prevent small problems from becoming big and keep big problems from getting out of hand. A number of firms offer kits especially assembled for dogs. A typical version includes twenty or more items veterinarians consider important: eyewash, a styptic to stop bleeding, antiseptic powder, special ointment, hydrogen perox- ide, an oral syringe, sterile cotton and applicators, gauze roll, sterile pads, tape, and more. Many pet shops sell these. If you prefer, you can make your own. Three firms currently produce ready-made kits: Pet Medical & Health Products, Princeton, NJ; Ryter Corporation, Madella, MN; and Dan Hill Products, Orlando, FL.

A dog can return from a hunt with small seeds caught in its eyes. As a first aid measure I carry a baby bottle with a soft rubber nipple filled with fresh-boiled, sterile water. Instead of using a handkerchief, I wash the eyes with the water. The nipple will not injure the eyeball and the clean water safely flushes away the largest seeds. I prefer sterile water over manufactured eyewash. It is cheaper and readily available. I also check a dog for burrs and foxtails every time we hunt, looking between the toes, in the ears, and around the tail. I carry cotton swabs and mineral oil for this purpose. The oil is used to soften foxtails and burrs caught in the ears and nose, reducing irritation until I can get the dog to the vet. I never try to remove obstructions in these areas.

OTHER ITEMS

When it is time to teach your dog to retrieve, you will need a couple of training accessories, a dummy (or buck) and a dumbbell. You can make your own or buy them ready-made, and if you shop around, you'll find several versions. Some have handgrips, some are propelled by powder, and still others are designed to throw. The "shooting" models, which propel the dummy quite a distance, are not essential in training a pointer as they might be when training a retriever. Hand-thrown canvas and plastic models are adequate, and at Black Point they've served us for years.

Dummies and dumbbells are easy to make, and you can certainly use a homemade version if you wish. For a dummy, which is not retrieved from the ground, you can use a stick, a section of dowel, a broom handle, or even an old sock or glove stuffed with rags. You can make a dumbbell as easily. It has raised sides so a dog can easily retrieve it from the ground. The easiest way to make one is to cut two squares from a 1 x 4 (two four-inch-square pieces). Cut a one-inch dowel or a section of broom handle into a six-inch length. Place one 4 x 4 square on each end of the dowel and attach it with a screw or nail (see Illustration 28). Later, when your dog needs a heavier dumbbell, make one with 2 x 4 ends.

Although a remote-controlled electronic bird release, commonly called a "popper," is expensive, it is an extremely helpful training tool (see Illustration 29). When you are teaching your dog to point, you do not want the animal to come in direct contact with the birds, whether they are tethered or caged, because a bad experience can change the way a dog looks at birds. If the dog injures itself on a cage, it may associate that injury with birds, thus creating a reluctance to ever point or retrieve again. An electronic release allows you to release a training bird before the dog reaches it. The fact that a bird takes to the air seems natural even though you use pigeons, a bird that does not normally flush. A popper can teach a dog to hold staunch on point as fast as any technique.

There are a number of makes available, from hand-operated units to electronic versions. The electronic models are the more practical since they can be operated from a distance, and distance is important. When a dog is racing full tilt across a field, you may not always be able to get within range to pull the hand-operated trigger before the dog arrives. If a popper seems too expensive to justify it's purchase, consider sharing cost and use with two or three friends.

CHAPTER NINE

Training Basics

Man and dog have been friends for a millennium, and during those years we've taught dogs to cooperate with us very successfully. A trained dog has better judgment than one that is untrained. It knows its conduct is governed by rules, accepts them, and feels secure. The dog applies those rules to new situations, and at the very least considers the fact that a new situation probably has its own rules. A well-trained dog will never be comfortable until these rules are discovered.

Early training goes best if you have a nonworking spouse who can help with your objectives. It is possible to raise a puppy in a home where both adults work and there are either no children or children in school, but "latchkey" conditions make it difficult. Empty hours lead to boredom and destructiveness, and it is harder to control such problems as housebreaking and chewing. If the family is away from 8 A.M. to 5 P.M., the pup has only an hour or two in the morning and a few hours at night for socialization. You should give it as much of that time as possible.

YOUR PUP AS A PET

There is considerable controversy over whether or not a puppy can be both a pet and a well-trained field dog, but there is no doubt in my mind that an intelligent pup can sort out the two positions, especially if the family agrees on common guidelines. Some of the best field dogs I know are family members on nonhunting days.

Since the entire family wants to play with a new puppy, the dog may seem more like a family pet than a developing hunter, but that's an illusion. From the first, one person must assume responsibility, keep a record of shots, evaluate health, and make certain the pup is brushed, bathed, and free of ticks and fleas. One person must also be responsible for his training, and since you are the one who will hunt with the pup, it stands to reason that it should be you.

You'll have fewer problems if you understand the Black Point system before starting and can readily grasp both the concept and the techniques. There is nothing mysterious about it. The approach is geared to the way a dog thinks and learns. The better you understand and read your dog, the faster training will progress.

SOCIALIZING

Psychologists refer to the process of getting an animal used to the companionship of humans as human/animal bonding. I call it socialization, but by any name it needs to happen early. A pup that is comfortable with humans and respects them has had pleasant people-experiences. Most kennels manage some socialization before they sell a pup, but you must finish the job at home.

Socialization begins the moment your pup arrives and is the first step in any training. In my opinion it develops best if your pup lives with you the first weeks. The normal interaction among you, the pup, and your family is the best of all early training. When you feed your pup, play with it, and comfort it, you are reinforcing human/animal bonding. A pup learns your moods, and a dog who does not understand its master's moods will never learn to relate.

A pup should consider training fun, and two factors go a long way toward creating this. The first is to separate the pup from the litter, which is self-evident since you've brought the dog home. The second is to keep the pup separated from other dogs for a few weeks. You want your pup's interest centered on you.

I call the rapport that develops now the pup's "focus." It is a psychological transference, an important secret training weapon on which you should capitalize. In its first days in the litter, the pup's life revolved around its mother. When it was weaned its interest switched to food and littermates. Now, the focus should transfer to you. The intelligent trainer will make this phenomenon one cornerstone of his training effort. The more time you spend with your pup in these early weeks, the closer your relationship.

Finally, a field dog should be friendly toward people and other dogs. It is sheer hell to hunt when one of the dogs in a party is hostile. A dog mean toward people will be mean toward canine companions; conversely, one with a good family experience is generally friendly. This is another plus for careful, thorough socialization.

UNDERSTANDING TRAINING BASICS

A pup's early months are among its most important. Canine character and habits become established in the first three. Then, between the fourth and twelfth months, the things you teach or don't teach, that you correct or overlook, establish the way your dog will accept all training that is to follow.

In the first weeks you should teach your pup to wear a collar, walk on a leash, and respond to three or four simple commands. It should come when it is called, respond appropriately to "no" or "don't," as well as to "stay," "heel," and whatever else is necessary to create a cooperative household pet.

Your pup will learn in two ways, first by associating the things you want it to know with pleasure or satisfaction, because of your encouragement. Secondly, your pup will discard those things you don't want it to learn, through discouragement; that is, through correction.

Training is broken into stages, and the basic premise underlying each centers on the following five points:

1. The cardinal rule is that the pup quickly learns it must obey, not occasionally but always.
2. Never give an order unless you are certain the pup can comply.
3. Be consistent.
4. Be gentle.
5. Keep training sessions short, interesting, and fun.

The most important factors are attitude and concentration. Together they are a major part of the game. You need to present an upbeat, happy attitude at every session. Your attention must be focused on your dog. You cannot let your mind wander. If you are dull and listless, your dog will be the same.

Your dog will also learn to read your moods. It will know when you are angry and when you mean business. The way you present yourself during training determines whether or not your pup will respect you, whether or not it listens, whether or not it learns. If training sessions are not important to you, they will not be important to your dog.

I can remember times when I've been angry, tired, or concentrating on personal problems. Each time the dog has sensed my mood and I've lost the animal's attention. The session has been wasted. When my mind isn't on training I postpone the session.

A dog has a short attention span, and a pup an even shorter one. The training sessions need to be short; with a young pup no more than ten minutes each. While each session should ideally be stretched to the full time, the length must be variable. Depending on the dog, rapport, and other circumstances, training can run from five to ten minutes, and the way you end each session is as important as the way you begin. It is best to quit while your dog is still interested, still learning, still doing commands correctly. I would rather end a session at seven minutes if a dog is doing what I want, than to be forced to quit at ten when it is tired and making mistakes. Your pup can sense what you want. Given half a chance, it'll comply and if it gives you one or two good command responses back to back, you may want to end on those. Your pup will remember success above all else.

It will understand what you want from three kinds of input, verbal, visual (hand and body signals, showing the dog what you want), and physical (pressure on the leash, lifting the pup to put it where you want). Visual signs will be extremely important when the dog takes to the field. One year down the road, when you teach "whoa," the pup will learn it both verbally and visually. You'll begin using hand signals early.

A DOG'S WORLD

There are more than physical differences between dog and man. A dog has its own behavior and value characteristics, and while you can train a pup without being aware of them, the better you know your dog, the faster it will learn. If you understand how your dog learns and how fast it absorbs knowledge, you may discover a little about canine language in the process—the meaning of your dog's sounds, facial expressions, and body movements. At the same time your dog is learning our language. Some dogs learn fast, some slowly; some can only absorb so much, and for others the sky is the limit. You must discover where your dog fits in. You will need to tailor the pace of your training to its abilities. Never pressure or push your dog to learn faster or do more than it is capable of.

If you pass a dog's breaking point, then you've lost the dog. It will become disinterested, displaying amazing passive resistance. It will not do anything wrong, but neither will it do anything right. The dog simply will not care—and will not learn.

FIRST TRAINING

No pup is born with a knowledge of the things you will teach, and some of it may even go against instinct. Remember, the pup is eight to ten weeks old—much younger than the age at which we begin teaching human babies. Anything new, even as simple as attaching a collar or a leash, can be frightening. The problem is partly one of scale. You are ten times the puppy's size. Consider how you might react if the situation were reversed. Imagine a collar around your neck, a towering giant tugging and shouting in a strange language. When communicating with your dog, bend so your face is at its level. Look into its eyes. I prefer being eyeball to eyeball. With eye contact you know when your dog is paying attention. The best trainers attach so much importance to attention that they will not proceed if there is the slightest distraction, and some hold one or two sessions just on eye contact. They kneel in front of the dog and gently hold the animal's muzzle until they are eyeball to eyeball. They'll try to maintain that contact for several seconds.

Dogs are creatures of habit. They like schedules and will quickly fall into a routine. Ideally you should work with your pup at the same time every day. Your dog will look forward to the sessions. Almost as if it owns a watch, it will be waiting.

And when you are training, gently, firmly and consistently insist on the same response each time you give a command. You cannot allow a dog to be inconsistent. You cannot let it ignore a command. If you are lax and inconsistent, the pup will become lax and inconsistent. Bad habits develop from poor training. They begin when you allow a pup to "get away" with a half-hearted response or ignore a command. These are the beginning stages of trouble.

In the early weeks, training ideally progresses without your dog realizing it is being trained. If you've become the focus of interest and if the sessions are fun, the pup will accept training time as play. When your pup has a substantial repertoire of commands, you can change the pattern and the way in which you present them. Variety keeps sessions from becoming boring.

Although I teach one point and when that is learned progress to another, I do not agree with those who insist that a dog can cope with but one detail at a time. With my method the familiar is reinforced as the new is introduced. I like to devote two-thirds of a session to the latest command and one-third to reinforcing old ones. Repetition is important. The more often a command is successfully repeated, the more automatic the response. You'll also find other times during the day to reinforce the commands, and the more you can do this, aside from training sessions, the faster the progress. Once you give a command be sure to enforce it.

Do not expect training sessions to advance evenly. There will be ups and downs. Your dog will have good and bad days just as you do. If you find your pup in a funky mood, ask it to perform a couple of easy commands, so you can offer praise; then end the session. Never threaten a dog. Sooner or later it will test you and you'll pay dearly. Testing leads to a lack of attention and then open rebellion.

WORDS

It is also important to realize that commands are only sounds. Your dog doesn't understand human language. It hears sounds and reacts as it thinks you want it to react. You can use any words—French, Spanish, Swahili, or an invented language—as long as you are consistent, but in our sport certain words have traditional meanings. Advanced training will go easier if, from the beginning, you use these in their proper context. Avoid words that may have another meaning later. The dog will only have to relearn those commands. Always show your dog what you expect. Your pup learns as much from what it sees you do as from what it hears you say.

Be sure your children remember this as they play with the pup. Like you, they must never use confusing words and must never countermand your training.

Do not use the word "down" on a nonflushing dog. Sooner or later it will create confusion, as the command, with flushing dogs, is used to drop a dog in certain field conditions. When I get a pointer for training, I sometimes test it on the word and discover to my horror that the dog drops flat on its belly. There is nothing uglier than a pointer lying on point.

"No" is also controversial because it has a sound-alike command, "whoa," a word never taught the first year. Many owners use "no" as a correction, to keep a dog from doing things they do not want it to do. Though "no" is pronounced "noh" and "whoa" is used in the longer "whoa-up", some trainers consider the terms to sound similar enough to be confusing. I'm not sure I agree, but I use "don't." It is less likely to be misunderstood.

IMPORTANCE OF VOICE

Tone of the voice is more important than words. Commands should be given in a gentle but excited voice. Avoid stern tones and never raise your voice. Save loud, challenging tones for times when you need to make an important correction. Too often I hear angry owners shouting and cursing at eight- to twelve-week-old pups. Pups that age are too young to realize their mistakes and are often corrected for things they have not yet learned. A heavy-handed correction pressures and intimidates a pup. In time the animal will become submissive, brow-beaten, even "case-hardened." High-strung dogs generally require especially calm, quiet handling. Never loose your temper. Apply too much pressure to a high-strung dog and it will panic, literally blacking out. To repeat myself: training should be fun for you and your pup.

Incidentally, if you want a far-out correction word, one dogs pick up on instantly, try "fooey." Say it once and you've got your pup's attention. I can't explain why.

CORRECTION AND PRAISE

A correction is the trainer's way of letting a dog know it has not followed a command. It should come immediately after the mistake. The first correction should be gentle, a change in tone of voice along with a chance for the dog to correct its action. I use a repeat of the command with the dog's name. For example, if the pup was told to "heel" and did not, the correction would be (in a voice lower in tone and more imperative than the original) "Rover, heel!" You should use the dog's name before every command to get attention. If a second correction is needed, repeat the command in a tougher voice. If you must give a third try, speak louder and add a tug on the leash. Only if a dog continues to ignore the command should you pick it up and place it where it is supposed to be. If you cannot correct a mistake immediately, ignore it. Never try to reprimand a dog later. The pup will never understand and will associate the correction with something it is currently doing. As a rule, training sessions go better and learning is faster if you can praise a dog more often than you correct it.

Praise, when your pup does something right, is more important than a correction when it doesn't. I do not suggest bribery and am not implying that you should create a mercenary. Food may work once or twice but will eventually backfire. Your pup will work harder for praise and respect.

One way dogs communicate is by acting, and when you "act out" or exaggerate praise the animal appreciates it. Praise is your pup's paycheck, and the bigger the paycheck, that is, the louder and more dramatic the praise, the harder it will work. A softly muttered "good dog" will get only halfhearted attention. If you are not demonstrative by nature, try to change your personality when training. A warm and well-meant "good dog" along with a friendly rub under the belly or along the ear goes a long way.

Before making any correction give your pup an opportunity to get it right unaided. Corrections must be consistent, fair, and never stronger than required. Never strike or abuse a dog. If you must get physical, pick the pup up by the loose flesh at its neck. This is the way a mother handles her offspring and the way an older dog proves dominance.

Where you train is as important as how. Select a site with few distractions. Your dog will not give you full attention any other way. There must be no ringing phones, no noise of autos, and most importantly, no extraneous people, or dogs or interesting or exotic scents. If for any reason—or for no apparent reason—a pup seems to dislike a training site and becomes nervous or uneasy, find a new place.

CHAPTER TEN

Training Your Pup

You can bully a pup into learning faster, but pressure backfires. A force-taught pup lacks intensity and will never be as good as one that learns at a slower, more natural pace. Begin training with two ten-minute sessions daily, one in the morning, the other at night. If your pup is a fast learner, add a third. There is no way to predict how long training will take, but as a point of reference, some phases should be completed in two or three sessions while others will require weeks.

You should concentrate on four commands the first two weeks. None require formal sessions since they are orders you'll automatically use: teaching the pup to respond to its name (and incorporating the name with "here" or "come"), to accept a collar, to get used to a leash, and to "kennel."

RESPONDING TO ITS NAME

Teaching a dog its name comes first because opportunities to teach this occur frequently. You simply use the pup's name every time you comfort, feed, or play with it. Teaching a pup to come when it's called is a natural part of the same routine since its name is used before every command.

Most kennel masters call their litters from the whelping box by clapping their hands and calling "come," "come on," or "here," so most pups are familiar with one of the three terms. Consequently, this training also does not require an organized session. Feeding and playing with the pup give you the needed opportunities.

While many trainers use "come," I prefer "here!" It has a more urgent ring. When you want to call your pup, clap your hands and say "Rover, here!" In training parlance a command is called a "cue" since it cues the pup to the expected response.

Begin by using "here" every time the pup would naturally come to you. At feeding time the pup is eager to respond because it is hungry. Instead of immediately placing food before the animal, call "here." When your pup comes, praise it, then give it the meal. The pup will quickly associate the command with food and praise. (Underlining my earlier comments: feeding reinforces both socialization and the "focus" concept.) When it is playtime, do the same thing. Call your dog using "here." The animal will come because it wants companionship and a little roughhouse, and when you praise it, you're reinforcing the desired reaction. Much early training utilizes common-sense situations like these.

LEASH AND COLLAR

You should fit the pup with a loose-fitting collar, and if it tries to scratch the collar off its neck, distract the animal with praise and petting. Make it wear the collar a few minutes, then remove the collar if the dog fights. Replace it later. Under the worst possible scenario it should not take more than two or three attempts to get a pup to accept a collar. If you plan to use dangling ID tags, do not attach them immediately. Clanking metal will only frighten an uncertain pup. You can add them in a week or so, after the pup is comfortable with its collar.

Next, attach a short, light-weight lead. A six-footer is right. Clip it to the collar and let the pup pull it about the floor. If the pup wants to bite, play with, or pick up the free end, let it do so. The pup should consider the leash as fun. Remove it after ten minutes and replace it later. Leash-breaking, like teaching a pup to wear a collar, is not difficult. It should require no more than three or four sessions. After your pup accepts the lead, pick it up. If the pup reacts by tugging or pulling, do not correct it. End the session. Repeat the procedure until the pup accepts the fact that you have control when you are holding the leash. Be sure to praise your pup as much as you can.

The first few times you walk with your pup, it may be frightened. The pup may rebel. It may sit, lie down, or refuse to move. It may even cry. Do not tug on the collar to try to make the dog cooperate. Pulling and shouting create panic, and fear can make a bold pup timid. Speak gently, lift the animal to a standing position if it sits, and try again. If the pup is still frightened, end the session. The pup's reactions will depend on your gentleness and its boldness. Some pups take to the leash instantly, tugging and ready for the new experience. Some do not. It is important that your pup look forward to these sessions. Training may be serious from your viewpoint, but it should be fun for your pup. An upbeat attitude, a happy voice, and a lot of praise will go a long way toward making that happen. When the pup is ready to walk with the leash, let the animal set the pace. Keep the leash loose and the sessions short. If the pup tires before ten minutes, stop.

KENNEL

The "kennel" command is the fourth taught without regular training sessions. Although I suggest using a portable kennel while the pup is in your house, remember: just separated from the litter, the pup will be frightened and lonely. Let it sleep beside your bed until it feels secure. When it's comfortable, generally within the first week, choose a permanent sleeping place. Whatever the site, whether portable kennel, basket, or box, refer to it as a "kennel." Begin training by carrying the pup to the sleeping area, repeating the command "kennel" in a calm, easy voice. Once it proves it knows the command and the proper response, never let the pup ignore it.

I know many owners feel that it is not important to make a pup kennel each time it is told. They are wrong. The day you let your pup off without complying is the day battle lines are drawn to see who is master. In time the situation can develop into open rebellion, a confrontation you should avoid. If the pup ignores your command, close the doors so it cannot escape, run it down, attach a lead to the collar, and then make it go to its kennel. Repeat the command several times, enforcing the response each time. Later, when you house the pup in an outside run, refer to that, too, as a "kennel."

HEEL

"Heel" must never be taught until a pup is comfortable with its collar and leash but should come before "stay," which usually means the pup is in its ninth or tenth week. You can hold sessions indoors or out. If your yard is large enough (and has no distractions), hold them there. You can also use a park or vacant lot. Some trainers begin with the dog in a sitting position. I prefer to start while the pup is walking.

You should always walk with your dog on the side opposite your gun. If you are a right-handed shooter, place the pup on your left. If you are left-handed, walk with the dog on your right. Give the command to heel as you pull the leash gently across your body, forcing the pup back. In heel position its head should be even with your legs. When the dog complies, give it lots of praise. Be consistent, sympathetic, and tolerant but never angry. If this is your first, second, or third session, remember, the little fellow beside you may not yet understand what you want.

Do not drag your dog. The leash should never be so tight that the pup is forced to lean into it to keep up. Never tug on the leash except when making a correction. When the pup is in the proper heel position, the leash should be loose. If the pup seems frightened, bewildered, or awed, abort the session.

Instead of using a short lead, I prefer a longer light-weight nylon check line, one about twelve feet long. I hold it with my right hand at six feet with the remainder coiled in my free hand. If the pup tries to break in front of my body, I twirl the open end in front of me. When the dog breaks the plane of my knee, it is hit in the nose by the twirling line. A couple of flicks and the most rambunctious dog will drop back to the proper position. Even a slow learner gets it right after two or three sessions.

Some trainers teach "heel" by walking a pup beside an older dog familiar with the command. They believe the older dog will train the younger one faster than the trainer alone. The idea has merit, but it's not something most hobby trainers can copy. Nor should you. Your pup can learn "heel" well enough on its own. At Black Point all dogs are taught singly.

As the pup becomes comfortable with the command, vary the speed of walking. Make the dog heel when you trot and when you walk slowly. Give the command as you walk in circles, S-shapes, and other patterns. If the pup follows with its head in the general vicinity of your leg, consider that excellent. Our objective is to make an obedient upland game dog, not an obedience champion. If a field dog follows in a reasonable heel position and does other commands in a workable manner, I consider it well trained. The precision you see in obedience trials is simply not necessary in the field.

STAY

Many books written to help people train household pets suggest a complicated series of stay-related commands such as "down," "sit," "stand," "stay," "sit-stay," and "down-stay." I've already discussed "down" in terms of springers, and none of the other terms, except a simple and direct "stay," make sense in the field. They may have validity if you want an obedience-trained show dog, but in the field they only create problems that have to eventually be corrected. If you have a flushing dog, you can teach it "sit-stay" (at five or six months) since that's the breed's standard delivery position on a retrieve. A pointer should stand on "stay." It should never be taught to sit. That command is reserved for flushing dogs (see Chapter 12).

"Stay" is a very important command for a pointer. It will lead directly to "whoa" when the animal is ready for field training. ("Whoa" is used to halt a dog that is in motion.) Then why not teach "whoa" now, instead of one year down the road? Because "whoa" is the most important word a pointer learns, and most owners who teach it early become lax in enforcement. If you teach the command to your pup the first year but have few if any occasions to use it, by the time field training arrives the dog will have to be retrained. Teaching "whoa" the second time is harder. I find it wiser to teach the pup to "stay," avoiding "whoa" altogether. Then, even if you become lax enforcing "stay," the dog will react to "whoa" with the necessary intensity when it is time to teach it because it is a new cue. The transition from "stay" to "whoa," is relatively easy.

Dogs are quick to copy, and you'll teach "stay" as much by action as by voice. It is important to combine the vocal command with a hand signal, because later your dog will be taught to respond to "whoa" on both voice and hand commands. Some trainers teach "stay" from a stationary position. I do not. Begin with the dog walking in heel position. Pull gently back on the leash, lower your hand in front of its face, say "stay," then stop. If the pup stops beside you, even for a split second, offer praise. I've insisted that a pointer should stand, (and it should), but if your pup sits or lies now, it is fine. Praise the dog as if it's done everything you wanted. You'll only make waves if you demand a perfect response the first time.

Repeat the "stay" command as often as you can in a ten-minute training period. Walk, give the command, then stop. At this point you're teaching by example, showing your dog what to do. Each time you say "stay," make a complete stop. Try this trick to speed the learning process: shuffle your feet just before you give the command, say "stay," then come to a full stop. The shuffling alerts your the dog.

At first, when your dog responds, if even momentarily, give praise. Do not expect the dog to hold long. As soon as it stops, being walking immediately. If you pause, the pup will become nervous and may move on its own. That only makes training harder.

When the pup is confident enough to respond consistently, you can teach it to hold for longer periods—even when you are not at its side. Begin by placing your pup on "stay." Step forward one or two paces, turn and face your dog. If the dog does not move, praise it. If it breaks, pick it up and place it on the spot on which it was standing. Repeat the command. Be sure to make eye contact.

RELEASING FROM STAY

It is as important to release a dog properly as it is to teach it to "stay." Once your pup has learned to hold, you must to teach it to be released. The release should be given from the beginning after each command: "stay"—"okay." The two work hand in hand. Initially you'll be close. Even so, never release your dog until you are face to face, making eye contact. Say "okay," and when the dog breaks, praise it. Begin walking immediately. Later, you can release the dog from longer distances just by repeating its name and saying "okay." It is important to use two tones of voice: a slightly heavier voice for the command and a lighter, upbeat tone for the release.

"Stay" is an important command, and you'll have to spend considerable time teaching it. Be patient, consistent, and demanding. If, in a week or so, the pup holds ten or fifteen seconds, consider that you are making headway. Repetition alone will extend the time. Vary the routine so it does not become boring, and each time try to increase the distance at which your pup holds. Before you are through the pup should understand the command, respond consistently, and hold firm at any distance. Continue working until your pup holds even though you are completely across a room or yard. It may take a month or more to reach this point. Don't be impatient. Don't give up. Your dog must hold consistently on "stay" before it can be taught "whoa."

As the distance increases, you should use the thirty-foot check line mentioned in the chapter on equipment (Chapter 8). Do not try to make do with a short leash. As you increase distance, you'll eventually reach the end of a short line, and without a lead the pup is beyond control. Even a dodo-headed canine will realize it can wander where it wants and you will have created a new set of problems that need to be erased.

EARLY GUN TRAINING

A field dog not broken to the gun is not worth its salt. At some point in early training your pup should become used to sudden, unexpected sounds similar to those it will hear hunting. Unfortunately, there is no consensus on how to accomplish this.

Some trainers begin firing handguns with 22 blanks when the pups are five or six weeks old and still in the litter. They reason that if the pups hear the noise as a group, the littermates will reinforce each other and none will panic. Few professionals, aside from a handful of southern breeders, use this method. Your pup has probably never heard gunshots. Obviously you'll have to introduce the dog to them.

Timing is everything. One shot fired early can ruin an animal. You should begin by conditioning the pup to unexpected sounds (though not gunshots) when it is ten or twelve weeks old. Since my dogs are either in kennels or in my house, I use what I have on hand. Guns, even blanks, are out of the question in a city. In my case the sudden noises come from pots and pans. I bang them together out of the dog's sight. The length and intensity of sounds depends on the dog. If a dog is frightened by the noise, stop or soften the tone. Once it accepts the gentler sounds, increase the decibels. If the pup's bold and quickly ignores the sounds, consider yourself lucky. When an animal reaches this point, there is little to be gained by repetition.

When your pup is four or five months old and is used to sudden sounds, you can try gunshots. Take the dog to a place where you can use a gun. If it is hunting season and the dog seems bold, you may even take the animal on a hunt accompanied by experienced dogs. To my mind, however, it is safer to begin with a handgun, blank shells, and a friend to handle the details. Let the pup run at the end of a check line, and if it seems excited and happy, distracted by the things in the field, have your friend—some distance behind you—fire a handgun loaded with blanks. If the dog does not spook and takes only a cursory notice of the shot, repeat it, bringing the gun closer. Try this on several different occasions until your pup accepts shots no matter where they come from.

Incidentally, no matter how well broken you think your dog is, protect it from July 4th. It is a difficult time. More pups have been ruined for all hunting by the sudden, unexpected fireworks than in any other way. Keep the pup with you on the Fourth, and if you even suspect a promise of fireworks take your dog to some remote, quiet place until the day is over.

Now, take the pup as many places as you can. Let it run at the end of a check line in a variety of spots where there are people, traffic, unexpected noises, and interesting scents. I take my dog to parks, shopping malls, and open fields. The dog is allowed to sniff, snort, and chase butterflies and small birds. During this time be sure to repeat all of the commands the dog has learned. You should be able to use commands such as "stay," "heel," and "kennel" several times a day, and the more you use these the sounder your pup will become.

These are important days. The pup is discovering its world, learning from the things its nose tells it, from the things that happen to it and from the mistakes it makes. A pup is like a young child. The more it has been around, the more self-assured it is. The more fun a pup can have in open fields that first year, the better bird dog it will become. There are such things as "delayed" instincts, natural reactions undeveloped inside an animal, and the more opportunity for field-running, the more these are brought to the surface. If you can arrange it, a pup should experience outings like these at least once a week.

TRAINING ON WATER

Pups should be exposed to water as soon as possible since at some point in life they'll be expected to retrieve over it. Any kind of water can be used, a small stream, a lake, or an ocean. It is easy enough to take your dog to the beach on a warm summer's day. The animal will be hot and the cool water will look inviting—even though the dog's never seen it before. Roll up your pants and wade in. You are your pup's God (really!) and it'll follow. Don't go far—about to the dog's knees. Let it splash around, becoming used to the idea. When it seems comfortable, put your hand beneath its stomach and gently float it into deeper water. The dog should instinctively begin swimming. If it does, let it swim for a moment, then guide it back to land.

Repeat exposure to water as often as you can. The worst thing in the world is to have an older dog meet up with water before it's learned to swim.

RETRIEVING AND FETCHING

I know every hunter likes to see his pup retrieve, and it is okay to let a young pup do a little retrieving just to amaze the gentry. You'll prove to yourself that the dog has a natural desire, and your friends will be suitably impressed, but do not overdo it. Too much backyard retrieving creates problems. I know trainers who let their pups play with dead birds. They think it makes the pup excited, but to me this is a serious mistake. A pup allowed to play with a dead bird may well respond the same way when it is old enough to hunt, and you'll face a lot of unnecessary work breaking habits the dog should not have learned.

It is good for your pup to learn to carry things in its mouth. The experience can be a plus when you begin retrieving training, but do not make a game of it. Above all else, do not hide things for your pup to find. One of the worst practices is to hide a training dummy or wings from a killed bird and order your pup to find them. I know, some hunters swear they've taught their pup to be a great, instinctive bird dog in just this way. Don't believe it! Nine times out of ten that game backfires and two things can happen: first, the trainer creates a ground-tracking dog instead of one that hunts via the air; and second, the dog learns to react to bird scent without pointing. And never ask a pup to retrieve such objects as soft rubber balls. There is something about elasticity that invites a pup to chew, and when a pup chews the objects it retrieves, that also leads to trouble. Incidentally, if you want to introduce the command "fetch," this is okay. You will use it later to cue your dog to retrieve in the field, and it's safe for it to be learned now. Be sure to repeat the dog's name before the cue, such as in, "Rover, fetch!" so that later you can cue the dog to "fetch" with its name alone. This avoids confusion in the field.

If there is a problem common to upland dogs, it is properly finishing a retrieve. Too many dogs drop a bird five or ten feet away, and their owners let them get away with it. If a dog purposely drops a cripple, it can mean real trouble. You'll end up chasing a downed bird across an entire field. Anticipate the problem. Teach your pup now that when it retrieves something, anything, it must bring it to your hand. When the dog does, tell it to "give," then offer praise—even if it has just retrieved your best slipper.

Trainers specializing in flushing dogs often feel it is important to train a pup to sit with a training dummy in its mouth. They believe this guarantees a more perfect delivery, and though I do not do it, I see their point. If you would like to try that with a spaniel, go ahead. It is not very exciting so limit yourself to a few short sessions. Do not bore the pup. Boredom could also lead to problems.

In the first year, retrieving is not important. If a pup takes to it, capitalize on it. If not, don't force the issue. Any dog can be taught to retrieve later, though no dog can be taught to point. When your pup is young, concentrate on developing its pointing instincts.

Once your pup has the basic commands under its belt, training should be expanded to include travel and playtime in the country. If possible, travel with your pup in a portable kennel so it will become used to one early. Whenever I take my pup, I put the kennel in the back of my pickup and tell the animal to "kennel"—which means to jump into the crate. The pup not only accepts the crate as normal transportation, but looks forward to it. It always means a day in the country.

You could take your pup hunting if you're with friends (see Illustration 30). The experience of running with trained dogs is good, but keep your pup on a check line. A lot of youngsters will point naturally, though not staunchly. Under no circumstances do you want your dog to point, break, then flush a bird and catch it. The check line should prevent this. If the pup catches you off base and points with the check line unattended, act immediately. You can try the "stay" command—though with the scent of a bird in its nostrils the dog might not respond. It is better to run down the check line as quickly as you can and regain physical control. Ask your partner to kick the bird out while you hold the dog. If you flush the dog's first point, pray that it happens when you can make a kill. A downed bird gives you something to build on. As a matter of fact, if you could take a young pup hunting, shoot nothing but the birds it pointed, and ignore any it flushed, the dog would almost train itself.

FIRST TIME ON BIRDS

The time it takes to train a pup is determined by the progress it makes in each stage. As a rule the dog should be reasonably trained—that is, firm on basic commands and bold and sure—in nine or ten months. An additional six months of intensive field training should have the animal ready for hunting.

CHAPTER ELEVEN

Testing Natural Pointing Ability

A majority of younger upland bird hunters put the cart before the horse. They insist a dog's ability to retrieve is substantially more important than its ability to point. They are wrong. Pointing comes first. It's not only at the heart of the issue, it is the issue. You can hunt from now to the twenty-first century and never shoot a bird if your dog can't point. The way it finds game, points, and holds staunch is everything—verse, chapter, and book. Dad said it in Chapter 1, and I'll emphasize it: the style and beauty of upland game hunting is all in your animal. If I hunted over a dog that was beautiful on point and so staunch it was a joy to watch, it would not hurt my feelings if the dog never retrieved.

Don't get me wrong. I like retrieving. It has a utilitarian purpose. It saves unnecessary walking and while we're all supposed to be such good shots we never cripple birds, a good retriever saves a lot of running, too. That is not under consideration. What I am emphasizing is that you can teach any dog to retrieve but you will never teach even one pointer to point. Pointing is either an instinct or a dog has no interest. You can come close with a "whoa-point," but even that is a mediocre substitute. It is trainer initiated. It lacks intensity.

You've probably discovered a little about your dog's pointing instincts by now. Perhaps you've fluttered a pheasant wing on the end of a string (see Illustrations 31 and 32) or taken the dog to a field, beach, or park to let it chase dickey birds, pigeons, or gulls. In short, you've seen the dog in action enough to know whether or not it has an instinct to develop.

Professionals take that discovery an additional step. When a pup is about a year old and nearly ready for "whoa" training, many will take the animal to a field to see how it reacts with live birds. The procedure can be done in two to four half-hour sessions and accomplishes a number of things. First, it lets you appraise your pup. Second, it introduces your pup to birds naturally and more effectively than days at the beach. And third, it lets your pup teach itself a little about the art of handling its new-found feathered friends. Every pup with a dab of instinct will flash point, that is, will briefly stand tail up, body erect, nose pointing toward a bird, but without training few will hold long. Two or three sessions on well-controlled birds can introduce a pup to the idea that there is more to pointing than a flash of instinct and more to handling birds than an urge to rush in where wiser minds fear to tread.

THE RIGHT EQUIPMENT

Not every professional believes in this phase of training, but those who do generally rely on an electronic bird release, a popper, because it is essential that the dog not reach the bird. It must flush quick and clean before the dog arrives. The pup learns one important lesson: that when it breaks point and pressures a bird, the bird flushes, and when the bird flushes the dog has no chance at it.

If you want to try my suggestion, I recommend an electronic release because it provides the greatest margin of safety. It is not the only solution— I'll mention others—but I think it is the best. During this session the pup is running on a "free-floating" check line, that is, with the line dragging unhampered behind. The dog has not been introduced to "whoa," and though it knows basic obedience, the only control you have—or want at this point—is an ability to release a bird before your pup reaches it. With a remote electronic device, no matter where you are in the field, you have that control. If you are not able to buy, rent, or share one, there are other solutions which, though not quite as good, can be considered workable. The check line is only an insurance policy, used as a last resort to prevent the dog from catching the bird.

For some, the second choice is a mechanical bird release, a rope or push-button-operated popper that resembles the electronic version. It is good but has drawbacks. Birds can only be released when you have the trigger in your hand. That means you must control your dog more and control partially defeats the concept. In the first place, you, the owner-handler, enter the picture, and it is better if you remain an observer. Secondly, because you are "on stage," the pup will not react naturally. If you use a caged pigeon, one confined on the ground, you must work your dog even tighter and be in closer control, and for all the reasons above this is not recommended. The instinct to point must be kept as natural as possible. In this case, the electronic release does it best.

I'm not in the business of selling electronic bird releasers. I do not own part of any company and make no retail sales, but if you are concerned about the cost of training a dog—hard-earned bucks spent for equipment, live birds, and more—there are a couple of ways to justify the expense. First, a professional would charge between $700 and $1,000 to train a dog, and a fully trained dog is worth $1,500 to $3,000 on the open market; more, if the bloodlines are right. If you spent $500 or so on equipment and resold it as used after you were finished, training would probably cost no more than $300. Now $300 for a dog worth five to ten times that amount seems pretty sound business to me. Sources for equipment are listed in the back of the book.

CHOOSING BIRDS

Pigeons are preferred, first because they are the best bird to use with a mechanical release, and second because they are the least expensive. If you cannot beg, borrow, or buy a popper, my second choice would be native birds, though the disadvantages are numerous. It is not easy to find an area with a supply of them. Use of the area may be limited by seasons. You cannot know if there are birds in the spot you've chosen. Finally, you cannot possibly control the birds if they are there. The important advantage is this: even if the area is flooded with wild birds, you can be certain your pup will never catch one.

In lieu of native birds, try captive-bred varieties. For this job I think pheasants are best. You can plant them in controlled locations, and if they are healthy, mature enough, and good fliers, you can be sure your dog has as little chance of catching one as it has a wild bird. Healthy captive-breds sixteen to eighteen weeks old should be good fliers, though a pen-raised pheasant will not flush like a wild one. Partly domesticated, it may hold longer and when flushed will lack stamina. You may also find a professional trainer willing to help. A check-out session should cost between $15 and $30 plus the price of birds. As a rule five to twenty birds are used. A professional will probably rely on homing pigeons.

Whatever your choice, never use hand-planted pigeons. If dizzied lightly, they will fly before the dog reaches them, and if controlled too much, your pup will probably catch at least one. I've seen it happen time and time again.

A new dog owner tells his friend, "Watch my pup point." He picks up a couple of pigeons and heads for the closest field. The birds are tethered, hobbled, or dizzied, and the pup is turned loose. It finds the first bird, points momentarily, and, before the owner can catch the check line, rushes in. If that pup catches just one bird, say goodbye pointer. The next time the guy tries the routine his animal breaks a little sooner, and before he knows it his dog will not point. Why should it? It is a lot more fun busting birds.

THE CONCEPT

However you do it, a few sessions should prove extremely interesting and helpful and the concept is simplicity itself: for a trainer it is time for observation, and for a dog, time for self-discovery. Your dog will prove, under field conditions, whether or not it is an instinctive pointer. Since you are still working with a pup, sessions should be short, not longer than thirty minutes, sufficient time for about four birds. Your pup could probably handle two or three sessions on a weekend, enough to build any pup's confidence. Probably the most important knowledge gained from the weekend will be this: your dog will discover a little about birds. It will learn that when it pushes, pressing to get closer, they fly; when it holds back, they don't. If it teaches itself that, consider the weekend a bargain.

THE SESSION

You'll need a large area to work in, a hunting preserve, a farmer's field, or public land. If you have a mechanical release, manual or electronic, position and load it without your dog spotting the location. Bring a blank gun. This is an excellent time to reinforce gun training as well. If you have two releasers, the training goes faster because you can move from one to the other, but two are obviously not essential. With one you kennel your dog while you reload and reposition the device.

Either way, place a pigeon in the release, then let your dog go with the long checkline attached. The dog should be running free, the line "floating" or dragging behind. When the dog discovers a bird and points, do nothing. Do not talk, do not interfere. Simply observe. As long as the dog holds its point the bird remains in the popper, but if the dog breaks, if it takes just one step, the bird is instantly released. And if the dog wants to chase the flushed bird, let it. Be sure to fire the blank gun each time a bird flies. It simulates hunting.

It is important to trigger the release substantially before the dog can reach it. Obviously, you must allow time for the signal to transmit, the doors to open, the bird to become airborne. You do not want your dog to arrive while the release is operating. If it is smacked in the face by one of the doors, the animal may equate its pain with the bird and may never want to hunt again.

I realize many hunters will not agree. They will insist a pigeon is not a native bird, a popper is not a pheasant, and the whole procedure is unnatural. In theory they *could be* right; in practice they are *wrong*. The procedure works, and "unnatural" or not, I've never had a pup who would not point an electronic release. I can say unequivocally that a dog who refuses to point a popper with a pigeon in it will not point a pheasant. In truth, after a couple of tries many dogs will point a popper and pigeon with more intensity than a free-running bird because they've learned that if they look cross-eyed or take one step, the bird in the popper flushes. A native bird will rarely respond as quickly. Neither pheasant nor Bobwhite quail like to fly. They are tight-sitting ground birds, and often a dog can take four or five steps before pressuring either enough to break. Train a young dog on birds like these and it'll quickly learn it can fudge. If it moves a little on one bird, it'll move more on the next.

That should not occur with an electronic popper. If your dog takes one step, press the remote release and flush the bird. After your pup has pressured four or five birds, it will discover that the longer it holds, the longer the bird remains on the ground. That is an important lesson.

With two or three sessions under its collar, that is, after releasing less than twenty birds, your dog should progress from a hasty, bust-'em-up pup to a slightly crafty, seminatural, eager-to-learn pointer. And if your dog points with some intensity and learns a little about the art of stalking birds, the animal has made an important statement. It has told you that it has a pointing instinct. It's said it is eager for "whoa" training. And it's proven the two of you are ready for Chapter 12.

CHAPTER TWELVE

Learning to "Whoa"

Your dog's first birthday is an important occasion. This marks the time that it stops being a pup, becomes "grown up," and is ready to learn the duties and responsibilities of a hunting dog. But a dog is not a machine. It cannot be programmed to be ready for advanced training on precisely the 366th day of its life.

When a pup is young, it is neither mature enough nor experienced enough to cope with the pressures of advanced training. Some canines mature as early as eight or nine months, and for others a year is too early. One year is a reliable average, and I strongly suggest waiting "full term" before teaching more than basic obedience. In the end, you are the only one who can sense the right moment, the only one who can be sure when your pup is ready and when it is not.

If the dog is alert, bold, confident, interested in the world around it and can respond to both criticism and new ideas with eagerness, it may be time. But if it is not all of these things, build confidence before embarking on the training I'm about to describe. Remember, whenever you start, the pup must have learned obedience. It must come promptly when called, be firm on "heel" on and off leash, and absolutely understand "stay." In addition, it should have proven its pointing instinct.

THE PROBLEMS OF "WHOA"

At Black Point field training for pointers begins with "whoa," the order to stop. Flushing dogs are ready for "hup" training, the counterpart to this, a little earlier. (See Chapter 13).

I do not know the history of the command, but it is commonly pronounced "whoa-upp," and I've always suspected it came from horse training where a similar word has a similar meaning. For an upland game dog it is at once the most important command and the most difficult to teach. It takes over from "stay," ordering a dog to stop. It is an invisible check line, giving you long-distance control. It must be learned before any dog can be staunch on point and certainly before a pup can be turned loose on birds. Flushing dogs are taught "hup," a command which is a logical extension of "sit"—"stay."

"Whoa" is difficult to teach because it goes against canine instinct. When a dog is running free across a field, it naturally expects to continue until it finds game, and when it scents a bird, instincts tell it to run the bird down. Like a check line, "whoa" imposes your will on the animal. It reminds it that it is not out for fun and games but for the serious job of finding birds. What it wants— and what its instincts tell it that it wants—are not important. For some dogs, especially ones that have had permissive training as pups, this is an unnerving discovery. It helps illustrate why an animal should be emotionally mature before you begin advanced training.

I know some hunters who let their dog race in uncontrolled to retrieve as soon as a bird is flushed, shot, and downed. The dog does not wait for a command, is not under control, and is not staunch. I've suspected this happens because the dog initiated the action. It works well enough and the owner sees no reason to change. Perhaps. After everything is sorted out, the bottom line in training is to create a dog that pleases you. If you're happy with a half-controlled dog, stick with it. But I wouldn't want to hunt over that kind of animal.

Control on point is essential. Unless a bird is wounded it will take to wing the instant a dog pressures it, and pressure runs contrary to all precepts of pointing. (The entire concept of upland game dog training can be explained in four sentences: The purpose of training is to teach a dog that the only birds that count are those its owner flushes. A dog must not push a bird until it flushes, but instead must reduce pressure, must hold back. Birds the dog breaks are lost game. The wise hunter does not shoot them.)

A finished, polished, reliable gundog is "steady to wing and shot." I'll explain that later (Chapter 16), but essentially it means a dog remains staunch on point through five distinct phases: (1) when its owner gives the "whoa" command, (2) when it is on point, (3) when the bird is flushed, (4) when the bird is shot, and (5) until the retrieve command is given. A dog that can do all of this is one you can be proud of.

"Whoa" not only gives you that control, but is the key to subsequent training. Your dog must thoroughly understand the command and must obey whether it is five or five hundred feet away, whether racing at top speed or standing on point. The command means "stop immediately"—not two seconds from now. The dog is expected to stop and hold staunch until released.

Some dogs learn quickly. Others require months. There can be no schedule since "whoa" training is divided into several steps, but as a rule a cooperative dog should become reasonably sure-footed in four to eight weeks. A stubborn dog, one that fights all the way, may require six months. Even in the extreme, this is not as bad as it sounds. Remember, you are working with ten-minute sessions three or four times a week. That means a brainy, cooperative dog learns in 160 minutes, about 2 ½ hours. A dog slightly less eager, one that requires two months, still does the job in 320 minutes, or 5 ⅓ hours. That's not bad, either. And if a stubborn animal requires the full six months, it's still not doing badly. According to my calculations, that fellow will have learned to "whoa" in 960 minutes: just 16 hours. It takes most kids longer to learn to play baseball.

PRELIMINARIES

Trainers have devised a number of ways to teach the command. Some use punishing collars and others half-hitches around a dog's loins. Still others use ropes and a few whips. Perhaps the largest number use a "whoa post," an upright fence post that requires two ropes and two collars (a punishing collar and a regular collar). The post and ropes let the trainer control the dog's movements. The regular collar is used to guide the animal. The punishing collar inflicts pain if the animal makes a wrong move. In theory, the dog is learning that when it "whoa's" properly, there is no pain and when it messes up there is. Again, in theory, the animal is not supposed to associate pain with its trainer. The dog can see the trainer in front. The object responsible for the pain, the post, is plainly visible on the opposite side. I've always wondered how many dogs really think things through that way.

I disagree with all such methods. If you can teach obedience without punishing collars and complex ropes, you can teach "whoa" the same way. And the easier it is for a dog to learn, the faster it learns and the better the relationship between the two of you.

Problems will develop if the animal was taught to sit during first-year obedience training. Teaching a sit-trained dog to stand on "whoa" adds an extra dimension, often demanding more patience than an owner cares to muster. Later, I'll tell you how to work around it. Again, only springers should be taught to sit, and they are not taught "whoa."

VOICES AND INFLECTION

The tone of voice is very important. Be sure you have eye contact; then give the command in a calm, even tone. If your dog does not respond immediately, or if it stops for a moment, then moves, do not raise your voice. Repeat the command and give the dog a second opportunity to get it right. If, in early training, the dog holds, even for one second, consider it a job well done.

One or two weeks later you can demand better compliance. As an example, your dog is still on the check line after a couple weeks of training. You give the "whoa" command. The dog stops briefly, then something catches its eye. It seems ready to break. Until this moment you've said "whoa" calmly. Now, you say it louder. The dog knows the new voice is a correction because it has a different tone and intensity. The dog gives you his immediate attention. Increasing decibels, greater intensity, and a change in tone are correction techniques that work well if not overdone.

Later, when the dog is on the long check line but running free (the line dragging), it will be ranging further afield. If it makes a mistake under these conditions, you must avoid the urge to give double commands, a common mistake so confusing it can undo a lot of good work. Typically, here's what happens: a dog is running twenty-five to fifty feet away when an owner yells, "Tiger, whoa!" Impulsively, Tiger keeps going. Instinctively, the owner shouts, "No! Tiger! Here!" The owner has just given his dog three commands, back to back—"whoa," "no," and "here," i.e., "stop doing what you are doing" and "come to me." At best that's confusing, and at worst, it takes the dog's mind off the original order. The dog forgets that it did not obey "whoa," and the owner has changed the name of the game. Instead of forcing the dog to stop in its tracks, the fellow is now running after his pup. The dog is in command. If the animal comes after all this, it thinks it's done exactly what its boss ordered.

TWO "WHOA" COMMANDS

A dog is taught to respond to "whoa" in two ways: to a verbal command (that is, when it hears the word) and to the hand (when the hand is raised). It is essential that your dog learn both because, when hunting, it will often range beyond the sound of your voice.

Consider this example: your dog is on point. The wind is blowing toward you. A bird flushes. Anticipating your dog may break, you want to prevent it. The dog cannot hear you but it can see your raised hand. The dog stops in its tracks. What might have developed into a touchy situation has turned into an event you can praise.

The command is always taught without birds and before a dog knows much about them. (To this point your pup has been exposed to live birds only for fun.) The rationale is simple: at some time during training your dog will have to be reprimanded, corrected by pulling on the check line, by stern voice, or by something more severe. If birds are involved, the dog may associate pressure and pain with them and will thereafter flinch every time it senses a bird. The dog will anticipate being jerked or yelled at; I mean, that it will think about those things and will develop a number of responses you'll have to train away. The dog may blink, loose attention, or worse. I'll explain these factors later. If "whoa" is taught without birds, the dog can only associate cause and effect with its trainer. Its bird instincts will remain intact.

THE TIME TO TRAIN

Training should be kept as natural and happy as possible. Let the dog progress at its own pace. Do not push. Be sure to hold sessions when they are convenient for you. Select a time and be consistent. Dogs prefer routine, so vary the time only in extreme circumstance. For example, if visitors or guests play with the pup immediately before training time, postpone the session. Give the pup time to calm down.

Teach your dog only when it is rested and at peak energy. Those who say, "Get your dog a little tired, then give the command because he'll be more cooperative," are wrong. A tired pup is "whoaing" because it is pooped. "Whoa" has become nothing more than a rest period, and it is easy to comply because the pup gets a chance to catch its breath. If your pup cooperates when it is full of vinegar, it will cooperate any time.

As throughout training, when your dog responds properly, give praise. A pat on the head and a sincere "good boy" can go a long way toward making your dog more cooperative and more receptive.

BEGINNING "WHOA" TRAINING

Early training is an extension of the "stay" training given months ago, and you are transferring your dog's response from the cue "stay" to "whoa" and then expanding on that. Start your dog on the short check line, in "heel" position; and after a little walking, give the command, "Tiger, stay," quickly adding "whoa." As with every command, use your dog's name first. Initially it will learn more by copying your actions than by understanding the command. When you say "whoa" be sure to stop. And instantly. If you don't, your dog won't.

EARLY LESSONS

(See Illustrations 34–38.)

The first sessions should go this way: your dog is on your left side (unless you are a left-handed shooter, in which case the dog is on your right). Walk with the dog in "heel" position. Lean forward, raise your hand in front of the dog's face, say, "Tiger, stay-whoa," then stop. The dog should stop exactly as it has been trained to do on "stay." If "stay-whoa" confuses the dog, try again. If the dog is not paying full attention, it may help to shuffle your feet just as you did when teaching "stay."

Watch your dog. It's tail is a sure sign of its feelings. If it is stiff, the dog is confident. If it goes down, the dog has cowed. Back off. You're applying more pressure than your dog can handle. Return to basics.

As the dog learns to obey the command, transpose the words. The order becomes, "Tiger, whoa-stay." Once a pup becomes reliable on this command, separate the words—"Whoa" (pause) "stay"—farther and farther, until you eliminate "stay." The amount of time required for this phase of training depends on your dog, but it should respond well to verbal "whoa" commands in two weeks.

Remember, all this time you are giving a hand signal along with the verbal order. This is important because once the dog responds reliably to words, you'll concentrate on the hand. I often begin this phase by lowering my voice gradually, phasing out the verbal command as the hand signal takes over. As with the verbal signal, you will eventually get to the point where the dog responds to the hand exactly as to voice. This kind of training can become boring for the most cooperative dog, and it pays to vary your approach.

RELEASING THE DOG

A dog is released with "okay" exactly as for "stay." In the beginning the dog will be by your side. After you've given the command, "Tiger, stay-whoa," delay the release only as long as you think it can hold. Say "okay," then begin walking immediately. If you've timed it properly, your dog held and you have something to praise: if it held for just one second, it did it right. Give the dog a full measure of praise.

Whether the dog is at your side or yards away, be sure you have its attention before giving any release. All too often a dog will stop instantly on "whoa," but its mind is someplace else. You can tell because its eyes are wandering. Never give a release until you've made eye contact. It teaches your dog to watch you. The animal is not always going to be in a position to hear your voice, or even your whistle. From the first, when you teach "whoa," teach your dog to check in visually.

And if your dog is required to keep its attention on you, you've got to give it 110% of yours. You cannot be standing in the middle of the field shooting the breeze with your buddy. You must watch your dog as intently as you expect it to watch you.

Incidentally, do not release a dog the instant you've made eye contact. If you give the command too quickly, your dog will believe that once it makes eye contact it is released, a bad habit for any dog. Never call a dog back after giving a "whoa" command. It is confusing. Instead, release the animal and cast it off on another run. Similarly, do not call it back after giving the release command. Even with a pause between "okay" and the command "here," a dog will quickly get the idea that release means to come to you. When you are hunting, you don't want that.

Most dogs are far more attentive than you'd suspect. Every move sends a message. Reach for your car keys, the pooch knows its time for a ride. Reach for a hat or coat, it knows it's time to go outside. Thus, if you pause before giving a command, the dog will not be anticipating a particular order, and not knowing, will remain intent, ready to hear or see exactly what you want.

MORE "WHOA"

It helps to talk to your dog while the dog is holding firm. You reduce tension and increase confidence by saying something encouraging—"Stay, that's a good boy, stay," for example. There will be longer delays between "whoa" and release as you increase the distance. Don't let the dog off the hook as soon as it's shown a willingness to comply. It must learn that once on "whoa," it is expected to hold until you release it. Remote commands are new and the dog may seem uncomfortable. If the dog softens, that is if its tail drops, shorten the distance and the time between command and release.

As with obedience training, the length of the sessions should be variable though never more than ten minutes. If you get a good piece of work—say one good "whoa" after a couple of half-hearted ones—you may accomplish more by quitting in five to seven minutes. Conversely, if you get a number of half-hearted attempts, you may want to go the distance. If you quit early, finish up by repeating commands the dog already knows. In this way you can "pyramid" its schooling, reinforcing previous lessons. And when you go for your evening walk, you can try two or three "whoa's" along with other commands, but be sure there is time for play. A dog must have time to relax.

TRAINING FOR DISTANCE

Once your dog is "whoaing" reliably at your side from the "heel" position, change to the long check line and begin training for distance. Give a "whoa" command (voice or hand); and when the dog responds, step forward one pace, turn, and face your dog. At first the dog may want to move with you but if you've laid the groundwork, it should hold. If the dog moves, correct it and try again. When the dog holds, step forward, give the release, and praise your dog. As with any training, your dog will progress in increments. Repeat training until your dog is firm and certain on short distances, then increase both the distance and the time your dog must hold firm.

CORRECTIONS

Never let your dog get away with anything incorrect or half-hearted without a correction, and until your dog proves it knows the "whoa" command and obeys more times than not, it should remain on the long check line. It makes correction easier, but when training progresses to the point that the dog is running farther than the length of the check line, you have a new ball game. Though the line is attached to its collar, you are not in immediate control. The line is "free-floating," or being dragged behind your dog. The situation must be handled differently. If the dog does not stop, mark the spot at which you gave the command with your hat, a handkerchief, anything. Then stop the animal any way you can. Run down dog or check line, whichever you can reach. Lift the animal and carry it, walking briskly to the place where you gave the command. Put down the dog and go through the "whoa" series face to face. Usually lifting a dog off the ground is better than dragging—no matter the circumstances. Lifting tends to disorient a dog, and believe me, it remembers.

If a dog continually refuses to obey, even after it's been air-lifted a couple of times, try picking it up by the scruff of the back and shake the dog gently. It is uncomfortable and humiliating. A dog treated to this a couple of times rarely forgets.

THE IMPORTANCE OF REPETITION

In the first days you need to be forgiving. It is entirely possible your dog may not understand though you feel it's had every chance to catch on. Whether it makes a half-stop or doesn't stop at all, give it several chances. If the dog still doesn't understand, return to "stay." Work with that until it does well, then add "whoa" and repeat the training just described. But once you know your dog understands the command and proves it can respond, successful repetition is important. The dog must not be allowed to make mistakes. Each time it repeats the command successfully, it is one step closer to an automatic response. With "whoa," compliance must be perfect.

Training for distance is based on the same concept. Each time you take one step farther from your dog, each time you delay release a few seconds more, you are reinforcing the desired response. But there is a reverse side to watch for. Each time you delay release you are inviting a mistake. That's only natural. The longer a dog stands, the more nervous it becomes. It knows it's in the field for some reason and is eager to be off. Be stubborn. Make the dog hold. Talk to it, reassure it—"good boy, stay. That's it, stay, good boy." If your dog is soft, insecure, and uncomfortable about "whoa"—and the tail will tell you—reduce the time it must hold.

Timid dogs are always hard to teach and difficult to keep intense, but timidity is not unusual. I'd guess there are more timid dogs than bold ones, and if you have one, take heart. That trait by itself is not a drawback. You can make a dog bold by praising it and by progressing at the dog's speed, not yours. You can apply more pressure with an older animal, but a timid pup needs to brought along gently.

CONTROLLING A SITTING DOG

Some dogs, and most commonly those who have been taught to sit as a part of obedience training, will insist on sitting on "whoa." It is not a pretty sight for a pointer and must be trained out. That can be a difficult, time-consuming job, especially if the dog is stubborn but soft.

The common approach has been to prop the dog on its feet, time after time after time. Sometimes the procedure worked, but many dogs never got the idea. At Black Point we've developed a better way. Though not original, I do not know who invented it. I've seen several trainers use versions and it is worth recommending. Run the check line from the collar under the dog's chest, between its legs, then to your hand. If the dog tries to sit on "whoa," lift the check line. The action literally hoists the animal by its own petard, driving the point home. I guarantee the most flagrant sitter will quickly become a confirmed stander.

WORKING FOR STAUNCHNESS

When your dog is comfortable with "whoa" and is holding firm, it is time to train for staunchness, that is, to teach the dog to hold even when a bird breaks. A lot of trainers make an error here. They'll use feathers, wings, anything that smells like a bird because they believe it makes a dog more intense. I suppose it does, but there is more against the idea than in favor of it, and my argument returns to the point previously made—about not using birds in any phase of "whoa" training. Your dog can transpose negative pressure into a dislike for all birds. In short order, you've created a problem dog. Avoid birds and you avoid possible problems.

I prefer to use "the hat trick." It is as close to real birds as you can get. Again, this is done before birds have been introduced. The dog is still on the check line, and it helps if you have a second person to control the line.

When the dog is some yards away, give it a "whoa," and while it is standing, walk up to it. Without letting the dog see your actions, drop your hat in the grass in front of it. With your friend holding the line, kick the hat. I don't care what breed or how well trained, when the dog sees the grass wave and the hat move, it'll think it's a bird. If the dog is going to break, it'll do it then. The dog will want to go for the hat just as it would go for a bird, and the point of the trick is this: your dog cannot associate a jerk on the check line with birds because there are none.

THE FINAL TEST

A good field dog must learn that it should continue working when released. It is not expected to return to your side. You can begin by giving "whoa" commands when the dog is twenty-five or thirty feet away. Release the dog and cast it in a direction away from you. If it comes toward you, give it another "whoa," then cast it off again. If the dog gives any kind of compliance, praise it. If not, give it another opportunity.

When the dog is in the field, holding firm on "whoa," talk to it if it is close enough. Say something like, "Stay. Steady, steady, easy boy. Good boy." Keep your voice calm. You may be able to approach close enough to stroke its sides, and if you can that is good. But watch your dog's reactions. If it softens, back away. Let it remain on "whoa" for a few seconds, then release it.

CHAPTER THIRTEEN

Introducing the Flushing Dog

Anyone into bird hunting, even the newest and rawest recruit, realizes there are two kinds of upland game dogs, those that point and those that flush birds. This is the kind of trivia you absorb almost automatically, and it should be equally obvious that while flushing dogs are popular, on this side of the Atlantic pointers predominate.

Flushing dogs are not as common here as abroad, and three spaniels, Boykins, Cockers, and springers comprise the entire U.S. list. Boykins are up and coming though unrecognized by the AKC Cockers can be superior hunters, but are bred here most often as pets or for bench competition. English Springer Spaniels are the breed most American upland game hunters demand when they want a flushing dog. They outnumber cockers ten to one in field trials competition, and all others, even remotely related—Labs are one example—are considered retrievers.

It is not easy to suggest why the once popular flushing dog is now less popular than the pointer, but one probable reason is that they are more demanding to hunt over. Flushing dogs were probably at their prime when game was caught with nets, coursing greyhounds and falcons. Guns changed all of this. They made hunting more leisurely, and for the laid-back and relaxed, shooting over a flushing dog is anything but slow. A gunner must be constantly within range. With a pointer you can call your shots.

Aside from those deep into trivia, this distinction is important to people for only one reason: not only are pointers and flushers hunted differently, but in many ways they are trained differently as well.

Much of the material in this book applies to both. Most chapters have been written so that no matter which you own, the suggestions will be valid and helpful. From sections on buying pups, housing, and health to those on diet and field trials, the information applies equally, but at certain places the road divides. Some training techniques apply specifically to the pointer and others to the flushing dog. As an example, Chapter 12 is a pointer chapter. Flushing dogs have no interest in "whoa." And this section is exclusively for the owners of flushing dogs. Pointers have no interest in "hup."

Here I suggest specific techniques for training spaniels, from the earliest obedience, at eight to ten weeks of age, to the time your dog is ready for advanced "hup" training, at about ten months. Chapter 13 is also concerned with spaniels. It focuses on advanced "hup" training.

FLUSHING DOGS

In practical terms, the English Springer handily outnumbers Boykins and Cockers. Other spaniels are pointers though their name implies otherwise. The Brittany is an example. Several years ago a grassroots group removed the appellation "spaniel" from the Brittany's name. Setters, several breeds that sound as if they should be included with flushing dogs, are also pointers.

In the field the spaniel's style differs from that of a pointer and offers a wealth of characteristics many hunters appreciate. It is an unusually enthusiastic, energetic, happy dog, and its choppy style of running is unique. At work a spaniel appears to be leaping from one trampoline to another. It quarters with precision and hunts with real enthusiasm, running wiith its head erect, its tail high and flashing. The spaniel tracks airborne scent first, double-checks the ground, and like a Mountie, gets its quarry. It is a natural retriever.

The training schedule differs from that for pointers for these and other reasons. The name of the spaniel's game is obedience. It works closer to its hunter than pointers and instead of holding staunch once game is scented, is expected to flush the bird—even capturing one is not discouraged if the dog can accomplish it in the first two or three feet.

A pointer ranges farther and can work its field almost as it wishes. If it has learned its lessons and is staunch, it'll hold a bird on a solid point until its hunter arrives. But when a spaniel is out of range, its hunter is in serious trouble. The dog may flush birds wildly, as out of control as a five-dollar watch. The good spaniel must learn to be happy and effective within gun range. Much of its breeding has been toward that end.

EARLY TRAINING

For these reasons, the spaniel's training schedule is unique. Paralleling the pointer in the beginning, it differs as the dog grows. The schedule is neither as complex nor as involved as that facing a pointer, and it is shorter. A spaniel is taught less because its job is different and its instincts make some of the training easier and faster. A well-bred spaniel should quarter naturally and retrieve instinctively. If it doesn't have a bred-in enthusiasm to chase birds, to flush them, to race to one that is downed and retrieve it, it is not a sound, well-bred spaniel. A sound spaniel needs very little retriever training and seldom requires force-training.

This is not to say spaniels are perfect. After all, you are training dogs, not breeds. Each animal is different, and while there may be problems, most are minor. The most common is sloppiness on retrieve: a spaniel, even with a strong retrieving instinct, may drop a bird on its return or may not bring it precisely to hand. Fine-tuning can eliminate both headaches. You should neither worry about nor anticipate these problems while your pup is young.

The basic obedience training is the same for pointer and spaniel. The information in Chapter 10 should be followed exactly with one addition: pointers are not taught to "sit." Spaniels are, and at an early age. You'll begin basic training when your pup is eight to ten weeks old and will continue through the fourth month. In this time you should work on the essentials, basics every dog must learn. "Sit," "stay," and "here" are especially important for spaniels and should receive a special emphasis. You can begin preliminary "hup" training in the fifth or sixth month and advanced "hup" training when your dog is ten months old. Though we begin training pointers at the same age, they have several months of "recess" before intensive field training, time in which to to run, play, and build boldness and interest. For them the rigors of advanced training, "whoa" and staunchness, do not begin until they are one year old. The spaniel is introduced to field training earlier.

BASIC TRAINING

To be friendly, happy, and easy to live with, it is important that your dog learn the five or six essentials of basic obedience: to accept a collar, to cope with a leash, to come when called, to go to its box or "kennel," to "heel," to "stay," and, for spaniels, to "sit." These are commands that keep you in control of your pup and provide the groundwork for field training. I prefer to develop obedience to a point of reasonable control by the fourth month—not perfection, for the animal is still young—and then, with the groundwork established, introduce the first stages of "hup," letting a pup develop its instincts naturally.

Many amateurs feel that rewards—cookies, snacks, and kibbled food—motivate a dog to learn faster. Not so! They only create a monster, a spoiled dog that will end up demanding sirloin and caviar. I expect a dog to do what I tell it with nothing more than praise and encouragement, and if you begin this way, offering substantial praise each time your dog does something right, it will be happy. Just remember: praise is your pup's most important reward. Your dog will learn faster if praised each time it rates it than if you delay praise and offer it in lavish amounts though only occasionally.

TIMING THE SESSIONS

Beause you are beginning with a very young pup, sessions should last no more than ten minutes. If you have an opportunity, schedule two a day, the first in the morning, the second in the evening. If you cannot separate training by several hours, limit yourself to one per day.

USING A WHISTLE

Ordinarily, you would not introduce the whistle until your dog is ready for field training, but since you will introduce preliminary "hup" training with the command to sit, you may wish to introduce the whistle at that time. The Roy Goonia whistle suggested in Chapter 8 is a good choice.

THE RELEASE

No command should be given without a release, and the verbal release for "sit," as for "hup," is "okay." With the whistle it is two short blasts. You must be sure to at least give the verbal release each time you free your dog from "sit," "heel," or "stay." If you wish to use the whistle, be sure your dog knows what two short blasts mean; then vary the release, sometimes using the whistle and sometimes the voice.

BEGINNING

Early training should progress at a slow, easy pace. There must be few, if any, pressures. In the first weeks, your dog should not realize it is being trained. Let the sessions be fun, times your pup looks forward to. Your pup is not in school. Don't consider the lessons "training." You are simply establishing good daily habits.

Be sure to read Chapter 10 and begin with the four initial steps—getting your dog to wear a collar, to accept a leash, to come when you call "here," and to "kennel." The schedule is as valid for a spaniel as for a pointer, and the time table is too. You should have your dog comfortable with its collar and leash in a few days.

The training schedule, as all that follows, progresses in a series of small, close-knit steps. Do not break this rhythm. Dogs cannot cope with major jumps, and to expect a pup to consider that once it has learned "A" it can leap to "B" is to not understand the canine mind. Dogs do not reason, at least not in that way. As an example, once you teach your pup to sit at your side you cannot assume it will hold at a distance. Distance is an entirely new game. When you reach one plateau, the next must be treated as a new subject. It will be the same with advanced "hup" training. Though your dog proves it can hold firm, introducing a live bird, or shooting one, will create a new dimension.

It is as important for a spaniel to learn the "kennel" command as it is for a pointer, and the reasons for using a portable plastic or aluminum kennel as an early bed, given in Chapter 10, are equally valid. The method described there should be used.

By the tenth or eleventh week you should be ready to introduce "heel." Remember, a dog is always walked on the side opposite the gun. If you are a right-handed gunner, your dog is on your left, and if you are left-handed, the dog is on the right. Follow the instructions in Chapter 10.

Some trainers do not spend much time teaching spaniels to "heel." They feel the dog's place is not with its trainer, but in front, hunting. While I agree in theory, "heel" is not a difficult command to teach and is extremely helpful. In the field it helps to keep a dog under control. I would suggest including it.

SIT COMMAND

Although "hup" is the traditional field command that makes a spaniel sit, I do not use the cue with a pup. My reasoning is the same as that given for delaying the introduction of "whoa" with pointers. It is common for an owner to become lax with commands in the early months; you can almost bet on it. For this reason I suggest starting your dog with "sit." If you are lax in enforcing compliance with "sit," your dog will not lose intensity. You can substitute "hup" without missing a beat. The two words are so close in tone and inflection that, when it is time to change, "hup" comes as no surprise. I know. I've taken dogs familiar with "sit" but not "hup," substituted the word, and had them comply the first time out.

There are two reasons. By the time you make the substitution your dog has had considerable training. It's been conditioned to sit on command. It is used to watching you and copying your actions; and when it hears the short command, though this is not familiar, it sees you react and follows. There's rarely a need for transitional training, and if it is necessary, one or two days does it.

SIT: PHASE ONE

"Sit" is introduced with your dog at your side. The initial phase can be taught in your house or in the backyard. At first it should be presented as a voice command only. Give the command "sit" and immediately press down on the pup's hindquarters. Once seated, the animal can stand as soon as it wishes. As it rises, give the release command, "okay." Couple this with much praise. The objective is to make the dog associate the command with squatting on its haunches and rising with "okay." You may find it easier to kneel initially. It puts you at your pup's level and is less frightening for the animal.

After a few days the pup should sit without hand prompting and you can stand. In a week or two it should sit promptly on command and hold for a few seconds, rising only when you give the release. If not, continue training.

After using the voice command for two weeks, you can introduce the whistle. There is no reason to delay, you'll be using it in the field. With the dog still at your side, give the command to sit verbally and follow as promptly as possible with one short beep on the whistle. If the dog seems confused, press on its hindquarters as a reminder, forcing it to sit. Once seated, release it with "okay" and follow with two short beeps on the whistle. Two short blasts are a universal command to "continue as you are." Repeat the lesson.

Several sessions later reverse the order in which the commands are given. Use the whistle first and follow it with the verbal command. As your dog gains confidence, make the verbal command softer and softer until it is eliminated and the dog sits on the whistle alone. Once the dog is familiar with both commands, vary the routine. Use your voice alone occasionally and the whistle other times. Repeat a week or more until the dog responds promptly to either cue. During this phase of training, try making your dog hold in a seated position for longer periods, increasing the time before release a little every few days. In the end, the dog should remain seated for twenty or thirty seconds.

SIT: PHASE TWO

Once your pup demonstrates it can sit at your side on voice and whistle, you should teach it to respond while walking. It is best if you do this in the yard. Attach a short check line and walk with your pup in heel position. Say "sit" and stop. The dog should stop beside you and immediately sit. If it seems confused, shuffle your feet before stopping. This helps alert the dog to the coming command. If a further reminder is needed, press down on the hindquarters to make the dog sit. If the pup responds, praise it. Your dog deserves it. This is the first time it has been ordered to sit while walking, and this is a new ballgame. Once the dog understands the response, continue training a few days to condition the animal, to set the response, to make the actions automatic. It should require about two weeks to complete phase two.

SIT: PHASE THREE

(See Illustrations 39–42.)

When the pup proves it can sit at your side and when walking, you can begin training for distance, teaching the pup to remain seated as you are farther and farther away. Attach the long check line and begin with the dog in the heel position. Give the command to sit using either voice or whistle. When the dog sits, take one long step forward and turn to face your dog. Do not let the animal move. If the dog is nervous, speak gently to calm it. If it moves, return it to the spot it was supposed to be in. Make the dog sit, though not long. Return to your dog. Do not release the pup until you are in front of it. Make eye contact, give the release, and praise your pup. Repeat the lesson.

Once your pup proves it can hold staunchly at one pace, increase the distance—a pace or two every two or three days—until you are several yards away. You will probably need several weeks to reach maximum distance. To this point you have not released your dog until you have returned to its side. You can now try releasing it at a distance. Give the command "okay," then call the dog to you with "here."

STAY

As you teach your dog to hold while sitting, you should introduce the word "stay." In the early months it is used to help keep a pup firm while sitting, and later, in the field, it can be used interchangeably with "hup" to keep a dog staunch. The technique is explained in Chapter 10.

You should also follow instructions for introducing your pup to the gun. It is nearly impossible for city dwellers to do this directly. I realize you cannot fire a blank gun—I can imagine the wild scene that would follow—but beating pots and pans together is the best substitute. It is a good way to introduce a high level of noise at an early age. When you have time for a weekend outing bring a gun along.

THE FIRST PHASE OF "HUP"

The two most important commands your pup can learn at this age are coming when called, i.e., "here" and "sit." You should reinforce these at every opportunity. They are the basis of "hup," and the better your dog learns them, the quicker it'll accept advanced "hup" training. When you go for a drive, at feeding time, when you put the dog out or bring it in, call "here" and make the dog respond promptly. Have your dog sit before each feeding, before entering your car, and before it comes in or goes out. The more often you can repeat and enforce these commands, the more automatic the response, and if your pup learns to respond without question, "hup" and related field commands will come naturally.

INTRODUCTION TO RETRIEVING

You should be able to determine at an early age whether or not your dog has the instinctive urge to retrieve common to spaniels. Once comfortable in your house, your pup should begin mouthing and retrieving objects, and if it does, do not discourage it. Ask the pup to bring them to you (calling "Rover, here") and offer praise. In time you'll be able to send the pup after objects— no rubber balls please—introducing the word "fetch." When you do, remember to preface the command with the dog's name, that is, "Rover, fetch." When you begin hunting, months from now, you do not want your dog cued to retrieve only on the command. With other hunters around that could become confusing. Sending your dog off with its name and the command to "fetch" gives you one leg up. Eventually you'll drop the cue, sending the dog on retrieve by name alone.

After your dog is comfortable retrieving objects around the house, introduce it to the bumper or dummy. Either buy or make a small one and let the dog hold it. Once the dog seems comfortable with it in its mouth, teach holding it several seconds before release. When you accept the bumper, be sure to use the release command, "give," and take the dummy with a positive action so your dog realizes you are in charge. Make the dog know that you decide when to hold and when to release. Be sure to give lots of praise. If your dog spits the dummy out, make it open its mouth and replace the dummy. Make the dog hold it a second or two. And if it tries to release it early, replace the dummy and make the dog hold it a second or more.

Once your dog is comfortable holding the dummy, try frozen birds. I suggest pigeons because they are small and easy to hold. Begin by placing a frozen bird in the dog's mouth. If it holds it a second or two, take it out and give praise. As the dog becomes comfortable, make it hold the bird longer and eventually get it to walk with the bird in its mouth. If it is also possible, buy a live bird, tether the feet, and hide it in tall grass. Let your dog discover it and sniff it out. A natural, successful introduction to live birds builds confidence and maturity.

An alternate suggestion is to take your dog to a local park or a similar place where wild pigeons congregate. If you can—and in some parks it is not legal—let your dog run free. It won't catch the birds and cannot injure them, but the experience will do a lot. If you live near water birds, seagulls or, other shore birds, this also provides an opportunity for your dog to chase game, have fun, and build a background of happy prehunting experience. You must also expose your dog to water. See Chapter 10 for suggestions.

Let your dog have as many varied experiences in its first ten months as possible. Take the dog to the beach, to shopping malls, and to open fields. Let it ride with you in your car. The more your dog discovers, the better its rapport and the greater its confidence. When your dog is ten months old, you can celebrate by introducing it to the advanced "hup" training in Chapter 14.

CHAPTER FOURTEEN

Spaniels: Advanced "Hup" Training

The flushing dog that can quarter with confidence, jump game reliably, and drop on a dime is a beautiful sight and the command that accomplishes this is "hup." It is unique to flushing dogs. Since the only dogs that can do this on our side of the Atlantic are spaniels, the terms "flusher," "flushing dog," and "spaniel" will be used interchangeably throughout this chapter.

BASICS OF "HUP"

"Hup" is a field command, one you and your spaniel will use as long as you hunt. It is to the spaniel as "whoa" is to the pointer: the most important of all commands. It has several uses and is a verbal "check line" that keeps you, the owner, in control. A spaniel must know the word as thoroughly and automatically as a pointer does "whoa."

You can understand that when a dog is on scent it becomes intense. If but partially trained, it may forget its owner (and most previous training). The only thing on a young, half-trained pup's mind is the bird. "Hup" training changes that. After graduation, you, the bird, and your dog become a triumvirate. Your dog remains intense but remembers. You regain command. "Hup" training is the crash course that brings a dog under tight control without reducing its desire to hunt.

As I've said many times, spaniels can be taught at a younger age than that at which pointers are introduced to their counterpart command; but because "hup" runs contrary to instinct, training is a long and difficult process. You introduced the basic concept of "hup" (first as "sit-stay," then as "stay") when the pup was young; and now, at ten months, you'll polish the edges. I've divided the procedure into several natural and progressive phases because it is easier to describe and follow. The total process will probably require two to four months, and your dog should be about one year of age when training is completed. The dog will then be ready for hunting, though not for trails competition. Additional polishing is required if that's your objective.

USING THE WHISTLE

Although a whistle is never used with "whoa," it is with "hup." Some owners tell me they've heard a "two-beep" call, a long trilling whistle to get the dog's attention and a short "beep" to order it to "hup." Not so, at least not for spaniels. Readers who believe this are confusing a whistle pattern occasionally used with retrievers. Those dogs run far afield, and a long preliminary trill is often used to get their attention. Since spaniels are never more than twenty to twenty-five yards away, there is no reason for warning or attention-getting preliminaries. You can be certain your dog will hear the single, short whistle command that orders him to "hup."

THE RELEASE

No command should be given without a suitable release, and the release for "hup" is the same as that used for many other commands. Verbally it is "okay," and with the whistle, two short blasts. In your dog's world this is the universal signal to "continue as you were." It has a number of uses from urging your dog on during a retrieve to casting the dog off once it changes directions. If you have not introduced your dog to the whistle, begin now.

If you introduced your dog to the whistle while it was young (see Chapter 12), skip to the paragraph on "repetition." If not, follow the steps outlined here. For the first week give the "sit-stay" command verbally; then as promptly as possible, back it up with a short blast on the whistle. The second week reverse the procedure, introducing the command with the whistle, giving the verbal prompt second. By the third week you should be able to vary the command sometimes using the whistle alone, and occasionally, the voice. Repeat the lessons and by the fourth week your dog should be well broken to voice and whistle.

UPLAND GAME DOGS

If you are going to have a gun dog you might as well own a superior animal. This Irish Red Setter is typical of the stylish upland game dog.

An upland game dog does it all, locating game as well as retrieving it.

WHICH BREED

The English Pointer is a far-ranging breed that is often handled from horseback.

German Shorthair, FC and AFC Erdenreich's Neika Ptarmigan owned by Dave and Linda DeGere, Mill Valley, CA. An extremely popular breed, the Shorthair has power, endurance, and speed, while being tractable and well-tempered.

Viszla, a Hungarian pointer bred to be an all-around game dog.

The German Wirehair Pointer has excellent ground-tracking abilities, is an excellent retriever, and a near-perfect pointer.

The Weimaraner is fearless but can be hard to train.

The Pudelpointer can be traced to the Barbet, an early pointing breed.

The Brittany, a popular dog that is excellent for more restricted hunting. It is an excellent pointer.

The English Setter, an especially beautiful, stylish breed with an excellent reputation.

The English Springer Spaniel, one of the best flushing breeds, in action.

The Irish Red Setter. Though not a common dog with upland game hunters, it is a stylish, hard-working breed.

CHOOSING A PUP

All pups are cuddly and cute, and you must look beyond appearance when making a final selection. These are German Shorthair Pointer pups.

When checking a litter, choose pups that are bold and curious.

German Shorthair Pointer pups. Testing for alertness and interest.

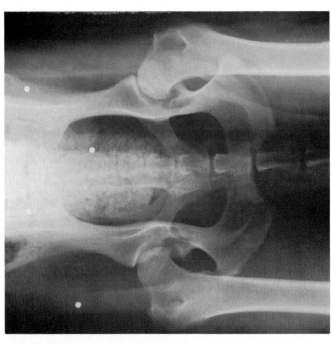

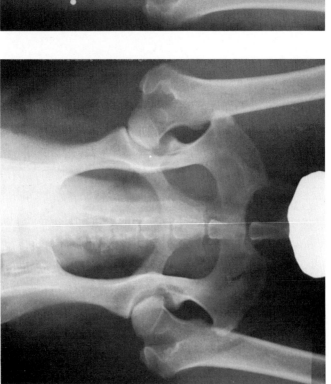

This photo of hip dysplasia shows typical development on a Weimaraner. The radiograph on the left shows the Weimaraner at age 2; the photo on the right at age 4.
(Courtesy of The Department of Radiological Sciences, School of Veterinary Medicine, University of California, Davis)

HOUSING YOUR DOG

A nice backyard run. The door is full height and the run is large enough for the dog to get exercise. The overhead is protected against sun and rain.

A prefabricated run showing the door. It is the full height of the run, about six feet, and slides on an overhead track.

A closeup of the manner in which pipe can be set into cement. The wire is mounted directly to upright pipes with special clips.

A commercial run showing the way in which dogs are separated. The uprights, made of pipe, are set in the concrete flooring.

A typical doghouse after use. The chewing of the wood is typical. It would be better to protect the exposed edges with metal.

EQUIPMENT

The checkline should be attached directly to a nylon collar. Tie plastic "ski rope" to the D-ring, then heat the edges of the knot. The line will not loosen.

A blank gun such as this is a handy item as a training tool.

Not every dog requires a pinch collar, but bold animals often do in early training. They should be used sparingly and often just one or two applications are all that is required.

A bark limiter is a handy device if you have an outside dog that barks chronically.
(Courtesy Tri-Tronics)

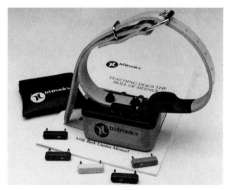

A canteen is an important item on a hunt. It allows you to water your dog, even when in the field.

Constructing your own dumb-bell. Nail two square ends, 4 × 4 inches, to a dowel. The dumb-bell raises the dowel above ground so a dog learning to retrieve can get his mouth comfortably around it.

An electronic bird releaser is a handy device. This illustrates how realistic the releaser is—the bird flushes naturally yet cannot be caught by the dog.

EARLY TRAINING

Exposing pups to the real world. The owner has taken them to a trials so they can meet people and other dogs. This kind of interaction makes pups bolder.

Testing a pup's instincts by moving a pheasant wing in front of the animal. The pup should not be allowed to catch it. The test checks a pup's instincts and interest in pointing. Do not do this often, and stop after two or three good responses.

A perfect response—front paw up, the pup is ready to spring. Do not let him catch the wing.

WHOA TRAINING

Begin whoa training with the dog at your side, in "heel" position. As with this dog, the animal will be insecure during early training. Note the tail, a certain sign of insecurity.

Praise is important, especially with an insecure dog.

The checkline remains on as you work for distance. Once the dog holds well at your side, move back a little at a time.

Increase the distance, even beyond the length of the checkline.

Continue to move back, far beyond the length of the line. Throughout the training the trainer and/or handler should be the focus of the dog's attention, as shown here. At this point you go off the checkline—for whoa training only.

HUP TRAINING

Begin hup training with the dog at your side and gradually increase the distance at which he holds. Here, Mike takes two steps from the dog.

Gradually increase the distance. Hup training is always taught with the checkline attached.

Still more distance.

Proof of the pudding. Holding on hup, in the field and from some distance.

QUARTERING

Casting the dog off to the right with a combination of voice and hand signals.

Casting the dog to the left with a combination of voice and body signals. The body angle alone makes it easy for a dog to understand what you want.

Working with planted birds. The dog makes a perfect flush. A springer can catch or trap a bird if he does it in the first two or three steps.

Many springers sit up on their haunches when marking a fallen bird.

MAKING A RETRIEVE

A Springer doing its job.

A perfect retrieve. When taking the bird, remember to use the command "give."

BIRD HANDLING

A homemade pigeon cage. Made of one piece of 1/4" wire, the ends are bent with a lip and fastened with wire clips. The pigeon is inserted, and the cage is secured with rocks placed on the lips. A gentle kick then frees the bird.

Using a pigeon in a popper. The bird is not restrained in any way except by the canvas sling. Place the bird in the sling and close the metal doors.

A sequence showing how to put a pigeon to sleep. A humane, temporary method. Tuck the head beneath one wing.

Place your hands around the bird, turn it upside down and rock gently.

The immobilized pigeon. In time it will awaken and escape before a dog gets close.

An alternate method of immobilizing pigeons by crossing the wings. Begin by holding the bird upright by its wings.

Cross the wings.

Wrap the right wing beneath the left. This is not painful to the bird.

Gently lower the bird into the grass. The bird can be freed at any time by the handler.

Hobbling a pheasant. Use soft wool yarn since it is the most humane. Tie one foot with a clove or half-hitch.

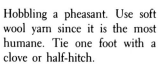

Tie the other foot in the same manner. The feet should be about two to three inches apart. This allows the bird to be mobile to escape yet constrained enough for a dog to find. They can also pick the yarn in time.

HOLDING POINT

Bring the dog to the bird from an angle. In the beginning keep the checkline in your hand, as shown.

In the beginning the dog may be insecure. If so, take time to reassure him.

When approaching a dog on point, be sure to come from one side or the other so that your approach is not a surprise.

After whoa, if the dog moves at all, release the bird. Releasing the bird from a popper has a very natural appearance.

FORCE TRAINING

Place the checkline around the dog's neck.

Familiarize the animal with the bumper. Place it in his mouth. If you must, if the dog is reluctant, force the bumper into its mouth.

Make the dog hold the device. If he begins to lower his head, tap him gently beneath the chin. This keeps the head raised. With his head raised he is less likely to drop the bumper.

To make the dog retrieve from even a short distance, place your hand under the collar and over his head. You can guide the head side to side with the thumb and small finger and force it forward with the heel of the hand. In addition, the tension of the collar on the throat helps training.

When a dog refuses to open his mouth, you may have to place the tip of the ear against the D-ring and pinch. This should be used only with severe cases.

Teaching for distance. At first hold the bumper an inch or two from the dog and make him reach toward it on the command "fetch." The bumper is held at head level.

Once the dog learns to retrieve at head level, slowly lower the bumper, first an inch or two below head level, then lower and lower toward the ground.

When the dog retrieves well near the ground, switch to the dumbbell. First, familiarize the dog with the new object.

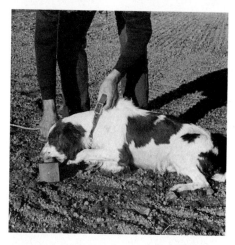

Place the dumbbell on the ground. At first you may have to tap the device with your hand to get the dog to pick it up.

Working for distance on the ground. Place the dumbbell farther and farther from you, making the dog go to it on each retrieve.

Introducing a frozen bird. Frozen pigeons are used because they are easier to hold and retrieve. Move from frozen birds to fresh-killed.

Walking the dog with a bird in its mouth. It is important that the dog become used to this. Initially, some stop when they have the first bird in their mouths.

Teaching a dog to retrieve from the ground. At first the bird is placed close, then progressively farther away.

The finished retrieve. Teaching a dog to retrieve the heaviest of birds, in this case a cock pheasant.

Completed force training. A dog will retrieve anything its master commands.

STEADY TO WING

When teaching this phase, the owner/trainer should be close to his dog. His partner kicks the grass, flushing the bird.

HONORING A POINT

The dog in the foreground is on point. The one in the background has been stopped with whoa, teaching him to stop whenever another dog points.

A dog should honor a point with as much enthusiasm as he does when pointing.

FIELD TRIALS

Field trials are becoming very popular. Men and women participate. Here a woman handler controls her dog while her male gunner prepares to flush a bird.

At a National Shoot-to-Retrieve trial, dogs are allowed to break to shot. The second handler in the brace keeps her dog steady.

Two handlers and dogs, which form a brace, start with one of two judges on horseback. Birds are planted before each brace departs.

Dogs are judged on several things: finds, retrieves, obedience, ground race, and backing. The dog with the highest points is the winner. Winning points can be accumulated for Championship status.

Judges compare scores of the dogs they've just seen. Helpers who plant birds wear gloves to avoid leaving a human scent.

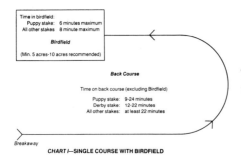

Time in birdfield:
  Puppy stake: 6 minutes maximum
  All other stakes   8 minute maximum

Birdfield

(Min. 5 acres-10 acres recommended)

Back Course

Time on back course (excluding Birdfield)

  Puppy stake: 9-24 minutes
  Derby stake: 12-22 minutes
  All other stakes: at least 22 minutes

Breakaway

CHART I—SINGLE COURSE WITH BIRDFIELD

This chart shows a single course with a birdfield.

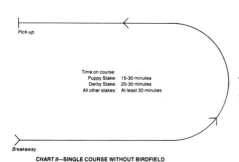

Pick-up

Time on course:
  Puppy Stake: 15-30 minutes
  Derby Stake: 20-30 minutes
  All other stakes: At least 30 minutes

Breakaway

CHART II—SINGLE COURSE WITHOUT BIRDFIELD

This chart shows a single course without a birdfield.

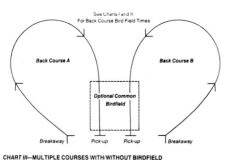

See Charts I and II
For Back Course Bird Field Times

Back Course A

Back Course B

Optional Common Birdfield

Breakaway   *Pick-up*   *Pick-up*   *Breakaway*

CHART III—MULTIPLE COURSES WITH/WITHOUT BIRDFIELD

This chart shows a multiple course without a birdfield.

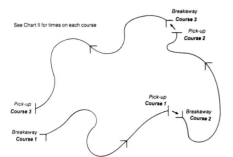

Breakaway
Course 3

Pick-up
Course 2

See Chart II for times on each course

Pick-up
Course 3

Pick-up
Course 1

Breakaway
Course 2

Breakaway
Course 1

CHART IV—CONTINUOUS COURSES

This chart shows a continuous course.

ELECTRONIC COLLARS

An electronic collar and components. The plugs at the side can be changed to vary the intensity of the stimulation. The hand-held transmitter can activate the collar for electrical stimulation and sound.

The collar electrodes. Plugs on the side can be changed to vary the intensity and should be tailored for each dog.

The collar should be loose enough to allow two fingers between the collar and the neck.

A Pudelpointer with an electronic collar. The collar is worn with the battery unit down and the antenna pointing upward on one side.

A FEW FIELD CHAMPION DOGS

Winner of the 1983 Norden Award: Rocky River Buck, a male English Pointer owned by Irv Mohnkern, State College, PA, and handled by Gerald Tracy, Broadbeck, PA.

Winner of the 1985 Norden Award, Warhoop Express Liz, an English Pointer female, owned by Lester C. Shepard, Conroe, TX, and handled by Gordon Hazlewood, Navosta, TX.

Winner of the 1986 Norden Award, Mickette, a female English Pointer owned by Robert Mickolyzck, Milford, CT, and handled by Bruce Jacobs, Middletown, CT.

A champion German Shorthair: FC and AFC Erdenreich's Neika Ptarmigan. Owners, Dave and Linda DeGere, Mill Valley, CA. (AKC-GSP Gundog of the year, 1986)

REPETITION IS THE SECRET

There are no shortcuts and no substitutes for thorough training. Repetition and patience are the entire secret. The only way your pup will learn to respond consistently to any command is by repeating the same training day after day after day, always insisting on an identical response. Never release your pup by calling "here." Always use "okay." Give lots of praise.

CONVERTING "STAY-STAY" TO "HUP"

"Hup," the command to sit and stay, gives you total control in the field, the ability to stop the dog when it is off leash, when game flushes, when it is sidetracked by a rabbit, and when you need to stop the dog. Obviously, the command must be thoroughly learned. When your dog was young you used the command "sit-stay" as a substitute. Now it is time to introduce the real thing.

If your dog learned the command thoroughly as a pup it should ready for advanced training. The transition to "hup" should be easy.

Attach a short check line, walk your dog in heel position. Give the command "hup" and stop. Since the words sound similar, many dogs accept the switch immediately, especially since their trainer also stops. If your dog does not, begin walking again with the dog in heel position, give the verbal command to "sit-stay," and follow it immediately with "hup." Within a few minutes your dog should be familiar with the term and you should be able to demand as prompt a response with "hup" as with "sit-stay."

If your dog is familiar with the whistle command as well, try a few joint commands using a vocal "hup" and then the whistle, just to familiarize the animal with the change-over. By the end of one day your dog should be as comfortable with the new word as with the old.

When your dog proves it can sit consistently and hold confidently at a distance, you can try something I'd never suggest with a pointer. Release your dog, call the dog to you, and while it is running toward you give it a "hup," with voice or whistle. It should stop immediately, and if it does, give lots of praise. The dog has earned it. The reason you should not try this with a pointer in a similar stage of training is that when pointers work a field, they should be constantly running out, away from you. You do not want to confuse them, to order them to return when released. A spaniel works close, and the order is not contradictory. Varying the way you give commands helps to make training more interesting and fun for your dog.

PHASE ONE: QUARTERING

(See Illustrations 43 and 44.)

When your pup has proven it can hold firm in a sitting position at any distance, it is ready to learn advanced field work. Unlike a pointer, who can literally follow its nose, a spaniel limits its hunting to a series of forty-yard runs, each twenty yards or so to the left and right of its owner. The dog continues this zig-zag pattern until it finds game or until the area has been thoroughly investigated. The pattern is called quartering and is one of the things a spaniel is bred to do. It can only be taught in large areas, and you will probably need to move your classroom to a field. I prefer one without game. If your dog finds birds, you must interrupt training, diluting valuable sessions. Aside from this consideration, you can use almost any area, a park, a vacant lot, or a farmer's pasture.

Training should go quickly because you'll capitalize on your animal's natural instincts. Your pup has both an inclination to be close and, when seeking scent, to quarter into the wind. You will utilize both. Ultimately, you'll walk straight while your dog ranges from side to side, twenty to twenty-five yards, but in the beginning, when you must show your dog what you want, your path will be anything but that. Be sure to attach the long check line.

Begin at one end of a field. Plot an imaginary line that will carry you straight down the center. Turn to the right of this imaginary line, and with your right hand cast your dog in that direction. When the dog moves, blow two short whistle blasts indicating "continue on." In this phase of training, you'll be teaching your dog three things, to quarter and to follow hand and whistle signals. Let your pup run ahead, and when it's a few yards in front, turn 180 degrees, crossing the imaginary line in the opposite drection.

As you change directions call your dog by name adding the command "over," that is, "Rover, over!" Point the new course with your left hand and send the dog off with two beeps of the whistle. If the dog doesn't follow, coax it. You will be identifying directions with your hands, the right hand moving out at shoulder level from your body when you want the dog to go to the right and the left hand moving away from the body in the same manner when the dog is cast to the left. Six or seven turns up the field should comprise one training session. Each time you change course, indicate this by changing your body angle, turning toward the new direction. Always call your dog by name, adding the command "over." Initially, quartering is triggered visually, so be sure your pup sees you. When it turns to the new course, reinforce the move with two blasts of the whistle, the order to "carry on." In the first days of training, the dog does not have to go a full twenty yards. You only want it to turn from side to side, to learn that it is expected to hunt in this fashion.

If your dog will not turn when it is called, stop, use its name and repeat the command. Avoid calling it to you. If you call "Rover, here!" the dog has to come all the way, and that's not what quartering is about. Try to make the dog correct its mistake. Commonly, a dog does not obey because you do not have its attention. If you call with sufficient enthusiasm, your dog will hear its name and will realize it is about to receive a command. If it still refuses to change direction, try "hup." That should receive the dog's immediate attention. When it sits, you can change direction, releasing it. The dog should follow. If all else fails, run down the check line and give it a tug. Once the dog complies stop for the day. Repeat the same training the next session.

Although quartering sounds complicated, it isn't. You are training your dog to work like a windshield wiper, sweeping a field from side to side. It is important to remember that the best dog does not work in straight lines. The dog is not cast straight out to an imaginary bumper where, like a pinball machine, it bounces twenty yards to the opposite side. Instead, the dog angles slightly to the left and right so that while it is twenty yards out, your dog is also several yards in front. A dog does not need to cover every foot of ground. It can pick up scent on every side.

In the first week you must show your dog what you want. Some young animals like to be close to their owners and respond better when near. If your dog is like this, keep it close at first, then gradually train it to work farther from you. You will rarely have serious problems. Once a spaniel understands, it will work a field naturally.

In the beginning, let your dog run almost any pattern if it's willing, and praise it each time it changes direction. The routine is new, and you can only demand precision and obedience after your pup thoroughly understands what you want. Be patient, gradually demanding compliance, gradually reducing your own side movement as the dog continues its movement. In four to six weeks you should be walking a reasonably straight line while your dog is ranging the full twenty to twenty-five yards from side to side.

Do not attempt to change directions if your dog is about to reach a clump of grass or a bush it seems ready to investigate. It may have scent and you're only asking for disobedience. Wait until the dog loses interest and/or is ready to turn. Then give the signal to "go over."

Whether you are using whistle or voice, remember to vary the intensity with the distance. When a dog is close, speak in a normal voice. Shout only when it is farther afield.

In England a series of sweeps or casts across a section of field is called a beat, and it is important to keep your dog moving. The dog should work its beat at the fastest pace comfortable for it, even if you trot to keep up. Never let the dog slow at the end of a cast and never let it run far afield. The dog should check in visually each time it changes direction, and if it stops before a cast is completed, give the command to "hup," then cast off the dog again. When you reach the end of the beat, you can both rest.

If your dog should flush game during practice, handle the situation as if it was an actual hunt. Once a bird flushes, control the dog with "hup" and make it hold though you have no gun. When you release the dog, do not let it go after the game.

PHASE TWO: VARYING TERRAIN

By the time this phase of training has been completed, your dog should work a field consistently, but terrain affects performance. In some areas, in flat, grassy fields for example, your dog can quarter with the precision of a trials champion, though in other areas the dog may be harder pressed. In the west there are lots of stubble fields with numerous windrows. The spaniel asked to hunt against these must continually leap over tall-cut, drying stalks, bouncing up and down like a pooch on a pogo stick. Force the dog to abide by tradition and it'll be bushed in ten minutes, but let it hunt a looser pattern and it'll remain fresh. The point is this: before insisting on by-the-book perfection, use your head and let your dog use his. Be a little forgiving and you'll both have fun.

In the U.S. spaniels are often considered "ditch" dogs, and Springers especially are hunted this way. In this terrain, too, you may need to be forgiving. If your dog jumps a bird in a ditch, you cannot expect the dog to hold firm at the bottom. The dog knows it's expected to retrieve, and there is no way it can spot a downed bird sitting in a hole. The sensible dog will climb to the top. This is not disobedience.

In England spaniels are taught to hunt a lot of punishing cover, brambles and gorse for example, because that's where the game is. Here, they rarely work rough country, certainly not in field trials. This considered, if terrain in your area has low thickets, thorny bushes, and similar cover, you may want to train your dog to include them since these are likely areas for birds. One way to teach a dog to work brush is to throw a dead or frozen bird into one. Two or three tries should make an animal willing to inspect every thicket.

PHASE THREE: ADVANCED RETRIEVING

(See Illustrations 45–48.)

Once your dog has learned to quarter, it is time to move to birds. As with a pointer who has proven staunch on "whoa," it is time to make the classroom as real as possible. You introduce birds for three reasons: to teach your dog to hold though tempted by game, to reintroduce the gun, and to teach the dog to retrieve. The three fit naturally together. By now you should have discovered your spaniel is a natural retriever (See Chapter 13). You've tested the dog as a pup, let it retrieve small objects around the house, and perhaps had it hold a bumper. Retrieving is a much more natural instinct for spaniels than for pointers where, to a degree, it has been played down in favor of other attributes. This is one reason pointers are often force-trained while spaniels rarely are.

The traditional command that sends a spaniel on a retrieve is "back," a movement of the hand (up and away from the body) and two short beeps on the whistle signaling the dog to go in the direction indicated by your hand. If you prefer, you can substitute "fetch," a word used with pointers and my choice. Either term is satisfactory. Be sure to use the word you prefer plus the hand and the whistle (two blasts to "continue"). In time you can even train your Spaniel to respond to body English, a flick of the hand will cast the dog off and a step back will tell it to work closer.

Whether or not you begin phase-three training at home, depends on several considerations, space and whether or not your dog has been introduced to the gun being among them. Either way you'll be working first with dead birds. I've discussed birds, choices, costs, and selection in Chapter 15, and if you read that chapter you will have an idea of where to find birds, how much to pay, and how to hobble and control them. You do not need an electronic popper. They are used to teach a pointer to be staunch on point and to provide a safety valve that releases a bird before the dog can catch it. Spaniels are different. You'll need many more birds than for a pointer. A pointer is expected to do no more than find game, hold staunchly, and retrieve. It can be trained with as few as twenty or twenty-five birds. A spaniel will require two to three times that number.

You can begin with a training dummy or with frozen pigeons. A dummy, if properly thrown, hits the ground much like a bird. Pigeons are also suggested because they are small and readily available. Do not use live or freshly killed birds because this phase of training is designed only to get your dog familiar with carrying a bird. A frozen pigeon is preferred because it is small, compact, and easy to carry.

If you introduced your dog to birds while it was young (see Chapter 13), you can go directly to the training below. If not, take a few minutes to accustom your pup to the feel of a bird in its mouth. Place a frozen pigeon in its mouth and let it hold it for a second or two. Repeat this two or three times until the dog is comfortable with the taste and feel of a frozen bird. Then move to the training below.

You should work with a partner. At home, position your partner five to ten yards away. Give the "hup" command, and when the dog sits, have your friend throw a frozen bird or dummy in a high arc so your dog can see it. Release the dog, send the dog for it, and then coax the dog to pick up the bird or dummy and return to you. If space is constricted, do not continue this long. Your dog will quickly master the situation and, if continued, will anticipate the throwing. The dog will have learned a little trick—one tiny part of retrieving—but will no longer be learning new things. Move to a field and switch to frozen birds. Throw the first two or three without shooting over them (to avoid complicating training), and if the dog is consistent and bold, fire blanks over those that follow.

If you are training in a field, send your dog on a quartering pattern with your partner nearby. When the dog is making its left-hand cast, have your partner throw a bird or dummy—unseen by the dog if possible—to the right. Coordinate the toss so that the dog is just completing its cast and can turn in time to see it falling. Fire a blank and give the command to "hup," either with voice or whistle. The timing is critical and the reason simple. You are anticipating a mistake—before your dog can think of it or make it. You give the "hup" command as the dog turns. It sees you and the bird, and while it thinks "run," it hears your signal. Before it can instinctively bolt, it has been ordered to sit. It sees what it assumes is game, yet realizes it is expected to hold. If it breaks, you can now correct it for failing to follow a command. In your dog's mind the correction is not connected with the bird.

At first, do not make your dog hold long. To do so is to ask for trouble. Once the dog proves it is firm, release it. As training progresses increase the time it holds. Be sure to fire a shot over each bird.

Training sessions should be short, just long enough for your dog to retrieve three frozen birds. In five or six days, that is after three weekends, it should have the idea firmly in its mind and should retrieve with confidence. If it doesn't, give the dog more time. When it is consistent move to live birds.

PHASE FOUR: LIVE BIRDS

(See Illustration 44.)

Throughout this phase of training you've had your dog on a check line as your partner threw frozen birds. You can now plant live birds for your dog to locate. The first few should be pigeons. If you've read the chapter on "whoa" training, you'll recall I suggested hobbling pigeons with cardboard. Do not attempt this with spaniels. They work closer to the birds and may catch or trap one that is hobbled.

Have your partner dizzy two unfettered birds by holding them upside down a few seconds. Place them in the grass in different places (without the dog spotting them). Immediately release your dog. Start the dog quartering, and as each bird flushes, give the order to "hup." Do not shoot the first two. If the dog holds well, you can shoot the third one. If it does not, and many do not hold on their first birds, return it to the spot from which it moved and make it hold. Repeat training without shooting birds, until the dog holds consistently.

Do not kill the first live birds. It is wise to let them go for a number of reasons. When actually hunting you may not be able to shoot every bird your dog flushes—sometimes you'll be out of position, sometimes you'll miss, and sometimes the birds will be illegal. A dog quickly learns that once a bird is shot, if the dog holds it'll have an opportunity to retrieve it. Your dog should also learn that this is not always true. It requires more control to stop a dog on a flush in which game escapes than when a bird is downed.

The only way you will achieve success is by repetition. Keep your dog on the check line. Plant two birds at a time, four per session; begin quartering and keep the end of the check line in sight. While you want the dog to be "free-floating" or independent, you must remain close enough to be in control. The moment a bird is airborne, give the command to "hup." If you think your dog will break, repeat the command with more force. Give the dog a chance to correct itself, and if you still think it will move, tug the check line. You do not have to flip the dog. If it moves, bring it back to the point at which it was sitting and make it hold. Keep the dog there thirty seconds or more.

When your dog goes out to retrieve its first bird, give it time to decide what the procedure involves (see illustration 48). Do not become anxious if it seems to sniff and nose the bird. It may only be deciding how to pick it up. Keep your voice excited and praise the dog. Coax it to pick up the bird—we call it "sweet-talking"—praising the dog when it does ("that's right, good boy"). Try to get the dog to come to you with the bird in its mouth. Be patient. If you can get it to do this once or twice without pressure, it'll become a more natural retriever.

If the dog drops the bird, try to get it to pick it up. Again, "sweet-talk" the dog into complying if you can. If you can't, call the dog in and send it out again—using either "back" or "fetch" as the command. Coax the dog to pick up the bird. If it refuses, go to the downed bird, make the dog open its mouth, place the bird in it. Close its mouth and make it hold the bird a few seconds. If the dog seems confident, take a couple of steps back and call it to you. The dog should come with the bird in its mouth. Remember, each time you take a bird, do it with a positive action and always say "give." If your dog picks up the bird but will not bring it all the way, take it off birds and teach it to come promptly.

If you will take time to read Chapter 15 (Moving to Birds), the section on retrieving offers additional tips. Though written for pointers, the ideas work well with spaniels. One of the objectives of shooting pigeons first is to give your dog an opportunity to retrieve warm, fresh-killed birds that are easy to carry. Once the dog is comfortable with them, to move to larger birds. The dog should learn to handle big birds, then pheasants and roosters, as well as cripples. You can use quail, pheasants, or whatever is available in your area. The most common sources are explained in Chapter 15.

OTHER TIPS

If, during training with live birds, a dog finds scents that indicate game you have not planted, you'll have to use your own judgment as to how long the animal should investigate. Since this is still a training session, it is better, in my book, to move the dog quickly toward the planted birds. A dog allowed to worry a scent in training will do so in the field, and a "worrier" is the worst kind of dog to hunt over.

Some professionals begin distance training by placing the dog on the thirty-foot check line, allowing it to immediately break after flushed game and to chase the game to the end of the line. There the animal is unceremoniously dumped. I do not suggest this. If anything can cool a dog's interest, it has to be rough handling. I prefer to prevent the mistake. In the beginning I stay close to the dog. The first times a dog scents game and sees birds flush, it will probably try to break. Talking may calm the dog. If not, a tug on the line should keep it under control. If it insists on moving, tug on the check line, say "hup," and make the dog sit.

If your dog breaks, you must run it down, catching animal or line, whichever you can reach. Dump the animal unceremoniously, lift it off its feet and bring it back to the point at which it was given the command. Make it sit until released. Let it think about the correction. If a dog breaks even after a tug on the line, it is showing that you have not spent sufficient time on earlier stages. Return to basics for a week or two.

You will reinforce your dog's understanding if you can use "hup" at every opportunity. Make your animal sit before it kennels in the field and before it crosses a road. You'll find many other opportunities.

Spaniels are not often gun-shy, but if yours is nervous around guns, you must reassure the dog before continuing. While there are several ways to accomplish this, the best is to let the dog run free in a field with game. Rabbits or dickey birds, that is, sparrows and other nongame birds, are ideal, because the dog cannot catch them. When the dog is yards away and intent on the game, fire a round of blanks. If it ignores these, fire more. If the dog seems gun-shy, try again another day.

Another approach is to wait until your dog is very hungry, then fire a gun while it is eating. In most cases a ravenous dog will ignore shots. Fire the first round from some distance, and if there is no adverse response, bring the gun closer. If you use the gun as a signal for mealtime, that too will often help gun-break a nervous animal.

By any name, well-trained spaniels make beautiful hunting companions. Friendly, stylish, birdy dogs, they deliver a unique shooting experience. To take full advantage of one you must learn to read it, to know when it has a nose full of game, to be ready when the bird flies. A good spaniel makes that easy. On scent its ears go up, its tail wags, and it moves cautiously closer to its quarry.

As they are natural hunters, so they are natural retrievers, and it is rarely necessary to do more than introduce one to retrieving as I've described. Seldom do you need to force-train a spaniel. The breed just does not require it. Once your dog has been trained to retrieve, and does so, though perhaps not to your standards, hunt with it one full season. The dog should improve noticeably through practice alone. If any fault remains at the end of this time, it will probably be that your dog does not follow through on delivery. It may not hold the bird from the point at which it is picked up to the moment it brings it to your hand. If this is your problem, you can partially force-train your spaniel to hold. Follow the suggestions in the first segment of the chapter on force training. A week or two spent on this should make a near champion of him.

CHAPTER FIFTEEN

Moving to Birds: Staunchness and Retrieving

Until today the only time your pointer pup has seen game was when it chased dickey birds in a park and rabbits in a field, or when it went hunting with an older dog. Training has been without birds purposely so the pressures would not create a distaste for them. Now that your pup has proven it can point and hold, it is time to focus on birds for a couple of reasons. First, there is no other way to polish staunchness. Secondly, it is time to introduce your pup to the job of retrieving. The line between training and hunting is becoming blurred. The classroom is becoming real.

This is an important distinction. You've been training your dog in the abstract. Now, you'll teach it to hold firm and/or retrieve with the scent of birds in its nostrils, to hold while you flush game and after it has flown. When this phase of training is completed, your dog should be ready to hunt.

The addition of birds changes the story. A dog on point has one thing on its mind, the bird. You have to retain control by establishing a rapport so your dog knows it's there for something other than its personal pleasure. This phase of training literally rearranges its thinking. When on point, the three of you—your dog, the bird, and you—become one. Your dog is still intensely aware of game, but you are in control. Pointers should first be taught to hold staunch on "whoa," and pointers and spaniels can be taught to retrieve following the instructions in the latter half of this chapter. Spaniel owners should also read Chapter 13.

FACTORS TO CONSIDER

Previous training could be done anyplace, in your backyard, a vacant lot, a park, or a field. When you go on birds, you obviously need more land, a place with birds or with room to plant them and to shoot in. In parts of the country such land is plentiful, and federal acreage such as that under Bureau of Land Management control can be used. In other states it is more difficult to find and choices are limited. Some states have space set aside for field trials, and it is possible to use this. You can train your dog wherever public hunting is permitted, and in a pinch you can arrange with local farmers to rent a back pasture.

Regulations vary, but in many states training is tightly controlled. In California, for example, field training is allowed with a training permit (cost: $2 per person and $10 for organizations) plus a valid hunting license for each person involved. Information is available from local Fish and Game offices. Domestic birds can be used much of the year, and all game must be tagged.

While it is common to use dummies when teaching retrievers, they are not used with pointers and springers at this stage. If you want a fully polished retriever, the type demanded in competition, you'll have to include a further phase called "force training." A "force-trained" dog is completely under your control. The process is traumatic and should not be attempted unless you demand the perfection required in field trials. It is not for everyone. Most hunters will be satisfied with a dog that retrieves as reliably as a graduate of this chapter, and you should consider this: train your dog as I suggest, and if you are not satisfied force-train it later. A dog should never be force-trained until it's had at least one year of actual hunting experience.

A TWO-STAGE PROCESS

Two procedures—training for staunchness, literally, polishing a pointer's ability to hold firm, and an introduction to retrieving—have been combined here. This is because, for a pointer, initial retriever training flows naturally out of procedures used to teach staunchness. You incorporate retrieving when your pointer is advanced enough to shoot over. Again, spaniels are taught their special form of staunchness during "hup" training, and the owners should skip the first half of this chapter. The section on retrieving can be of help.

If pointer owners have followed my method, their pups should be firm and confident enough to accept the pressure that comes with birds, but it is important to know precisely whether or not yours is ready. If you've tested your pup with the hat trick, and it's shown any timidity, by backing away, dropping its tail, or lying down, your dog is telling you it is not confident. It needs additional "whoa" training away from birds. On the other hand, if the dog came through intense and eager, or if its tail dropped when you corrected it but came up when you petted it or spoke to it, the animal is showing it understands. It's intent. The excitement remains. Your dog is ready for birds.

CHOOSING YOUR BIRDS

Almost any choice will have disadvantages. Wild birds are ideal though rarely available. On the plus side they are exactly the game your dog will be hunting, and their reaction is the same in training as when hunting. They are wary, will not hold as captive birds do, and will flush long before the boldest dog can get to them. On the debit side, there are seasons when wild game is not available or cannot be hunted, sexes that cannot be shot, and most importantly, you cannot count on them being in the right field, certainly not in sufficient numbers, when you're ready for training.

A trainer needs to control his environment. That means in training stages he must plant his own birds. The solution is captive-bred birds available year around, and there are several choices. At the top of my list are pheasants, quail, chukar, and pigeons. Any work well, and your selection depends on the kind of training equipment available and the amount of money you want to spend.

The first five or six birds your dog finds are critical. Even if the dog breaks point, it must not catch them. If it manages to run one down, it will try again and in short order becomes a "buster." This is a habit nearly impossible to break. Nor do you want to kill the first birds. If you down a bird, training stops while the dog is sent after it and the timing is wrong. The solution is to use the right birds, the right equipment, and the right techniques.

Pigeons are popular, though recommended with reservations. On the plus side, they are small, compact, fast, rarely caught, and inexpensive. On the debit side, they are not a ground bird and do not react as game birds. Uncontrolled, one will flush immediately. You can hobble a pigeon, but it won't act like a ground bird. You can flop or dizzy one, but it may come to its senses, flushing before your dog arrives, or it will remain so woozy it cannot flush, which is worse. The solution for all the above is a mechanical training device. The best is the electronic bird release, commonly called a popper. It is designed for pigeons, holds one until you release it, and makes a pigeon flush like a game bird.

There are two types of releases, mechanical and electronic. The concepts are similar. A bird is placed in a canvas sling hooked to spring-loaded arms. When the arms are closed, the canvas holds the bird humanely. The mechanical popper is released by hand. In most cases a ten-foot cord is attached to the release arm and placed on the ground downwind of the popper. The drawback becomes obvious: there are only two places at which you can release a bird—at the cord or at the device. If you are not at the right place at the right second, the dog may beat you to the bird.

That could be disastrous, because a number of things may happen: (1) Your dog may injure its paws or nose trying to get at the bird; or (2) it may free the bird and catch it. Either could affect the dog. If the dog injures itself, it may not want to go after birds again—it may associate its pain with the bird, not the device—and if the dog catches the bird, it may develop into a "buster."

The electronic popper uses a battery-controlled release activated by a hand-carried transmitter and it is the ne plus ultra. Many professionals use them because they eliminate foul-ups. Birds can be freed up to half a mile away, and your dog can never beat you to the popper. The bird can always be released before the dog is close, and that's its most important value. The units cost $400, and I've suggested that two or three hunters buy one, sharing expense and use. A mechanical unit is less expensive but is harder to find. Both are good; neither is essential.

Nonprofessional trainers have other ways to control pigeons, and the best, a system we've used on occasion, requires a simple wire "flop" cage. Made from from a sixteen-inch square of one-half-inch wire fencing, the cage should be assembled according to illustration 49. Cut the corners, then bend the four sides at right angles to the top until the center is deep enough to hold a pigeon, about four inches. Secure the corners with simple wire clamps. In the west we call these "hog rings." The sides should each have a one- or two-inch lip bent outward at ninety degrees. Place a pigeon inside, put the cage on the ground, and hold it in place with rocks laid on the four lips. Their weight prevents the pigeon from escaping. While the dog is staunch on "whoa," kick the grass, edging close enough to reach the cage. One kick usually topples the cage, releasing the bird. As with the automatic popper the pigeon flushes realistically.

If you do not use a popper or cage, I recommend captive-bred game birds. They are not as wary as the wild variety and do not flush as quickly, but they have an authentic scent.

In the spring, fourteen- to sixteen-week training birds are generally available. At that age Bobwhites cost $2.75 to $3.50. Chukar, not found everywhere, range from $4 to $5.50. Pheasants are available in most parts of the country and priced between $5 and $6. Beyond sixteen weeks, prices increase, week by week, as the birds mature and the farmer invests more in feed. Pigeons are the least expensive birds, costing $2 or less. You can seldom rent homing pigeons, that is, birds that will return to a keeper's loft to be reused. The birds you buy will be considered "killed." Whether they escape or are shot, the birds are yours. In most areas you'll find sources under *Game Birds* in the Yellow Pages. If you live in a major city such as New York, Chicago, or San Francisco, try suburban directories or those of surrounding rural areas.

Do not consider these birds as keepers. You are not buying meat. As with other equipment you've purchased, these are training devices. A certain number must be allowed to escape. They are part of the cost of training. It would be a mistake to attempt to shoot, kill, and keep every one. Using the recommended two birds a session, with eight to ten weekends required for the complete training, you will need 32 to 40 birds. The birds will be purchased over a number of weekends, and with luck you will be able to kill and keep at least half.

CONTROLLING BIRDS

Whatever the bird, it must be constrained in some way, caged or hobbled long enough for the dog to find it. If you use pigeons, I strongly recommend an electronic releaser (see Illustration 50). You may need the safety of a quick release in early training. You could also use the flop cage. Both are humane, though the cage is more restrictive and provides less freedom when releasing.

Some hunters prevent pigeons from flying by putting them to sleep, that is by dizzying them and placing their head under one wing (see Illustrations 51–53). This is not reliable. The pigeon may wake and flush before the dog arrives, or might be so dizzied it cannot break and will thus be caught. Some hunters immobilize pigeons by crossing their wings (see Illustrations 54–57). Other hunters attach a cardboard trailer or "flutter" to a pigeon to slow its flight and reduce the distance it covers. Pigeons hobbled this way can often be reused. Still other trainers clip the wings. No methods are as reliable as a popper. To reiterate, if you do not use a popper or flop cage, choose another bird.

In many ways upland birds are easier because they can be planted without equipment. At Black Point we hobble our birds, tying their feet with a length of wool, the loosely formed type used in knitting (see Illustrations 58 and 59). This is as humane a method as possible. It temporarily restrains a bird yet can be removed by the bird itself if it is not shot. When the wool becomes moist it breaks, and dry, a bird can pick its way free in a couple of hours. When the bird is dizzied and placed on the ground, the hobble will keep it in the vicinity long enough for your dog to find it. Use two birds and plant both before beginning each session.

Staunchness training requires two people, you and a helpful friend. While you are with your dog, your friend should plant the birds in separate areas some distance apart. He should hobble each, dizzying it by holding it upside down and briefly swinging it in circles. Place it in good grass cover and mark the area. If some natural marker is available—a brush, hillock, or rock—use it. If not tear off a clump of grass as a marker. Do not make the visual signals obvious. You would be surprised how quickly a dog can spot signs, and if your dog does it will use vision instead of its nose from then on. If the training site is small, plant the birds one at a time.

While your friend is placing the birds, condition your dog with two or three "here" commands and three or four "whoas." It is important to do this before every session. It reminds your dog you're in control, checks its responses, and helps calm it. If the dog does not do well on four "whoas," try a couple more, and if it still refuses, stop the training. Put your dog back on "whoa," without birds, until it does better. If it responds, it is ready for birds.

FIRST TIME ON BIRDS

(See Illustrations 60–63.)

The first time you work your dog on birds, everything is new. The dog has been taught to "whoa" and hold but has never understood the reasoning and, more to the point, has never been tempted by real birds. You should be as close to your dog as possible for control and confidence. After your partner has placed the birds, bring your dog, holding the check line about halfway along its length, into the wind. Check line the dog toward the first bird. When it points, indicating scent, give the "whoa" command. Hold the check line to prevent the dog from creeping. Remember that the temptation is tremendous and that the dog's never faced it before.

Work your way to your animal, approaching from an oblique angle; that is, from the side. Never come from the back or from a blind spot. Let your dog know where you are at all times. It gives the animal confidence and reminds it you are in control. Talk to it, telling it to "stay, stay."

If the dog takes a step, give a firm "whoa." Hopefully it will hold firm. If it lifts one foot, give a tug on the check line and say "whoa" with more authority. If you must repeat yourself several times while tugging on the line, the dog is not ready for birds.

I do not allow my dogs to break immediately after a bird flushes and prefer to be as close to them as possible. In that way I don't have to use the check line to dump a dog if it runs. A dog is extremely tense on point, and talk and petting helps build confidence, but each dog responds differently. Some remain so tense on point you can literally lift the hindquarters while the front feet remain on the ground, immobile. Others soften. If the tail drops and the dog relaxes, back away.

When you talk to your dog, use a calm, even monotone. Avoid signs of anxiety and hysteria. Too many first-time trainers make the mistake of letting their nervousness show in their voice. They think their dog will break and their nervous, high-pitched voice conveys that to the dog. If you think your dog will break and show it in your voice, your dog will surely break.

As your partner approaches the bird, continue to control the dog, either with a hand on the collar or with the check line. When the bird flushes, say "whoa" and hold the animal to reinforce your command. If the dog struggles to break free, keep it beside you with any amount of force, but do not make the dog hold long, initially no more than a few seconds. The dog should be released soon after the bird is airborne. Repetition will get the dog to hold longer. Never let your dog chase a flushed bird.

There are several reasons for not shooting the first birds. I do not want to get into retrieving while the dog lacks the confidence to hold firm for any length of time. Staunchness comes gradually and is more important. There is plenty of time to teach retrieving.

Many trainers who use pigeons fire blanks when the birds flush to get their dogs used to the sound of shots. I do not do this because I want the dogs to associate shooting with an order to "fetch." I assume a dog has been introduced to a gun before this.

If the dog breaks during the first session and tries to run down the bird, it needs a severe correction. Give it a strong tug on the check line and bring it back to where it should have been standing. Since the bird has flushed, try the hat trick. Throw your hat where the bird was, then kick the grass. Ninety percent of all dogs will lock into a point instantly because they still smell the bird. Give the command "whoa" and make the dog hold. Keep the dog there for a minute or more because you must make it understand that it is being punished for failing to "whoa" and not for chasing birds.

You can make or break a dog on these early sessions. If it is not sufficiently confident, the pressure of making it hold with a bird in its nose can have serious effects. At the worst, the dog may figure hunting birds is no longer fun. The dog could lose its intensity. It might give up. Be gentle. Never manhandle a dog.

On the other hand, if the dog raises a paw to step and, when given a "whoa," puts it down without moving, keeping its tail erect, be happy. This indicates that the dog knows the proper response. If your dog gets it right on the first or second bird, consider that you've had a good session.

If your dog gives you a good session on the first bird, do not rush things. I'd suggest that you forget the second one, though I know most owners won't. You've driven a considerable distance to find a place to train, and to quit after one bird seems as if you're not getting your money's worth. I understand the feeling, but believe me, you would be money ahead if you closed shop and headed home. Your dog will remember that one successful "whoa." But if you don't want to follow my suggestion, at least stop training for an hour or so. Turn your dog in another direction and relax. Have lunch. Do anything to distract the dog, then go after the second bird—and pray the response is as good as the first. Never use more than two birds per session.

Take your dog out the second weekend and repeat the training with two more birds. By the time you've gotten to your fourth or fifth bid, your dog should understand the routine. It should point and hold well, and you may not have to continue to use "whoa" as a precautionary aid. After pointing, the dog may hold on its own. If it does, use "whoa" only as a correction, at times when the dog seems likely to break. If the dog forgets, and all dogs will now and then, one good "whoa" should bring it back. The longer a dog holds after a bird flushes, the more staunch it will be on point.

You should check line your dog on the first three or four birds, and if it is doing everything right, let the line be "free-floating," that is, dragging after the dog. If the dog still does everything right, holding well on voice commands, you are on your way. If you've been using pigeons and a popper, you can switch to game birds.

ELIMINATING HUMAN SCENT

After your dog has handled five or six game birds properly, it is time to make things difficult. You've been planting birds by foot, and a dog soon learns it is easier to track a bird following foot scent than airborne odors. The next bird should be flown in. Hobble the bird as before, flop it—that is, hold the bird's body while it flaps its wings until it is tired (this lets you control the distance it flies)—then, without allowing your dog to see, toss the bird in the air and let it fly. The bird should go no more than fifty to one hundred yards and will remain near the landing site. Wait twenty minutes or more for the bird to regain its strength; then send your dog after it. Some trainers are even craftier. To eliminate all chance for human scent, they handle their birds with gloves, flying them in exactly as described above. The dog now faces a tougher job. It is as close to real hunting as it can get.

REUSING BIRDS

To this point you have not shot birds, and allowing game to escape after one flush may seem wasteful. With common sense precautions you can work flushed birds a second time. Mark the spot where the bird landed, and with your dog on the check line, turn in the opposite direction. Make the dog heel and walk away. If the dog has any birding instinct, it'll remember and try to go after the bird. You must keep the dog from cutting back. Some dogs forget quickly if distracted. Others are aggressive and will insist on going after a flushed bird fifteen or twenty minutes later. You must distract your dog. Walk in another direction, make the dog stay and rest, and when you think it's forgotten, cast it in an opposite direction. If the dog tries to circle back, call it to you. If it doesn't, redirect it toward the bird and work the bird as new game. Whether you use new birds or old, don't overwork your animal. Two birds and four tries are enough for one day.

Many trainers also reuse pigeons and have invented several methods to achieve their goals. In one system the trainer attaches a piece of cardboard to the pigeon's feet before placing it in the popper. The cardboard trailer keeps the bird from gaining altitude, and it will land fifty to one hundred yards away. The bird can be pointed a second time, and this is an excellent way to teach a dog to hold firm on a flush. Be sure to use knitting wool so that the bird can break free. A few trainers hobble pigeons with a complicated arrangement of rubber hose and rope. I've never discovered an advantage in this and do not recommend it.

Never let your dog get into the habit of chasing a flushed bird. It must learn that when one flushes there should be no further interest. Once hunting, that is the way it must be. In many states you cannot shoot female birds, and not every bird pointed will be male. Your dog must learn that some are allowed to fly free. There is no better time to begin than now.

RETRIEVING

Some trainers feel that, since a pointer or setter is bred primarily to locate game, this kind of dog is probably short on the ability to retrieve. It is true that some breeds—and the Brittany comes to mind first—do not like to carry game and are difficult to teach to retrieve well; but that charge is not generally true. Nearly every pointing breed likes to pick objects up and carry them around, even bringing them to their owner, and most game dogs enjoy it. The German wirehair and shorthair are examples.

Consequently, most trainers feel a pointer or spaniel can make a damn good retriever, though there is not much agreement on when to begin, how the subject should be taught, or how polished the game dog should be. A number of trainers begin with organized sessions when the pup is only a few months old. Some start with canvas dummies, tossed by hand or shot from a hand-operated catapult, and others use dead birds. One school suggests using cast-off pigeons, those dying a natural death, because the dog cannot develop a taste for game birds through them. Another school recommends fresh-killed game birds because it gives the dog a chance to work through any distaste for feathers. Still another says that when you begin training you toss out canvas dummies with the command "gone away," which means the bird has flushed and there is no retrieve.

I do not agree. You don't have to spend a lot of time teaching a dog to retrieve irrelevant garbage. Almost every breed has a natural retrieving instinct, and when there is something important to retrieve, yours will learn what to do. If you introduced your pup to the idea of carrying things in its mouth when it was a few months old, you can delay further training until you're in the field. I also question the command "gone away." To a dog it means, "don't do anything," and that's redundant. If you don't want your dog to react, it is better—and easier—to say nothing and teach the dog to hold.

At Black Point, retrieving training for pointers begins the moment you know your pup is staunch, normally one-third to halfway through staunchness training, either at the time you switch from pigeons to game birds (if you started with a popper) or after the dog has successfully held through six or seven birds that have been pointed, flushed, and freed.

Either way, your pup knows about retrieving. During preliminary obedience training I suggested that you might let your pup retrieve a few things, more as a game than anything else, and I recommended you not make a big thing of it. Human nature being what it is, I realized as I wrote that retrieving is a great way to show off a pup; many owners overdo it. Most pups brought to Black Point for training have had a full dose of retrieving, and some even know the command "fetch." There isn't a dog I've seen—and if you've followed the book to this page, I'll include yours—that hasn't been initiated into the mysteries.

So much for background. Months ago your pup learned a little about retrieving. It hasn't forgotten, and now, partially through staunchness training or upon completion of "hup," you've reached the point where you can incorporate everything. Your dog is obedient, it comes when you call, and it holds on point; the next step, naturally, is to kill a bird and let the dog retrieve it. Your pup has worked the field, found birds, seen them fly, and up to now, has come away empty-handed. This is the payoff. From this moment and for as long as you hunt, you will kill the birds he finds. His reward: to bring them to you. That may not sound like much, but this is what your dog was bred to do. Centuries of training culminate in this act. Believe me, your dog is aware of it.

THE FIRST RETRIEVE

Plant birds exactly as before. Attach the check line and let your dog run free. When your dog points, get as close as you can. Have your partner flush and kill the bird as you keep your dog firm. If you can, place yourself in front of your dog to one side, with your hand raised. Talk to the dog. Tell it, "Steady boy, hold it! Good boy! Stay." The fact that you are beside the dog as well as your voice and your raised hand should keep it on point. Do not release your dog the instant the bird falls, but make the dog hold a moment; then quickly give the command to "fetch" and cast the dog toward the downed bird.

In most cases your dog will find the bird without trouble. It may nose the bird a moment, but chances are excellent that it will pick the bird up. When it does, immediately call its name, say "here," and be sure the dog comes toward you. If the dog brings the bird a couple of feet and drops it, coax it to go back to the bird.

Some dogs have little instinct to retrieve. If yours is like that, go to it, open its mouth, say "fetch," and pop the bird in. Make the dog hold it for a second; then quickly remove it on the command "give." Pet and praise your dog. You may have to go through this procedure with two or three birds, but be persistent. Once the dog is familiar with the idea of holding a bird, it will be easy to teach it to bring one to you.

If your dog refuses to hold birds, open its mouth, place the bird in it, and make it hold for a second. Then, remove the bird. After a few tries the dog should be comfortable holding the bird. Now throw it a few feet away. Tell your dog to "fetch." Make the dog go to the bird. If your dog drops the bird after retrieving, coax it to go back, pick it up, and return to you. Once the dog has the bird in its mouth, call your dog. Hearing its name often has an element of surprise. Your dog may come running, forgetting it has a bird in its mouth.

If your dog repeatedly drops the bird, there is another trick that often gets results. As soon it has picks up the bird, put your hands above your head, clap them together, and call the dog by name. The movement of your hands above your head will get the dog's eye. It will look at your hands, and that brings its head up. It is almost impossible for a dog to drop a bird with its head up. Back away as your dog approaches—this makes the dog carry the bird farther—and when the dog is close, turn to one side, plant your feet and swing into the dog with your hand at mouth level. The minute you feel the bird, say "give." Remove the bird and praise the dog.

If the dog is slow to bring the bird to your hand, do not confuse the issue with compound commands. You are working with three commands— "fetch," "here," and "give." Never tell the dog to "drop it" when it's not doing what you want. If it drops the bird and walks off, in its mind it's complied. Obviously, that's wrong. When you want your dog to come, say "here" and be sure it does. If you want it to "give," make it bring the bird to your hand. Take it from the dog promptly and gently and give plenty of praise.

And when you take the bird, do not get into a tug of war. Make the dog release it on the command "give." If you get into playing games over who is going to keep the bird, your dog will either think it's a game and play tug of war or develop a condition called "hard mouth." At its worst, a hard-mouthed dog can crush a bird's ribcage and mangle it. You should be able to expect your dog to return the bird in the condition in which the dog picked it up.

If the dog will pick up the bird but does not come to you, return to the check line. Shoot the next bird, give the command to "fetch," and check line the dog to you. You may have to do this three or four times, but if you are patient the dog will get the idea.

Do not be satisfied with a halfway retrieve. Do not let your dog drop the bird and walk away. If it tries, coax it into picking it up, then be ready to receive the bird. Do not let the dog end a session with a dropped bird. The dog will remember.

For pointers, retriever training should begin after eight birds have been used to introduce staunchness. Since the complete process outlined in this chapter requires nearly forty birds, your dog will have an opportunity to retrieve fifteen to thirty. Most will learn in that time, though some dogs do not respond to this type of training. Some do not like to handle birds, do not want one in their mouth, and refuse to retrieve. If your dog falls into this category, you may have no choice but to try "force-break" training. We'll get into that next.

CHAPTER SIXTEEN

Advanced Retrieving and Force Training

Force training is probably the most controversial part of dog training, a diffi-cult procedure, full of pressure for the trainer, and traumatic and frightening for the dog. Many trainers feel the price is questionably high. Some believe only a professional should attempt it. Others insist that any owner with persistence can do it. A few consider it unnecessary. The objective is to make every dog a reliable retriever. Professional judgment is clearly divided.

You must be able to read your dog, to know whether or not praise, sweet-talk, and coaxing will achieve faster results. If you think your dog is a candi-date for force training, you must know whether or not you are applying too much pressure, the proper amount, or too little. You must know when to begin and must realize that, once started, the process cannot be stopped in midstream. If you are the least bit uncertain about your dog or your abilities, consult a professional. A good trainer can tell whether or not your dog is a candidate and whether or not you should attempt the process at home.

Even at Black Point, we are divided. Dad feels every upland dog should be force-trained. He says every animal is better for it. I do not agree.

Labs and other retrievers have but one priority, which is a deep-seated, in-bred instinctive urge to retrieve. Normally they only require polishing. In comparison, pointers are bred to find game and only incidentally to retrieve. Not every pointer has the same drive. In some cases interest can be kindled with kindness, coaxing, and repetition, and in others a dog not only lacks willingness, but fights every step of the way. If the owner of the second animal wants his dog to retrieve, it will come only after a clash of wills.

Professionals are divided over the value of force training precisely because it is so rigid. Some refuse to consider using it on any retriever. Those that cannot be taught naturally are eliminated from hunting. Other trainers use the procedure only on uncooperative upland game dogs. Still others insist force training is nothing more than polishing. They recommend it across the board.

MAKING THE DECISION

Before you settle into the last camp, consider a few factors. A dog should never be force-trained until it is two years or more of age. After that, the training can be given at almost any age. At Black Point, I've successfully put six-year-olds through the course.

Your dog should have completed obedience training, the basic field course described in previous chapters, and should have had at least one season of hunting. A dog that has completed field training may come out a sound, staunch pointer and still be less than a polished retriever; most dogs should be given an opportunity to build on their natural instincts before force training. A season of practical hunting experience can often change dogs from timid, uncertain boobs into cooperative tigers. Others balk. I prefer to coax and polish the first type: the latter are force-trained.

At least three problems seem to indicate a need for immediate force training. A dog may retrieve but not hold a bird long enough to be delivered. The bird may fall from its mouth on the way in. The dog may bring the bird to the owner, then spit it out shy of the target. Contrary to appearances, none of these dogs are candidates for force-training. As a rule, if a dog is willing to pick up a bird, you can make a retriever of it. If you fail, the problem is either obedience or trainer error. In both there are faster, less traumatic solutions than force training.

It is wrong to believe that the size of a dog's mouth has much to do with the problem. Some Brittanys have surprisingly small mouths, many about no larger than a big rat's mouth, but they can pick up any bird they choose and so can your dog. It may take an animal with a small mouth more time to decide how to get a handle on the bird, but that's natural. If you see your dog worrying a downed bird, be patient, and do not assume the dog is playing games or figuring out a way to get a free dinner. The bird may be alive, kicking and scratching the dog's face. You cannot know what's happening. Most new retrievers make two or three attempts before picking up their first birds. If you become anxious, if you shout, you'll confuse your dog. The dog will not know whether to stay, come, or retrieve, or even if it's going to be reprimanded on its return. If your dog is slow yet gets the job done, praise the animal. With experience it'll become more adept. If, on the other hand, the dog is obviously shaking the bird, crunching it, and trying to eat it, you must stop it immediately.

TEACHING A DOG TO HOLD

If your dog picks up a bird but only brings it partway, the problem is that either (1) the dog refuses to come; or (2) the dog is not holding the bird long enough. If the problem is the former, take the dog off birds and spend two or three weeks on obedience. Put the dog on the check line and make it come promptly every time you call. If the problem is the latter, solve it with patience. When your dog drops a bird, get it to pick the bird up with coaxing; then slowly call the dog to you. Give the dog lots of praise and "sweet-talk," ("Good boy. That's it. Here.") If its head drops, try two things. First, give a loud command: "Hey, watch it!" or anything else that comes to mind (except "here"). The unexpected sound of your voice will make your dog look around. To do that it must lift its head, and when it raises its head, it cannot release the bird. Then raise your hands over your head and clap. Call to your dog. Waving or clapping your hands helps keep the dog's head up. If you can coax the dog to hold the bird long enough, you'll get a successful retrieve. The minute the dog is in front of you, take the bird (with "give"). Do not make the dog hold it. Lavish the dog with praise.

If you can get your dog to bring two or three birds, you have something to build on. If not, you'll have to spend time teaching it to hold.

You can do this in your yard. Return to frozen birds. Toss one a few yards away, give the command, "Rover, fetch," and when the dog has the bird in its mouth, call it to you. If it drops the bird, go to the dog, put the bird in its mouth, and make the dog hold it. If the dog begins to lower its head, tap it lightly under the chin. This should raise the head. Then stroke the dog gently on the throat. Rubbing its Adam's apple makes its tongue contract, and swallowing helps keep its mouth closed. Repeat for two or three weeks and your dog should be willing to hold.

If your dog drops the bird at your feet or a few yards short of your hand, the problem is trainer error. This usually happens because a trainer is too quick to take the bird. He accepts it the instant the dog arrives. The animal anticipates a hand always being there or quickly realizes that once it jettisons the bird it can go hunting. Either way, it releases the bird farther and farther away, and if an owner permits it, the dog wins. Make your dog bring the bird to your hand; then delay accepting it. Make the dog wait several seconds for the command to "give." If you become unpredictable, the dog is forced to wait because it never knows when the command will come.

FORCE-TRAINING BASICS

(See Illustrations 64–78.)

If sweet-talking, cajoling, and straight forward commands do not work, and your dog either shows no interest in retrieving or refuses, you have no choice but force training.

Force training is a lengthy process. Once started, sessions should be held twice a day, every day. A professional may be able to compress the training into six weeks, but at home the process requires a minimum of eight to twelve weeks. Once begun, your dog does nothing else. You will get a better response and your dog will learn faster without diversions. There is no playtime, no chasing bouncing balls. And most important of all, there is no hunting. You are working with a dog that has shown no desire to retrieve. Do not confuse the issue.

Timing is most important. You should begin force training in spring or early summer so your dog finishes before hunting season. Inevitably, a dog graduates from force training with a temporary dislike of its trainer. You do not want to go directly to hunting with that attitude. Let the dog forget the pressures. With a few weeks of R & R, play and praise, your dog will again become your buddy. The worst possible scenario would be to go hunting before training is completed. If you shot a bird, there would be no way that the dog could equate half a course with what is expected of it in the field. You would lose ground.

THE THEORY OF FORCE TRAINING

Force training is a combination of psychological and physical pressures, a clash of wills, a test to see who is master. A dog is being trained to do something it does not want to do. The trainer must remind the animal that only what he, the trainer, wants is important. The dog must learn it has to comply. Part of the technique involves the application of psychological pressure, part of it involves the application of pain. The pain is neither intense nor prolonged and is used only in the beginning—only when the dog refuses to cooperate. It makes a stubborn dog open its mouth; and in a Pavlovian sense the dog learns to anticipate pain, then discover that if it follows orders, there is none. In a matter of a week or two the threat of pain alone makes the most stubborn dog cooperate.

Different trainers inflict pain in different ways. Some step on a dog's feet, others twist nails or ears. None of these are my style. I see no reason to be brutal. I'm reluctant to inflict pain. My first choice is to substitute pressure for pain. It is applied through the collar. I place my hand beneath the collar, lifting the animal just enough to limit its breathing. The pressure is momentary, and lasts only long enough to prove who is boss. It works for most dogs, but a handful of naturally stubborn animals continue to fight. The only answer is more pressure. I place the tip of one ear against the D-ring sewn on the collar. One thumb is used to press the ear against the ring. I can monitor the pressure and give no more than is required.

Force training can be done in the smallest yard. Many trainers begin on a training table. The theory is this: a dog is disoriented when it is above ground. It is uncertain, less bold, more tractable, and more cooperative. I agree with the theory but not with the table. In most cases it is unnecessary. If you use a table you must devise a way of restraining the dog. Commonly, a short lead is clipped to an overhead cable. You cannot keep a dog on a table long. Sooner or later you have to come to the ground, and as far as I am concerned, it is better to begin there if you can. In most cases you can. Only the most stubborn, intractable dogs need disorientation, and sometimes changing the environment works as well.

Not long ago I had a dog that had been abused on early retrieves. It refused to cooperate because it had discovered refusal was less painful. I started training on the ground and got nowhere. Then I realized the dog had never been in a house. I brought it to my office and for two weeks went through force training there. The environment was so threatening the dog was afraid to fight back. It did it my way, and by the time we got outside was cooperating.

Most of the time I work outside, on the ground. I stand beside or in front of the dog and am strong enough to physically keep the animal under control. If a dog becomes panicky, I back it into a corner. Since I am holding the front end, it has no place to go.

EQUIPMENT

Dogs are taught to retrieve with dummies and dumbbells, artificial objects used precisely because they are not birds. Any pain or pressure the dog experiences is associated with dummies and dumbbells and not birds. When a dog graduates, it is still intense and ready to hunt. For a number of years nothing was commercially available and trainers made their own. Some used boat bumpers; others made objects from wood, burlap sacking, and even old socks. In recent years plastic dummies, also called bumpers and bucks, have been available from sporting goods stores and mail-order sources. They are available in yellow, red, white, and black—colors more important to a retriever than an upland game dog.

You will need two devices for force training. One is a flat buck or dummy, which is used to teach the dog to hold things in its mouth and for early "fetch" training. Secondly, you'll need a dumbbell, which is used to teach the dog to pick up objects from the ground. Wooden dummies are also available, and if you prefer, you can make your own.

The dummy or buck should be the same thickness end to end. It can be made of plastic or wood, about two inches in diameter and long enough to extend beyond the sides of your dog's mouth. If you choose a commercial plastic buck, you'll find them available in two sizes, 2" × 12" and 3½" × 12". I would suggest the smaller version, and for colors recommend yellow or white. You want the dog to see the device from the first toss to the time it falls to earth, and both colors can be readily seen against the sky, in bushes, and in grass.

You will also need a dumbbell. It has large ends and a smaller center so it is easy to pick up. It is used to teach a dog to retrieve game from the ground. You can buy one ready-made or make your own. If you make your own, use a soft, nonresinous wood. See Chapter 7 for instructions on how to make your own.

Whether or not your dog retrieves, you should know by now that you do not have to say anything to get it to chase after downed game. Natural retriever or not, your dog is always ready to chase birds. Whether you toss a ball or shoot a bird, it's ready to go. You do not have to say a word. With force training, however, a cue or command is necessary. The most common is "fetch." Your dog is probably familiar with it, having heard it when a pup. If you prefer another word, use it. Whatever you choose, be sure to use your dog's name first—"Rover, fetch." When you start hunting, you'll need to use the dog's name. There would be chaos in the field if every handler simply told his dog to "fetch." By the time most dogs are ready for hunting, they've learned to retrieve on their name alone. Now, however, be sure to say, "Rover, fetch," every time you put the dummy in your dog's mouth, and later, when you train for distance.

After the dog has the dummy in its mouth, you must also have a command to release it. Some trainers use "leave it" and others, "let go." I prefer "give." Do not allow your dog to release the dummy until you have spoken that command.

Since force training is traumatic and heavy with pressure, the dog's reward—praise—must be prompt, plentiful, and effusive. It must be given every time your pup holds the dummy and every time it releases it. It is also a good idea to reassure your pup by petting it behind the ear, on the shoulder, or under the belly. Avoid touching its face. That's where you have been applying pressure; and to make your hands do both—inflict pressure one moment and provide reassurance the next—is only confusing.

FORCE TRAINING

Training advances through a series of steps, each repeated until the dog accepts it confidently. Because the first month or more is the most traumatic, sessions must be short, no more than five minutes twice a day. Each step should be repeated no more than three times per session.

Insist on longer sessions and you risk pushing your dog to the breaking point. If this happens, you'll know it. Dogs resist passively. They do nothing wrong, and nothing right. They seem to say, "I don't care. What ever you do is fine with me." At that point you've lost your dog. It is no longer learning. Give the dog a day's rest and then try again with less pressure.

FORCE TRAINING: PHASE ONE

Attach a sturdy nylon collar with a large D-ring. Begin on the ground, and use a table only if the dog cannot be controlled. Start each session with a short series of obedience drills—"whoa," "heel," "hup," and "here," for example. These help to calm the dog and establish a mood for learning. Then, with the dog at your side or facing you, begin phase-one training.

Place the flat buck, bumper, or dummy within easy reach. Put one hand under the top of the dog's collar, against its neck. If you are left-handed, use your left hand. If you are right-handed, use your right hand. Position your hand so three fingers are on the head. Your thumb should be on one side of the face, your small finger on the other. This allows you to turn the dog's head left or right, to press the head forward, and to lift the collar if it becomes necessary to apply pressure.

Steady the dog's head with the hand inserted beneath the collar. Hold the dummy with the other hand. Place it in front of the dog's mouth; say, "Rover, fetch," and press the dummy against the dog's jaw. If your dog accepts the dummy, reassure the animal with "hold it." Make the dog hold the dummy for one or two seconds. Remove it with the command "give." Praise your dog. Repeat three times and end the session.

If your dog refuses to open its mouth, you have two choices, to use pain to force it to its mouth, or to force the mouth open physically. In the latter, press the top lip inward against the upper teeth. If the dog tries to bite, it will literally bite itself. When the mouth opens, say the dog's name and "fetch," and insert the dummy. Make the dog hold it a moment (reinforcing this with "hold it"); then remove the dummy with the command "give." Praise your dog, repeat three times, and end the session.

The third method, suggested only for extremely stubborn dogs, is to place the tip of the ear near your thumb, against the D-ring. Using your thumb, press the ear against the ring, and when the dog opens its mouth—and believe me it will—say, "Rover, fetch." Insert the dummy and release your thumb. Make the dog hold the dummy for a moment, prompting it with "hold it"; then add the command "give." Immediately remove the dummy. Praise the dog. Repeat three times and then end the session.

Occasionally you may find a dog that will open its mouth but refuse to hold the dummy. You can hold its closed mouth with your hand if you do not hamper its breathing, but if it fights, attach a two-foot cord to the dummy. Insert the dummy in the dog's mouth and immediately wrap the cord around the muzzle. The dog will neither be able to open its mouth nor drop the dummy. After two or three sessions the dog should get the idea and should hold the dummy on its own.

Repeat the method of your choice twice a day. After three or four sessions the dog should accept the bumper without fighting. If not, continue until the dog freely opens its mouth on command. At that point reduce the pressure by removing your hand from its collar or your thumb from the ear. It will probably take seven to fourteen days for your dog to accept the dummy on its own and to hold it several seconds. At this point repeat the sessions for another week or two, extending the time the dog is asked to hold.

It is important to use a soft, friendly voice with all commands, and be sure to say "give" each time you remove the dummy. Never let your dog decide when to let go. You should make that decision, whether the dummy is held one second or thirty. Command the dog to "give" and remove the dummy in an obvious way so the dog knows you are in charge.

If your dog drops the dummy, it will most often lower its head first. To prevent this, tap gently under the chin. It keeps the head up, prolonging the hold. Reinforce this by saying, "Hold it!" As long as the dog holds the dummy, talk to the dog, give it confidence. Rub its neck to make it hold longer, and say things like, "Good boy. That's it!"

Occasionally in early training, a dog will develop a fear of the dummy since it is associated with pain and pressure. If this happens, you'll be able to see it developing. Your dog will open its mouth, appear to want to go for the dummy, then back away. The dog is uncertain. Change the dummy. Use another color or shape. You can substitute a glove, a stick, or even a sock filled with rags if that is all you have. The object is not as important as the fact that it is different and that the dog will accept and "fetch" it.

FORCE TRAINING: PHASE TWO

Once your dog accepts the dummy with confidence, you can teach it to "fetch" at a distance. Initially, you may again have to resort to force. Insert your hand through the collar as above; then hold the dummy about one foot from the dog at mouth level. Give the command, "Rover, fetch," and push the dog's head toward the dummy. The dog should open its mouth, but if it refuses, press the dummy against its lips. The dog should then open immediately. If it refuses, try pressure at the collar or pinch its ear. The moment the dog accepts the dummy, remove your hand, eliminating pressure. Make the dog hold the dummy for a moment, command "give," and remove it. Praise the dog and repeat three times.

Repeat the training several days, and as soon as the dog is willing to "fetch" on command at a distance of twelve inches, remove your hand from its collar or your thumb from its ear. Hold the bumper farther away. Make the dog go for it. Repeat this for a week or more until the dog is confident; then move the dummy still farther away. When the dog is again confident, increase the distance again. In several weeks the dog should be willing to take several steps to retrieve the dummy. Through all of this the dummy is held at mouth level. You can now begin lowering it so the dog not only has to step forward but must also lower its head. The dog should move for the dummy on command, but if it seems confused, put your hand back in its collar and force its head toward the dummy. Remove your hand as soon as the dog is confident. Gradually lower the dummy, an inch or so at a time. Within two weeks it should be just inches from the ground.

FORCE TRAINING: PHASE THREE

It is now time for a change. Many trainers go immediately to the ground, but I prefer to change the pace, to give the dog a breather, a "summer vacation." I think it is good for dog and trainer. Place the dog on a check line and begin by holding the dummy at some distance. Make the dog come to it; then step back two steps as soon as the dog has it in its mouth. Say "hold it" to reassure the dog. At this point most dogs are nervous, and yours may think you mean "stay." It is not a serious mistake if the dog does. Repeat this two or three times, and as soon as the dog seems at ease, it is time to teach it to walk with the dummy in its mouth. Walking builds confidence.

A dog will invariably spit the bumper out the first time it is asked to walk. Stop the dog, pick up the dummy, repeat the dog's name, and command "fetch." Put the dummy in its mouth and make it hold. Resume walking. If the dog drops it a second time, give its collar a jerk, make it "fetch," and walk again. Repeat as often as necessary. When the dog does it right, even for a moment, be generous with your praise. Within a week the dog will be holding and walking confidently. You can read the story in the tail. In the first, uncertain days, the tail sags. Your dog is fearful. Gradually the tail comes up, and the dog is walking beside you, full of confidence, the dummy in its mouth.

At that point, vary the routine. Hold the dummy some distance away, command, "Rover, fetch," and make the dog come to you. When the dog has the dummy, make the dog stay. Walk away, then call "here." Make the dog come to you. When the dog is confident with these maneuvers, it is time to go to the ground.

FORCE TRAINING: PHASE FOUR

Change now to the dumbbell. Again, place your dog on the check line. Your first move is to introduce the dumbbell to your dog. Hold it near its mouth, give the command to "fetch," and let the dog hold it for a minute. A dumbbell has a different shape and feel, and your dog should have at least one familiarization session. Some dogs accept the dumbbell immediately, others need time. The first session may be confusing. Often a dog will take one of the big ends between its teeth rather than the center. That does not matter. Your dog has done what you've ordered. Give plenty of praise.

When the dog seems confident with the dumbbell, place it on the ground directly in front of the animal. Even though your dog has retrieved a dummy from near ground level, the first dumbbell may create confusion. You cannot put one on the ground, give the "fetch" command, and expect instant success. At Black Point I find I usually have to put my hand on it. That often makes the difference. Occasionally a dog will inadvertently take hand and dumbbell, and if yours does, do not complain. The dog has done everything you asked. If the dog will not pick up the dumbbell, put your hand through its collar, say, "Rover, fetch," and press its head toward the dumbbell. Put the dumbbell in the dog's mouth and give praise. It may take a week or more to get your dog to retrieve a dumbbell placed directly in front of it on the ground. When the dog can do that confidently, try for distance.

FORCE TRAINING: PHASE FIVE

Trainers are divided on the best way to accomplish this. Some feel you should walk in front of your dog in full view, place the dumbbell on the ground, walk back to the dog's side, and give the command "fetch." They feel it is wrong to throw the dumbbell because it makes training a game. I do not agree. What's wrong with making learning fun? It is difficult enough to motivate a dog, and if you can accomplish it by a few tosses of the dumbbell, that's to the good. I like to excite my dogs with talk. "You want this? O.K. Let's go for it," I tell them. In a couple of days they are eager for this part of the training. Repetition will remove any idea that what we're doing is not for real.

At first, toss the dumbbell a few feet. Give the command to "fetch," and if the dog retrieves with little hesitation, offer plenty of praise. Some dogs are insecure the first time they are asked to retrieve from a distance. If your dog's tail is down, it is insecure. Toss the dumbbell, then walk with the dog. You may have to go all the way the first time. If that's what it takes, do it; and when the dog has the dumbbell in its mouth, offer praise. It is not that the dog does not want to retrieve, but that the dog is uncertain. It has had a lot of pressure and needs reassurance. The first time many dogs return on tiptoe, as if walking on eggs. If yours does that, give plenty of praise and reassurance as long as the dumbbell is brought. In two or three days the dog should be much more confident.

In a week or two the animal should be willing to retrieve a dumbbell several yards away. If your dog seems bewildered as the distance increases, try shorter distances until confidence is achieved. Since this has become fun, much of the pressure built up in earlier sessions is dissipating. Your dog may even be so eager you do not need to give the command to fetch. Using the dog's name may be enough. At Black Point dogs become so experienced at this that when I remove the dummy from my truck, they are eager to take it from my hand.

FORCE TRAINING: PHASE SIX

By the time your dog has successfully retrieved the dumbbell at distances of ten to fifteen yards for a week, you can move to frozen birds. As in many other cases, I recommend pigeons because they are small, compact, and easy for the dog to handle; but if you prefer, you can use small quail. They have many of the same advantages. You can do this phase of training at home.

Though I know the dog will fetch, I retrace steps, placing the first couple of birds in the dog's mouth for reassurance, to let the dog become familiar with the feel of them. The first day the dog is simply asked to hold the bird and then to walk with it. Most dogs will do this, but if yours drops the bird, you must go through the procedure used with the dummy. Pick up the bird, place it in its mouth, and make the dog hold it a second or more.

Now you must also repeat another pattern used with the plastic dummy. Even though your dog knows what to do—in terms of a dummy—you cannot throw a bird, give the command to fetch, and expect anything to happen. Your dog may not do it. It is apples-and-oranges time. To your dog, holding a bird in its mouth is different than picking one up from the ground. You must familiarize the dog all over again. As with the first dummy, hold the frozen bird a foot or two away, command the dog to fetch, and make the dog take the bird from your hand. Most dogs will do this without much persuasion, though some balk. If yours refuses, place your hand beneath its collar, hold the bird a foot away, give the command to fetch, and as before, force the dog's head to the bird. Invariably the dog will accept the bird. The dog should become confident in a few days.

Now you can try tossing a frozen bird on the ground. Most dogs will go after it, and if yours does, repeat this two or three or four sessions; then increase the distance. If your dog refuses, work with the bird in your hand, increasing the distance as you progress. At some point you'll be able to place it on the ground. As with the dummy, you may even have to place your hand on the bird the first time out.

FORCE TRAINING: PHASE SEVEN

Once the dog retrieves frozen pigeons from some distance, gradually substitute larger birds, ending with a hen pheasant and then a cock. When the dog is confident on large frozen birds, it is time to move to fresh-killed birds.

Once again the size of the bird is important, and in the beginning the smaller the bird, the easier it is for the dog. The difference between a frozen bird, which is compact and stiff, and one just killed is the difference between putty and a sharp stick. A fresh-killed bird is limp. It hangs unpredictably from the mouth. A dog must become used to the feel of it and must learn to walk with it. The first birds should be pigeons or quail.

I place the first birds in the dog's mouth, and if the dog seems confident by the end of the first day, I toss birds the second day. If the dog retrieves those, I use still larger birds on the third day. In all of this training you are not yet shooting over your dog. You have not yet killed a bird in front of him. If the dog balks at any point, stop and work on that segment until the dog seems confident; then, and only then, move to larger birds.

FORCE TRAINING: PHASE EIGHT

When your dog is firm and confident retrieving fresh-killed birds, it is time to kill the first bird. Again, use pigeon or quail. At first, plant just one bird at a time. If you use a pigeon, do not hobble it, but dizzy it as I've described previously. Obviously, these training sessions must be done in a field where you can plant and shoot live birds. Be sure to hold these sessions in the early morning while it is cool. Plant birds before your dog has time to run and become overheated. You do not want the dog so warm it is panting, racing with its tongue out. That adds an extra dimension: how is it to handle a bird and pant at the same time? It has never had to face that. Avoid the problem by starting while your dog is cool. Plant the bird, let the dog find it, and with your animal staunch on point, flush the bird and kill it. Tell your dog to fetch.

If the dog races to the bird and stands over it, do not panic. This is its first bird. If the dog doesn't do it quite by the book, give the dog the benefit of the doubt. Let the dog figure out how to pick the bird up, then coax the dog in. Often reassurance and praise will get a dog to retrieve the first bird better than harsh corrections. Once the dog has the bird in its mouth, watch closely. If the dog lowers its head, raise your hands over your head and clap to keep the head erect.

If the dog returns without the bird, give it a push toward the bird, and in a stern voice say something like, "Come on! You know better. Go fetch!" Send the dog out again. If that does not work, give a tug on the check line, and when the dog goes out, try again to gently coax it in. Most often, a dog like this needs confidence. If that does not work, go out to the bird, place your hand beneath the dog's collar as you've done before, and force the dog to pick up the bird. Let the dog hold it, then coax the dog to bring it in.

If a dog refuses a fresh bird at this point, it generally means you've pushed the previous training too far and too fast. The dog is not ready. Return to your yard and repeat earlier training; then return to birds later.

If your dog retrieves small birds well, move to larger ones, and if it consistently retrieves without a balk for eight to ten times, you can consider your dog to have graduated. It is important to realize that this does not mean your dog is perfect. Far from it. Most will still try to test you, and you must consider time and circumstances. If a dog balks when fresh, it's attempting to see how far it can push you. Don't let it get away with a thing, but if you've been hunting on a hot afternoon for half an hour without finding a bird and your dog suddenly finds one, that is another story. By then the dog is hot and panting, its brain literally dimmed by heat.. If it retrieves with its tongue hanging out and lets the bird fall from its mouth coming in, you will gain nothing by a temper tantrum. Do not berate your dog. Consider that the heat has gotten to it. It has shortened the dog's attention span. It's been a bad day for the dog. Pick up the bird, place it in the dog's mouth. Let the dog hold it a moment; then take the bird, release your dog, and let the dog cool off. If there is time, you can hunt later in the day. If not, try the next weekend.

Be patient. The first times your dog hunts after force training it will be uncertain and uneasy. Do not become the all-powerful white hunter demanding perfection. Let your dog relax. Let the dog enjoy the sport. As far as I'm concerned, it is a great pleasure to turn a fearful, uncertain dog, just out of force training, into a happy one. I want dogs to hunt because the sport is fun, not because they must. Consistency and perseverance will prevail.

CHAPTER SEVENTEEN

Steady to Wing and Shot

A dog trained steady to wing and shot is under the complete control of its owner. It will do all the things every well-trained dog is expected to do and more. The superiority of steadiness to wing and shot is like the superiority of caviar to roe. Steadiness training is the icing on the cake, the cream in the coffee, the college course that makes an upland dog as close to perfect as it can get.

I have presented steadiness training in two parts, both using birds. The first is an extension of previous staunchness training. That response is refined and reinforced. Your dog is taught to remain firm every time a bird breaks, whether it is an expected flush by the hunter, the unanticipated flight of a bird that breaks early, or the complete surprise of one neither dog nor handler were aware of—a bird suddenly airborne from an unseen side pocket. Steady to shot means your dog will hold absolutely firm after a bird has been shot. Steady to wing and steady to shot are coupled in training because both situations are common to hunting and can be found hand in hand in the field.

Many people feel this is the most difficult part of training because it expects a dog to really shape up, to become as good as it can ever get. I don't agree. The training is traumatic, though not as difficult as force training. Admittedly, it is not for every dog, but previous training has been designed to prove we're in control, that the dog cannot chase birds on its own, cannot flush birds when it wants, and cannot break after a bird until its handler gives the command. Teaching steady to wing is a logical extension of this (see Chapters 11 and 14). Consider it this way: the training I'm proposing focuses on the goals we've been working toward. It is a gradual reinforcement of the elusive concept we've been aiming at since "stay" training long ago when the pup was just a few months old.

Steady-to-wing-and-shot training is not essential. A dog well-trained in the previous steps can be hunted with pride without additional work, and a lot of hunters do just that. You can hunt your dog from now until the day it dies and be satisfied without the dog ever being steady to wing and shot. The dog will make an occasional mistake, but most owners can forgive. The final polishing simply anticipates the common mistakes and attempts to prevent them. If you want the perfect dog, a truly classy animal that is probably a cut above your neighbor's, consider this final training, and remember: there are no shortcuts.

Steady-to-wing-and-shot training is not polishing for the sake of polishing. It has practical applications. You may find yourself in situations in which the training pays off. Two examples prove my point. First, no matter how good a gunner, you are not going to kill every bird. Some will be out of season or the wrong sex, and others represent a clean miss. If your dog is steady to wing, it will not break. You will not have to call the dog back, run after it, or worse, lose control. Your dog will not move until released.

Second, consider that you are hunting a wooded area and, attempting a difficult shot, merely wing a bird. If your dog has not been trained to be steady to shot, it might break as the shot is fired and be beneath the wounded bird by the time it falls. You may say that is great, a plus for the "unsteady" dog. Not so. Every time a dog breaks unbid, it is teaching itself to repeat that failure. Uncorrected, it can lose its well-trained edge. With a dog steady to shot, you can spot your error, anticipate the situation, and release your dog early. Your dog will be almost as close to the bird as the dog who breaks early, and you'll retain the control that is so important. In time the disobeying dog will learn to anticipate action and will be out of control.

TRAINING BASICS

While training for steady to wing and shot is as beneficial for a pointer as for a flushing dog, it is not for a young, inexperienced animal. It is the last thing a dog learns. It must not be taught before "whoa," "hup," or staunchness. A pointer should be firm on all basics before it is introduced to steadiness training. It must walk at heel position on and off leash, come when called, "whoa" when commanded, retrieve, and have at least one season of hunting behind it. A dog should have completed staunchness training and have proven it can hold firm on planted live birds. If your dog is uncertain on any of these, go off birds and polish the less perfect phases before attempting a course in steadiness.

Steady-to-wing-and-shot training is not complicated. The key is reinforcement and repetition, working day after day with birds until your dog carries the idea of staunchness to its conclusion and response is automatic. A professional, working with a dog on a daily basis, should complete the training in two months, one month for steady to wing and the other for steady to shot. Working at home, no more than on weekends, obviously requires more time, perhaps ten to fifteen weekends. If your dog is staunch, it should get the idea of steadiness training the first two days. From that point on, repetition reinforces the response.

CHOOSING BIRDS

Training can only be done in a large field. In the beginning, you'll use pigeons if you can get them, and quail, pheasant, or chukar if you can't. I recommend pigeons because they are small and inexpensive. This is an ideal time to try homing pigeons. Not everyone will be able to obtain them, but some bird breeders will rent five or six birds to a trainer if they can be assured their birds will not be killed—and in training for steady to wing, the birds are not harmed. Homing pigeons are ideal because they flush and return to their base and are inexpensive.

If you cannot obtain homing pigeons, buy regular pigeons if you can. In most areas they cost between $2 and $3, the lowest-priced bird you can find for training. If pigeons are not available, choose the least expensive game bird. Quail are ideal because they are small, but your dog has had a year of hunting and the size of the bird should not be of primary concern. Pigeons can only be used once, but if your training area is large enough, game birds can be used two or three times. Let your dog point a bird and flush it; mark where it lands and use it again. Whether or not you use a bird the third time depends on its condition. You do not want to use one that is too tired. If your dog breaks, it might catch it, and you do not want that to happen.

If you use pigeons, you will need six for each training session, one dozen per weekend. If you cannot obtain pigeons, use three game birds per training session, six per weekend. Game birds can be flushed, marked, allowed to rest, and reused. The birds will be planted in the field, without your dog knowing the location. Pigeons can be placed in an electronic release or in small cages, or dizzied and planted in the grass. They can be hobbled and possibly reused, though I would not suggest this with any dog not absolutely staunch. The safest choices are the popper or electronic release or a wire cage. Game birds should be dizzied and planted as you've done previously.

Another possibility, suggested first for pups, is to bring your dog to a place where wild birds congregate—flocks of pigeons common to a park or shore birds found at a lake or an ocean beach. This is not a substitute for field training, but an extra step you can use to reinforce response between weekends. Place your dog on a check line, and as the flock breaks, give the command to "whoa." Make the dog hold. If it breaks, dump it with the check line and place it on the spot at which it broke. Make the dog stay. Repeating this several times—over a period of days—is extremely helpful.

STEADY TO WING

You should work with a partner throughout this phase of training. Attach a long check line to your dog's collar. Bring a game bag and a blank gun. Give your dog a few simple commands to calm its mind and focus it on training. "Whoa," "heel," and "here" are examples. If you are using pigeons, have your partner plant two birds—without your dog seeing—and place two additional birds in your game bag. Keep the others in reserve. Release your dog with the check line running free. When the dog points the first bird, be sure it holds steady as you approach. Have your partner approach the bird from a similar angle, but do not flush it immediately. The longer the bird can hold, the more training your dog receives.

Your position in relationship to your dog is important. With check line in hand, I like to kneel forward of my dog, at an angle left or right, so that the dog can see my partner, the spot where the bird is, and me (see Illustration 79). I face the dog with my hand half-raised.

Have your partner kick the grass, as suggested for the "hat trick." Rustle the grass as if a bird is there. If the dog is nervous, it may attempt to break, and you should be close enough to control it. Raise your hand, directly in its line of vision, and in a loud voice say "whoa." Your hand and voice are deterrents, and often your dog will hold because of them. If the dog breaks, grab the check line and dump the dog as quickly as possible. Bring the dog back to the point at which it broke, give the "whoa" command, and make the dog hold for several seconds.

Every time a bird is flushed, you or your partner should fire the blank gun. This is important since it simulates hunting and reinforces the dog's response to shot.

If the dog breaks as the bird flushes, dump the dog and bring it back to the original spot. Say "whoa," and make the dog hold. Remove one of the spare birds from your game bag without your dog noticing. Kick the grass near the dog and drop the pigeon. It will break immediately, simulating a wild flush. Make your dog hold while the bird flutters and takes to the air. If the dog breaks again, dump it quickly and bring it back to the point at which it was expected to hold. If you are using game birds, you cannot double up this way. You will have to let a bird flush, mark its landing, and use it a second time later.

Some people suggest electronic collars for this phase of training, and many professionals use them with difficult dogs; but a collar is extremely tricky. You must know your dog and its breaking point, and for this reason I do not recommend them. If you over use an electric collar, you can ruin your dog for hunting.

REPETITION

As I have emphasized before, if your dog is staunch enough before you introduce steadiness training, you should have few problems. Your dog may break at first under the pressure of live birds, but it should quickly settle down and begin to hold. At that point, training becomes a matter of repetition. Your dog is faced with one live bird after another until it is conditioned to hold each time one flushes, until released.

If your dog breaks, it should be dumped as quickly as possible. It will spring quickly to its feet to watch the bird, and if it still tugs on the line, attempting to pull you toward the bird as you shout "whoa" after "whoa," your dog is telling you something you may not like to hear. "You mean little to me," the dog is saying. "That bird is more important than any command you could give."

Immediately take the dog off birds and put it back on basic obedience training: "heel" and "here," then "whoa" and staunchness. Until you gain the respect of your dog, until it responds to a command because it knows that is what you want, you will never get an animal steady to wing. If it is not steady to wing, it is useless to attempt to teach it to be steady to shot.

In most cases the above will not happen. The common scenario is happier. You are in the field with six pigeons or three game birds. You'll use the pigeons once and the game birds two or three times. That gives you six to nine training sessions per day. If you plant three pigeons, two the first time out, and one later, and drop three more from your game bag, your dog has an opportunity to learn a great deal. Even if the dog seemed ready to break in the beginning, by the second weekend it should be holding firm. In another weekend or two it could be ready for the second phase of training.

STEADY TO SHOT

A dog must be absolutely steady to wing—that is, to all flushed birds—before it can be taught to be steady to shot; and if your dog has held firm while five or six birds have flushed, you can be sure it's ready to graduate. Yet—and this is hard for some to believe—just because the dog has proven steady to wing, does not mean it'll automatically hold when you kill a bird. Believe me, though a dog graduates from phase one and obviously understands what's required, it may still stumble when that first bird is downed.

The entire sequence—pointing, holding staunch, hearing a shot, and finally seeing the bird fall—is seen as something different. That makes live birds a new ballgame. Instinctively your dog will want to break and will, unless you're there to stop it. That's the point of this final phase of training: to shoot enough birds and restrain your dog often enough so that it not only has the idea ingrained that it must hold, but also has been made to hold often enough so that training will overcome its instinct to break.

The procedure is simple. You plant two birds, let your dog find one and then the other, shoot and kill each, and make your dog hold before it is released to retrieve. In the beginning you should not have the dog hold more than a few seconds, but as training progresses, you will increase the time until your dog holds a minute or more. As in phase one, you'll want to work with a partner who will help you plant, flush, and shoot birds, but there are three differences. First, the blank gun is replaced with shotgun and live loads. Second, your partner will do the shooting. You should be as close to your dog as possible. Third, while I recommended pigeons in phase one, I suggest game birds for this section. You can use and shoot pigeons if you wish, but quail or other small game birds are better; and at some point in training you should use the game bird most common in your area. The final phases of steady-to-shot training should be as close to a real hunting experience as you can make it.

The first day you should also bring a blank gun. Place your dog on a long check line. Give a few preliminary commands to calm it while your partner is planting the birds. Release the dog with the line running free, and when it points the first bird, make it hold a minute or two before flushing the bird. When the bird breaks, fire the blank gun and allow the bird to fly free. If the dog does everything as expected, holding firm until released, kill the next bird. If not, reinforce steady-to-wing training one or two times until the dog seems confident.

When you begin shooting birds, teamwork between you and your partner becomes especially important. As soon as your dog points a bird, you should position yourself in front and to one side of your dog, as described above. You want to watch your dog, not your partner. Again, have your hand raised so your dog can see it. You must carefully watch your dog so that the instant the gun is fired, you can sense the dog's reactions. The dog will be nervous, and if you sense it is about to break, stop it—with a loud "whoa" if possible and with the check line if not.

You will need some communication with your partner to determine what has happened to the bird. If you hear one shot, you can assume it has been downed; but if there are two, you need to know whether or not the bird has been hit. A terse, low-pitched comment will do the trick. "Got him," "Bird down"—anything similar will work. If you take your eye off the dog to look at your partner, or if he speaks in an excited voice, your dog will break.

After the dog has held for few seconds, send it on the retrieve, either with its name and the command ("Rover, fetch!") or with its name alone. Chances are your dog is so eager to go that the slightest indication of release is all it needs. Repeating the dog's name should do it.

Once the dog proves it will hold briefly before being cast off to retrieve, the remainder of your training is designed to reinforce that as you increase the time the dog is asked to remain staunch. From having your dog hold one or two seconds the first day, you will gradually extend to forty, fifty, or sixty seconds after several outings. When, after five or six sessions your dog consistently holds until you release it, you can consider the animal ready for graduation exercises. It is time to remove the check line.

TEMPERING TRAINING WITH REALITY

Once your dog is fully trained and steady to wing and shot, it's ready for any hunting you care to throw at it. It's been trained to remain on point, whether three minutes or three seconds, until you cast it off. This kind of control places a new responsibility on you. A dog reliably steady has advantages and drawbacks. If you are not a consistent shooter, you must learn to modify that control to meet varying hunting conditions. You must time the release of your dog with the results of your gun. If a bird has been crippled, the dog should be released much sooner than when a bird has been cleanly killed. But remember: a dog that breaks too soon may not mark the bird well. A dog that stands firm usually has an advantage. This dog keeps an eye on the bird and marks it better.

CHAPTER EIGHTEEN

Wrapping It Up

Once your dog successfully completes the long and varied training described in previous chapters, it should have become a slick, polished, well-oiled hunting machine, finely honed to deliver years of friendly, reliable service. Your dog should know his trade inside out and should perform well. But make no mistake: that animal is much more than a machine. It is as good a hunting companion as you'll ever have. It needs little in the way of refinement. But there is one aspect not yet covered: backing or honoring another point. That ability can transform a good dog into a great one.

In competition as in friendly hunting, one man's dog is expected to stop the instant another points, but not every dog does. Canines are jealous, highly competitive critters, and instinct tells the one minus a point to rush in and take charge. Obviously, this delicate moment is not the time for that kind of competitive urge. Two dogs, even a well-controlled pair, present too much pressure. At the least, a frightened bird will flush wild. At the worst, a canine battle royal may erupt. Training your dog to honor every point eliminates that scenario before it begins.

BACKING

Some dogs have a natural inclination to honor another's point while others must be taught. If your pup is sound on "whoa" it could be "whoa-backed"—

that is, forced to honor a point by command—until it understands and accepts the idea; but it is best to devote a little direct training to the concept. It is certainly a sound approach if you are considering field trials. A dog that must be "whoa-backed" in competition may or may not be marked down— that decision depends on age—but one that does it naturally generally receives more credit. In at least one association, trials-events backing is not a requirement for Puppy and Derby Stakes competition, but is basic in All-Age Stakes events.

CHECKING INSTINCT

Your first project should be a test to see if your dog has any natural backing instinct. Unless this is hunting season, you'll probably need a training permit as well as a hunting license. Regulations vary from state to state, so check with local Fish and Game officials. You'll also need a friend, a second dog, and, as with other field training, a few birds. Bring along a shotgun.

Tether, dizzy, and plant one bird so that neither dog knows its location; then have your friend cast off his dog. After the first dog is on point, release yours. Remember, this is the first time your dog has been in this situation, so keep a low profile. Give no commands. Remain silent. See what your dog will do. Once it spots the other dog, watch carefully. Most dogs will stalk catlike toward the bird, past the pointing dog. Some may move too aggressively, flushing the bird. A fieldwise dog stops short of that. If yours does, it shows a certain amount of bird savvy, indicating an instinctive backing sense. If not, you must start training from scratch, but that is not serious. Conditioning and repetition can make any dog a reliable backer.

Do not let your dog reach the bird. Once you've decided whether or not the dog has backing instinct, give the "whoa" command, end the session, and prepare for training.

The amount of training depends on your dog. A professional can do the job in a month or so. A hobby handler working only on weekends will need more time. You can probably teach a dog with some instinct in five or six weekends. One with no instinct could require sixteen to twenty. If training coincides with hunting season, sessions can be coupled with actual hunting. If not, you'll have to stage them. Either way, you'll still need a friend and a second dog.

TRAINING

There is no reason to repeat the testing above. If it is hunting season, you can use birds found naturally or you can plant some. Out of season, tether and plant a couple of birds as above. Give both dogs a warm-up, testing them on two or three "whoas" and a "heel" or two, just to set the tone of the session; then let your friend cast his dog off. When his dog is on point, release yours. Be sure to use the long check line. Whether or not you hold it depends on the confidence you have in your dog. If you think it may break even though you give a solid "whoa" command, hold the line. If you think the dog responds well, let it float. Bring your dog in at an angle to the bird. Do not walk the dog directly to it.

Once your dog spots its companion on point, watch closely. If the dog stops, give praise. If it wants to break, stop it. Give the "whoa" command even if the other dog is thirty to fifty yards away.

Keep your dog solid on "whoa," though the first time it sees another dog the urge to break may be overwhelming (see Illustration 80 and 81). Your dog will probably want to get as close as possible—a mixture of competition and jealousy is driving it—but you must hold the dog exactly where you gave the command. It often helps to move in front of your dog, kneeling slightly to one side. Look at the dog. Talk to it. Raise your hand. The sight of you and the sound of your calm, even voice should keep the dog firm, but do not let your eyes wander. If you take your eyes off your dog, it may bolt.

Tense moments will come when your partner flushes the bird and then shoots. The moment the bird breaks, your dog will want to break, and it will take all the control you can muster to hold the dog. Do not let the dog move. After the bird is shot, your partner will send his dog on a retrieve, and that will be your second moment of truth. Again, your dog will want to follow. Make the dog hold, though not through the entire retrieve. Once the other dog has the bird, release yours. Give it lots of praise and cast it off in another direction. Do not let the dog circle back.

Do not allow your dog to creep. If it stops on "whoa" and then inches forward, bring it back to the original mark and make it hold. Repeat the training as often as you can, certainly four or five times each outing. (You can do this in two sessions, two birds in the morning and two in the afternoon.) Each time your dog does it right, the animal should become more staunch. It should require less control. Repetition will teach it exactly what you want. Don't forget the praise. Praise is important.

The basic concept behind training is to teach a dog to react to motion, to stop the instant it sees another animal motionless. It doesn't matter whether the second one has stopped to scratch, to urinate, or to point. Backing is not an intellectual exercise. A dog must be so well trained that its response becomes instinctive.

RELOCATION

Relocation does not require special training, but it may help to understand the principles. The term simply means that your dog has found scent and established a point and that you've worked the area without flushing a bird. Now you want your dog to check new ground. A number of things may have happened. The scent may have been cold: the place may previously have held a bird but been vacated before your dog arrived. It could also have been an honest point: the frightened bird may have moved.

It is easy enough to tell your dog, "Okay, let's get on with it. Look someplace else," and then to cast the dog off; but if the scent is fresh and strong, you'll probably have to deal with a keyed-up canine. That can be tricky.

Some dogs can relocate game faster than others. Release one dog from a point, and it'll quickly pinpoint the bird. Others become so excited they literally forget their training. They barge in like a Sherman tank. I can't tell you what goes through that dog's mind, but I suspect it is something like this: the pup knows game is near and switches from using its nose to using its eyes. In the transition it moves too damn close. It literally stumbles over the bird, and gets a wild flush for its efforts.

That's the reason for a careful, calm relocation. If your dog is obviously tense, keyed-up, and nervous, talk the dog down. Use the softest, gentlest voice you can muster. Before sending the dog after a bird, tell it, "Easy boy, easy," and if the dog shakes nervously and tries to break, use a tone with more authority: "Hey! I said easy." Then continue talking until its nervousness disappears. When the dog seems relaxed, send it off. It'll have a better chance of finding its bird.

AFTER TRAINING ENDS

Once you have your dog pointing, holding, retrieving, and backing—well, it's pure pleasure to watch the dog work. The saddest time is the day hunting season ends. But let me tell you: this may be the end of outdoor sports for six or eight months, but it is not the last of the days you should spend with your dog. The important time is just beginning. A hunting dog is a twelve-month, 365-day-a-year joy, pleasure, and responsibility.

One of the most important decisions you can make is the one that deals with what to do with your dog when hunting season ends. With training over, with hundreds of hours invested, plus bucks for birds and more for transportation, you've reached the most important point in this or any other book purporting to tell you how to create a hunting dog. What you do, or don't do, in the off-season can make or break your dog.

Training never ends. If you ignore your dog, leaving it by itself in its kennel day after day, or if you relax on obedience, letting the dog have its way, you could start hunting next season with a dog half as sharp as yours is now.

When hunting season ends and you and your pup look forward to relaxed nights, keep the rapport you've built at a high. Continue to make your dog part of your life. Take the dog for regular walks. Give it exercise. Make it as much a friend as it was when hunting. Give it rides in the family car. And above all else, keep the dog sharp on obedience. As you go walking, toss in an occasional command. Make the dog "heel" from time to time, and when you cross a street, tell it to "whoa" or "hup" while the light changes from red to green.

When you go for a drive, make the dog "whoa" or "hup" before entering the vehicle; and if you can, bring along a portable kennel. A command to "kennel" is always appropriate. You do not have to work your dog as intensely as when it was training, but never let it forget. As long as your dog lives, a command is something it must respect.

And you should take time to keep your dog in field trim with occasional exercise on live birds. Get a training permit from local game officials if one is necessary in your state, and bring along a couple of friends. Plant birds and make your dog hunt by the book. Your dog will love it, and your friends' animals will benefit equally. Ideally, you should have sessions with live birds twice a month, but if that is difficult, do it as often as you can.

If minor problems develop, if your dog becomes lax on some particular phase of training, concentrate on that. When obedience drills are called for, go off birds and back on the basic commands "here," "heel," or "whoa." If you have any doubts about the abilities of your dog, this may also be the time for a professional evaluation. Most professionals ask a nominal charge for an hour or two critique. They'll go out with a few birds, run the animal, put it through its paces, and make an appraisal. If pointing or "whoaing" needs correcting or sharpening, they'll give you a full report. You'll know what to concentrate on and how to go about it.

Another good idea is to join a breed club. Most towns have a group of owners of your breed who meet monthly, hold outings, and talk about training and breed development. Everyone has a great time. Their "fun" days are excellent times for dogs. There are competitions, and there is always an expert available—a professional, or an amateur who is so sharp he should be professional. He'll be glad to help you pick up any slack. If your dog needs polishing, he may tell you exactly how to go about it. Keep your dog in condition during the off-season. You'll discover it pays important dividends when next year's hunting rolls around.

CHAPTER NINETEEN

Correcting and Preventing Problems

No dog does everything perfectly, but an occasional mistake is hardly critical. No two canines have the same intensity, and to be critical, each has some fault. If the problem is minor, with little effect on hunting, pointing, or retrieving, the wise owner may chose to live with it. If more serious, a hobby trainer can probably correct it. But when a problem is debilitating and deep-rooted, it may require a professional touch.

One mistake is not the end of the world; it cannot create a habit. Bad habits develop when a dog is allowed to repeatedly get by with a half-hearted or incorrect response. All it takes to prevent most of them is consistency, an awareness of how your dog is responding, and an insistence on the proper response each time a command is given. Much effort is required to correct a bad habit, and a good handler tries to anticipate mistakes. Prevention is the quickest and most permanent solution, and the best advice I can give is never let a bad habit get a foothold. Below are some of the common problems found in upland game dogs along with suggestions for preventing and correcting them.

BITING

Biting and overprotectiveness should not be allowed. With a little common sense you can nip both at first blush. A tendency to bite usually begins early, starting with the games people play with small pups. Tug of war is an example. Attempt to take a towel or glove from a pup and it hangs on. The pup may even growl. If you persist, the game develops into biting. A rubber ball has a similar effect.

Many dogs are protective of their food and will growl if you come too close. I train a pup out of that the first time it happens. I make an issue of it, dominating the pup so it knows it can't get away with growling, then try to never again place the pup in a position where it has to react over food. If it happens, the response is again corrected.

Too many owners think it is great if a dog growls when someone knocks at the door. A muffled growl, they reason, makes strangers believe the house is well protected. Even with that reasoning, "protective" growling is not a good idea. Never expect a dog to do double duty. If you want a guard dog, buy one. If a hunting dog growls in response to the doorbell, put an end to it immediately. If you don't, it will become a habit that carries over to the field.

Open hostility is equally serious. Sometimes an owner thinks it is cute and promotes it without realizing he is creating a vicious habit he'll come to regret. "Look, my dog is protecting me," he says, emphasizing that his bristling mutt is macho.

Well, macho is wrong. Though it may stem from natural instincts and the purest of motives, a sense of territorial rights and protectiveness, the response should never be allowed to develop. If a dog bristles in the house, put a stop to it. Outside, keep the dog on a leash, and if it growls at other animals, tell it in no uncertain terms to knock it off. Sure, many hunters insist that other dogs always initiate it. They say outsiders come up to their dog and growl. So what? If your animal growls in return, jump on him. If you are going to hunt with friends, your pup must learn to get along with humans and other dogs.

One day you are going to become involved in a dog fight no matter how careful you are. Some half-trained dog will rush over and begin chewing on your pup, and it will have to protect itself. Under those conditions don't fault your animal; it's only doing what it must. Be careful as you break it up, then try not to let it happen again.

Occasionally a dog is a natural fighter, aggressive and hard-tempered, and there is not much you can do. You can't train irritability out of an animal like that. The best you can hope for is to buy a short leash and hunt alone.

BACK-CASTING

Back-casting—a dog working behind itself instead of continually tracking ahead—is caused by trainer error: the trainer plants too many birds behind the dog, or lets the dog work the farthest bird first and then circle back toward the starting point picking up remaining birds along the way. Let a dog work back on a few birds, and sooner or later it'll figure that's where they are.

The solution is obvious. When you plant birds for any training session, plant the first close in, the second farther away, and so on. Back-casting may not be a bad habit when you hunt alone, but in trials competition a dog is penalized for it. Why let it start?

BARKING

The problem can be especially serious if you keep a dog in the city and have neighbors nearby. It is not healthy, and doctors now feel continual barking may affect the immune system. If you keep two dogs, a barker can make a nonbarker noisy. If your dog is kept in an outside kennel, the easiest solution is a bark-limiting electronic collar. It is self-contained, has a built-in switch, and gives a dog a jolt of low-voltage current each time it yaps. The current is not dangerous, and the collar is humane, providing just enough correction to break most dogs of the habit in a couple of days. There is even a fake, or dummy, "electronic" collar for a dog to wear after training—just to keep it in line.

BLINKING

A manmade problem, blinking usually develops when a soft dog receives harsh treatment during a point. It often comes after "whoa," at the moment you move to birds. It can also develop during force training. The dog gets a lot of pressure and not enough praise and associates all of its problems with birds. When it picks up bird scent in the field, its common sense tells it to forget it.

Sometimes you can ease a dog through the problem by reducing pressure, shortening training time, and bringing the dog back to pointing and staunchness slowly; but many timid dogs are too frightened for this to work. For them the only solution is to go off birds. Stop all training, since training is pressure, and let the dog build up a desire for birds. Let the dog chase dickey birds; then, when it seems to have regained interest and a sense of fun, reintroduce training. Return to basics. Bring the dog through the several stages of training all over again—with less pressure and a lot more praise. Try shorter sessions. It takes time to revamp a blinker, so realize you have a long project ahead. Most dogs will respond with patience, though some never recover. Take heart. Blinking is not always as bad as painted. More than one national champion has had a blinking problem along the way.

BUSTING

Sometimes called "bumping," busting occurs when a dog flushes birds on its own; and a dog that consistently busts birds is probably weak on pointing instinct. Sometimes it happens because a dog is gun-shy and does not want a bird close enough for a hunter to shoot, but most often it blossoms because a dog has so much instinct and drive it thinks it is fun to scatter birds.

Busting only develops after a dog is allowed to catch a bird. Prevent this, as I've cautioned throughout the book, and busting rarely becomes a problem. "Whoa" is the key. If a dog is fully trained, you can control it anyplace on the field, and you can stop busting the first time a dog breaks. If not, work on "whoa" first.

If a dog catches a bird, one solution is to take it off birds long enough for the memory to fade. Return to "whoa" and reintroduce birds under controlled conditions. Use a long check line and be sure that if the dog breaks, all birds flush before the dog arrives. This is the time when pigeons and an electronic bird release are especially effective.

An electric collar is the professional's answer, but you need to know your dog, as well as both the dog's and the collar's limitations. If the dog is under good control, "whoas" well, does everything you ask in the field—except when birds are involved—an electronic collar may be the solution; but if the dog's instinct and drive are on the fence, be cautious. Controlling a buster with an electronic collar is literally "going whole-hog." You'll create a dog that points staunch as a board or you'll lose the dog. We've tried this a number of times, and each time the dog has turned out to be super-staunch, but we're a little lucky and we're pros.

BLINKER-BUSTER

The worst problem, a blinker-buster combines both traits. The dog is inconsistent. Sometimes it will back away from birds, and other times it will flush them before the gunner can shoot. The dog is almost always gun-shy, and rehabilitation is long and slow. In some cases you may never erase the problem. It may be wise to send the dog to a pro for an appraisal.

Not long ago, a customer brought a female dog to me, and after a few minutes in the field I could see she was a blinker-buster. On each point she would hesitate and soften, then either back away or break the bird. In talking with the owner, I determined that the dog had been "whoa"-trained on birds. The fellow put her on a rope, and the minute she even looked like she was going for a bird, jerked the dog off her feet. She did not realize her owner wanted her to hold, and not understanding the command, assumed the bird was responsible. When she felt pressure on the line, she blinked. When there was none, she busted, hoping to beat the shot.

Her problem was created, compounded, and reinforced by her owner. He created the problem by training the dog on birds and reinforced it by shooting every bird the dog flushed. How was that poor animal to know she was doing wrong?

I don't know how many times I've said it. The most important point I can make in the entire book is this: if you shoot only birds that are properly pointed and ignore those your dog breaks, your pup will soon figure it out. The dog will say to itself, "Hey! We only get birds when I let my owner break 'em." At that point your dog will literally train itself.

A blinker-buster requires a lot of retraining. In this case, the dog was immediately removed from birds and put back into preliminary "whoa" training. Each time I worked with her, I tried to get her to trust me a little more. There were no birds, no thoughts of hunting. The two of us were simply in the field feeling each other out. She was relearning to "heel," to "stay," to "whoa," and to trust her trainer. I praised the dog every chance I could, and it worked. Her confidence returned and within a week she was happier than I'd seen her. She now looks forward to training and we're back on birds. I can walk up to her on point and talk to her and she holds.

CONSUMING BIRDS

Don't confuse crunching and munching. Chewing or mouthing enough to mark a bird is called "hard mouth" (see *Hard Mouth*), but if a dog eats one—feathers, carcass, and all—that is something else. Hunters talk a lot about it, but in my experience it rarely occurs. Only one thing causes it: the dog is hungry.

Before you condemn a dog, investigate. Is the dog skinny? Underfed? Has it been a long time since its last meal? Professionals find the problem occasionally near the end of a season. Their rental dogs have been worked hard, and even though they try to keep them fat by increasing food and caloric intake, a kennel master will sometimes misjudge and a dog will go to the field hungry. When that happens, the animal may eat one of the birds because it looks like a meal. The solution is as simple as the explanation. Give the dog a little food before you start. Nine times out of ten, if it's eaten before it hunts, it will not bother with birds.

CHASING BIRDS

Most of us like pups to chase dickey birds—field birds that can be any species from sparrows on. Young pups love the sport and should have as much opportunity as possible. It develops their birdiness—their in-bred birding instinct—and the good news is that most grow out of it. The bad news is that some dogs never do. The Brittany is a prime example. Unless stopped, most will continue to chase field birds throughout their lives. The best control is "whoa," and if your dog is firm on that one command, you can handle the animal. When the dog shags after a bird, give one loud, forceful "whoa." Repeat that a few times, and the dog will learn it can't get away with it. If you take charge quickly, the urge will pass. Soon the dog won't try. If you don't, it will become a deep-seated urge and when that dog fails to find game in the first few minutes, it may become bored. Once bored it'll change course to chase dickey birds. If that happens, you're in trouble.

CHASING CHICKENS AND LIVESTOCK

You may think your dog will never have a problem with farm animals because you live in town, but it is becoming increasingly difficult to find places to hunt, and many an accommodating farmer has opened his fields to hunters. Generally, there is no problem, because the farmer's livestock, from chickens to cows, are penned; and if you keep your dog on a leash when it's not hunting, nothing can go wrong. But if you'd like to teach a pup that although farm animals are friends, they are not game and strictly off limits, you can do so by letting your pup meet such strangers as chickens while the dog is young. If the pup gets a little aggressive, take it in hand. Teach it to leave that kind of animal alone.

If a full-grown dog chases chickens, correction is ticklish. If it's never met them before, a chicken is just another bird. To tell your dog "no!" and to punish the dog for what it's just been doing in the field, is confusing. Trainers who heavily discipline their dogs, make them carry chickens wrapped in wire, threaten them with carcasses filled with nails, or tie dead chickens around their necks are going about it incorrectly. What's a dog to think? Beat the dog and it may believe you don't want it to hunt birds. There is no way you can sit down for a question and answer session with your dog, so the best solution is as little punishment as possible. Keep the animal on a leash—or in a portable kennel. Circumvent the problem, don't bring it to a head.

The same solution makes sense when your dog meets an occasional cow, bull, or sheep. If yours is a farm dog, you can set parameters it'll understand; but that is asking a lot of a city dog. It rarely sees farm animals. It is better to keep it under control so a farmer has nothing to become angry about. If you can't, hunt someplace else.

EATING FECES

Thankfully, this is not a major problem, since only a few dogs do it; but it remains a mysterious, odious habit. Stool-eaters are not suffering from a dietary lack, as vets once thought. It's not hunger—the fattest dog may do it— and it is certainly not caused by boredom. There is not a lot you can do to correct the problem except to monitor the animal when it's in the field. Keep it under tight control or in a portable kennel when not hunting. If you could be with it continually, an electric collar might provide a workable solution.

GUN-SHY

Sensitivity to noise can be an inherited trait, though it is not common. If you see that a young pup is skittish and shy, don't buy the animal. Generally there will be no problem if you take time to properly introduce a pup to loud noises and guns, though gun-shyness can occasionally develop later.

New dog owners often create the problem. They take their pups out for a day and suddenly want to see if the animals are gun-shy. They fire a gun with the pooch standing beside them, and when it does not respond they think it has passed with flying colors. They do nothing more about introducing guns until it is time to put the animal on birds. Wrong, entirely wrong. The first time any dog faces birds is a difficult time. It's keyed up, churning with a lot of powerful, conflicting emotions. This is the first time it's put all the factors it has learned together, and there is an element of fear. An animal that a dog is not really sure about is just beyond reach. The minute the bird flushes, the dog is startled. That sets it's adrenalin pumping; and then, without warning, a gun blasts beside its ear. Can you blame the dog if it thinks the bird made the noise?

Once the dog blames the bird, any number of things can happen. It can become a blinker, refusing to get close to any bird, or it may become a buster—figuring, "Let's get the bird the hell out of here so there will be no more loud noises." Either way, the problem developed because the dog was *not* properly introduced to the gun—though its owner may swear it was.

If this happens to you, go off birds; let your dog run free until desire builds up, then reintroduce the dog to shot. Begin by banging pots and pans near its kennel. Try making noise just before feeding and then as the dog eats. Introduce guns only after your dog proves it can tolerate other loud noises. First use blanks, fired some distance away; then, if the dog takes this in stride, bring the gun closer. Once the dog has sufficient confidence, it may come around. Some dogs never do.

HARD MOUTH

The problem, defined as clamping down on a bird during retrieve hard enough to damage the carcass, is really a matter of degree. A few toothmarks are meaningless. Most upland birds have thin skin, and even the gentlest dog will leave punctures. A good dog will hold different birds in different ways. One that is not quite dead will be held tighter than one that has expired, and one wet and slippery will be held harder than one dry and limp. Before you charge a dog with hard mouth, be sure it is true.

If hard mouth is real, it is usually a manmade problem. In the case of young dogs, it often develops from playing rough—from tug of war, from tossing rubber balls, and from similar sports. I know: hardly a month goes by without one or more new clients reminding me, "I've done all of those terrible things and my dog doesn't have a hard mouth."

They're lucky. For every dog who has gone through that kind of training and come out gentle, there are five who haven't. If you play rough with a pup, you can almost see hard mouth developing. Stop early and you prevent the problem. Continue and you're creating a real headache. Once hard mouth develops, there is no certain cure.

Some trainers wrap birds in stiff wire. When a dog bites down, the wire pricks the mouth. I prefer frozen birds. They are cold and hard, and a dog doesn't like to bite on them. Repetition is the answer, and if frozen birds work for your dog, do it over and over. In time the dog may lose the habit.

Most dogs hard-mouth because their owners allow a delayed retrieve. When ordered to fetch, the dog runs to the bird, hesitates a moment or two, picks it up, and chews it a few times before returning. The best solution is to get the dog to return promptly. Send the dog on retrieve, and the instant it picks up the bird, call the dog to you. Don't let it delay. Get the dog moving instantly. If the dog is well trained, it'll come trotting—and it'll forget to bite. If you can get the dog to come promptly several times, it may get over the problem.

Hard mouth can also develop in an older dog, though for different reasons. If your dog has retrieved clean and well for a long time and then develops the condition, this probably happened because the dog has been nipped or spurred about the head by a half-dead bird. A big rooster has a lot of power in its legs and can rip a dog so viciously the dog will remember it for a long time. The dog discovers that one crunch with its jaws cures the problem. Return to frozen birds. They don't fight. Train with them until your dog forgets the attack.

JUMPING ON PEOPLE

You're right: a dog who jumps on people is a pure pest and ideally should be stopped while young. The problem usually begins because a young pup loves to see you and you're so damn tall it can't reach the important parts—your hands and face. It leaps to get closer, and you think it's cute. If you get down to a pup's level, you can solve the problem at the beginning. Kneel, let the pup lick your face and show you how glad it is to see you. Show the pup you're happy too, and if it jumps, pinch its paws.

Jumping can also be controlled later, though it demands more time. You can step on an older dog's paws (gently) every time it leaps, though a better bet is to give the dog a knee (gently) in the chest. Do it just as it's coming up, and if you time it properly, you'll send the dog spinning, totally out of control. After meeting up with a knee a few times, your dog will find another way to say "hello."

SOFTNESS

Natural shyness or bred-in timidity is best corrected while a pup is young. A pup that is socialized late, say in its thirteenth to fifteenth week, will require a little extra handling. Give the dog plenty of attention and praise. Shyness may also develop when a pup is five or six months old. It will become wary of the things you're trying to teach it. The solution is to build confidence. Spend more time with your pup. Praise it every time you can. Take it to as many places as possible, and let it do a variety of things. Expand its experience. By the time the dog is a year old there should be no problem.

If you have an older dog that seems soft, let it regress. Literally, let it spend some time as a pup, chasing dickey birds, running free. Add a lot of praise. Bring it back to adulthood and grown-up responsibilities as gently as you can.

TRAILING

Trailing develops when one dog works a field in tandem with another. Sometimes one animal is either not independent enough or the other is too aggressive. Other dogs are "head trailers." They are highly competitive and constantly want to know what the companion dog is doing. They can't hunt on their own because they are constantly checking the other animal. Obedience is the solution. "Head trailers" should be called back, corrected, and sent on their own way.

At still other times, one dog is older and obviously superior to the other. The first dog can find birds quickly; the second cannot. In this case two things can happen. First, dog B will probably copy the bad habits of dog A; and second, dog B will let dog A do all the work. It follows its companion, never exploring new territory. The trick is to end the relationship as quickly as you can. Work your dog alone for several weeks. Build its confidence. Let it discover it can find birds on its own. Praise it often.

Then spend some time on special training. Work a field with a buddy and second dog. Ask your partner to stick to one side of the field, and make your dog work the other. If your animal wants to trail the other dog, call your dog back. Correct the dog and cast it off in another direction. Be sure it does as ordered. Your dog knows what you want. It's not dumb. If it tries to circle back, set it straight. If it continually refuses, the problem is obedience. Take your dog off birds and work it alone on basic obedience—until you are absolutely certain it'll mind each and every time.

CHAPTER TWENTY

Seventeen Handy Tips

As I gathered material for the various chapters, a number of ideas surfaced. Some were techniques used daily at Black Point, and others tips I'd heard about, used occasionally, and almost forgotten. Most were easily assimilated into the book's various segments, but a few refused to be confined. Still others seemed worth repeating. Below are a number of handy tips you may be able to utilize when training or hunting with your dog.

1. BIRDS

Pigeons are an ideal bird for preliminary training, and though not the only bird used with a mechanical release, they are best. They are small, light-weight, and easy for dog and hunter to handle.

As training progresses, you will substitute upland game birds, partly because they are closer to the native species your dog will be be hunting, and partly because they hold and flush more realistically. Pheasants, quail, chukar, and Bobwhite quail are all suitable. Be sure to use birds old enough and healthy enough to flush and fly well. As a rule, fourteen- to eighteen-week-old birds are best. They are mature enough to fly yet young enough to be inexpensive, costing between $2.50 and $6. Captive-bred birds do not have the stamina of wild-grown natives and will often hold a little longer under pressure, which can be a drawback. A bird that holds may teach your dog to "creep," a trait certainly not desirable. Creeping can be eliminated by "whoa" training, especially with a mechanical bird release.

In most areas you can find sources for pigeons and other birds under *Game Birds* in the Yellow Pages. If you live in a major city, you may need to try suburban directories. Sources for bird-releasers are given in the back of our book.

2. MAINTAINING CONTROL

From the beginning, it is important that your pup consider you the top dog, the "alpha" leader of its pack. In the beginning that's easy, but as training progresses, most dogs will test their owners. If at any time your dog thinks it's time it became boss, you must change its mind. If you are playing a game and it runs off with a glove, a sock—anything—you must retrieve it; and if the dog growls, you must make it submit. This is canine law. If you do not follow through, you'll lose control. If, for example, your dog is sleeping on the couch and growls when you attempt to put it out, you must respond with positive action. If you don't, from that moment on your dog will assume it has you buffaloed. The dog will think it can lay there anytime it wants.

3. CORRECTION

A correction is the trainer's way of telling his dog the animal has done wrong. The most common correction is a repeat of the command and a change in tone of voice. If the order is ignored again, the voice becomes sharper. A third correction can include a tug on the check line. Initially, this need not be severe, but if a dog continues to ignore a command, the dog should be "dumped," that is, jerked off its feet with a stern and positive pull on the check line.

Never strike or beat a dog. Physical abuse teaches nothing. If a dog does not "sit," "heel," "whoa," or "hup" on order, run the animal down, grab it by the check line or collar, and bring it back to the spot where the order was given. Repeat the command and make the animal comply. When a dog needs a stern correction, do not drag it by the collar. Pick it up and carry it to the place where the command originated. Lifting an animal is an impressive correction, because once its feet are off the ground, a dog loses its sense of reality, becomes unsure, less bold, and more tractable. If the animal is young enough, you can lift it by the scruff of the neck. This is the way a mother moves her young and the way other pups prove dominance.

4. SUMMER TIPS

Each spring longhaired dogs should be given a summer trim, a close clip that improves cooling and minimizes the problem of burrs, foxtails, and such. A professional groomer can do the best job. Ask the cutter to clip the hair between the toes—to minimize problems there—and if the dog has feathers, clip them as well. While your pup may look more like a punk rock musician than an intrepid hunter, do not despair. It will feel better and require less care. The hair will grow back thicker and prettier than before.

Another good idea: if foxtails are a problem, put cotton in the dog's ears. This will keep annoying weeds out. Don't think your dog can't hear as well as without packing. It can.

5. A NEW BABY

If a new baby arrives after your dog, introduce the two with caution. Remember, the dog was there first and may feel certain territorial prerogatives. Reassure your dog. Never allow a dog and a small child to play unsupervised, and it is best to keep the two separated until the child is old enough to learn a few simple rules of conduct.

Chances are overwhelming that the dog will like and accept the child and will be fully trustworthy, but as long as there is the slightest risk, why take a chance? Young kids can do unexpected things. They can poke, pull, and prod in ways even a patient dog may not understand. You might not see the cause, but in a split second a dog can respond by nipping the child. Never risk scarring or the loss of a child's eyesight by assuming "everything will be okay." As dog and child grow older, there is plenty of time for the two to become bosom buddies.

6. OBEDIENCE TRAINING

Obedience commands are taught first, generally starting when a dog arrives. In most cases this is between eight and twelve weeks old. Training includes four or five concepts required for dog and owner to live happily together. A bird dog should not be taken to an obedience class. You can do better at home. Your dog will learn faster and with less pressure. If you can't teach your dog obedience, you'll never be able to teach "whoa," "hup," and other field commands.

7. OWNING AND TRAINING TWO PUPS

If you have two pups of similar age, do not consider them as a pair. They should be trained and hunted separately. If not, one dog will become dominant, the other subservient. There will be a constant sense of competition, and neither will develop completely.

8. PROFESSIONAL HELP

While anyone with patience and a reasonable temperament can train a dog, some phases of training are more difficult than others, and some owners may feel the need for temporary professional help. Some prefer to have a professional perform one phase of training or another, and other owners like to consult with a professional from time to time to see how they are doing. If you feel uncertain about any part of training, be reassured you can safely interrupt procedures long enough to consult with a local trainer.

Force training is an example. It requires a combination of patience, dominance, and technique not everyone possesses. Hobby trainers often bring dogs to a professional for this training. Unruly dogs that require the use of an electronic collar are another example. Using an electric collar demands an ability to "read" and understand a dog, and any owner short on this kind of experience may feel more comfortable with a professional.

9. PRESSURE

Pressure is the same as stress, and is also the professional's slang for training. As stress, it can develop in many ways, but most commonly from the attitude of a trainer or from frequent and/or decisive corrections. All training involves some pressure, and most dogs can handle quite a bit. But too much is bad. A dominant trainer demanding perfection and an immediate change in behavior can create pressures a dog cannot cope with. As pressure builds, a dog may fight back; but when it becomes excessive, the animal will crumble. The dog becomes extremely passive. At this point, it does nothing wrong, but neither does it do anything right. The animal seems to take an attitude that implies, "Do what you want. I don't care."

The best antidote for normal pressure is praise. A dog should be praised every time it gets a command right, and, as a general rule, the greater the pressure, the more praise the dog should receive. If a dog folds under pressure, and you can tell by the tail (it will drop), end training for the day and give the dog a few hours of rest, relaxation, and play.

If you apply too much pressure when working with birds, a dog may associate its problems with the birds. If that happens, the dog may refuse to hunt again. Excessive pressure can make a dog become a "blinker."

10. RABBITS

You do not want a dog to chase rabbits, but it is a natural instinct, and ten dogs out of ten have the problem to one degree or another. Most good bird dogs love their rabbits, and the primary solution is discipline. Once a dog has been "whoa"-trained, you should be able to keep it from running after them by making it "whoa"; but if a dog is a chronic rabbit chaser, you may have problems.

Years ago, when Dad was still an amateur, breaking a dog of chasing rabbit was difficult. The electronic collar had not been invented, and the only correction device was a light shotgun load of "peppershot," or rock salt. It did not harm a dog, but if the dog was hit, it stung. A couple of corrections with that and a dog was usually a confirmed nonchaser.

Dad had a female German Pointer that was addicted to rabbits. He tried everything and nothing seemed to work. One day an older hunter watched as dad attempted to control his dog. Finally, the man came over.

"I don't want to tell you how to handle that dog," he said softly, "but let me tell you a story. Years ago I had an English Pointer that chased rabbits. The first time she took out after rabbits, she came back in fifteen minutes and I beat her. The next time she took out after rabbits and came back an hour later. I beat her again. The third time she took off after rabbits and was gone two hours. When she returned, I got a strap and was just about to beat the hell out of her when I realized that poor dog might not be looking at the problem the same way I did. I asked myself, 'Is it possible that this dog thinks she is being beaten because she didn't catch the rabbit?'"

Some dogs break themselves. If you "whoa" them each time they break, call them back and correct them; they eventually realize what you want, but the precentage of self-trainers is low. A dog can be broken of chasing rabbits without an electric collar, and techniques include a couple that may seem like overkill. The first is to shoot the rabbit the dog is after and literally beat the dog with it. The other is to shoot the rabbit and tie the carcass to the dog's collar, making the dog drag the thing around for a day or two. Both ideas work, sometimes. They can also create problems. If you are going to shoot the rabbit, you'd better hit it (and miss the dog). If you miss the rabbit, the dog may think you are hunting just as you hunt birds—and that's the last thing you want.

The quickest and easiest answer in my book is an electronic collar. It is the greatest tool for anti-rabbit training ever invented. The punishment comes instantly, the minute the dog takes off. There is no mistake in the dog's mind. It knows what it's done—and what it is supposed to do. You can do this yourself. Training is quick—two or three rabbits and the dog should lose interest—but you must not overdo the punishment. Many people seek professional help because only one or two sessions are required—a cost generally less than the price of a collar.

11. RANGE

The term can be defined as the distance a dog works from its hunter. Big or wide-ranging dogs work a long way out, sometimes half a mile or more. Handlers traditionally work these dogs on horseback, though some trainers use three-wheeler cycles. Gun or foot-handling dogs work closer, two hundred yards or so away, and are controlled by gunners on foot. In the end, range depends on what you expect from your dog, and far too many hunters want their dogs closer than is natural.

It is difficult to say that a particular distance is a dog's range, but whatever distance from a hunter seems comfortable for a dog is probably its "natural range," whether that animal is hunting close in or far. If a dog is far-ranging, it is imperative that the animal be "in your back pocket," that is, completely trained, taught to respond instantly to "whoa." It is the only control you have.

Most often a dog will tailor its range to hunting conditions. In heavy cover, it will shorten up, working closer, and in open fields, it will hunt farther. If a field is bone-dry and the dog has a difficult time picking up scent, the dog may point its birds quite close, perhaps three to five feet away, whereas on a moist day, a dog may hit them at fifteen to twenty feet. Obviously, a bird pointed close is going to be spooky. That's not the dog's fault.

Control is the secret of being comfortable with a dog's range. If a dog knows "whoa" thoroughly and responds instantly, it is safe at any distance. If the dog works farther than you want, you can bring it in. It is always better to have a wide-ranging dog than a plodder, that is, one that works without intensity and close to its handler. You can always "hack," or control a far-ranging dog to bring it near. It is almost impossible to get a plodder to work farther away.

12. RETRIEVERS

Not all English Pointers retrieve birds. Many champion-level animals are not even allowed to touch one, and some have never had a bird in their mouths. Often the nation's finest pointers are run with a leashed retriever as a partner. After the pointer makes its point and the bird is downed, the retriever is cast off to make the retrieve. The explanation is this: a dog that has not tasted bird is more staunch than one that has. In championship matches every inch of staunchness counts.

13. RETRIEVING PROBLEMS

Force training, or as some trainers call it, force breaking, is sometimes considered the cure-all for retrieving problems, but just because a dog is less than perfect may not indicate a need for it. Ideally, force training is reserved for dogs without desire or interest in retrieving. The procedure, designed to make any dog a polished retriever, is long, difficult, and traumatic. The decision to attempt it should not be made lightly. Not every dog is a candidate, but one that graduates is a certain retriever, willing to pick up anything from birds to a wallet.

Not every dog is a natural retriever. The Brittany and English Pointer are not known as good retrievers. When a bird is pointed and shot, these dogs would rather find another than retrieve the one just downed. Such dogs may be candidates for force training. In comparison, German Shorthair and Wirehair Pointers are excellent. The Vizsla is also good. These breeds are less likely to need it.

A dog should only be force-trained if it refuses to retrieve or is extremely sloppy, although there is often an easier solution. For example, some dogs play with a downed bird or pick one up and run with it, like spoiled children. Brittanys are notorious for this. The problem generally develops from handler error. If a dog is responsive enough to come when called, the problem can be eliminated without force training. Take your dog off birds and work on basic obedience until the animal comes every time you call "here" or blow the whistle. Then go back on birds, and the instant your dog has its first bird in its mouth, call the dog to you. Many times a surprised dog will figure, "Hey, my owner wants me there right now." The dog will forget it has the bird and will run to you with it still in its mouth. If you can get your dog to repeat that several times, the dog may have solved the problem itself.

14. TIMIDITY

Timidity is a common problem and can usually be removed with a little extracurricular play. If a pup is "soft" or timid, let it chase birds whether they are pigeons found in a park, gulls on a beach, or native birds in a farmer's field. A few weekends of this can give a timid dog a surprising amount of confidence. Praise, as much and as often as possible, also helps.

15. FIRMING THE "WHOA" RESPONSE

"Whoa" is the most important command a pointer can learn. Through repetition, that is, insisting on the same immediate response each time the command is given, your dog will eventually understand what it means. At some point the concept will come together in the animal's mind, especially when you move from early training to birds.

The dog may figure it in a way similar to this: "Hey, when I hold a point my owner likes it. When he likes it I get to retrieve, and when I get to retrieve everyone is happy." When your dog reaches that point, it will become so staunch and reliable you may not believe it. You could be speaking with a hunting buddy when you notice your dog on point. Your friend will become excited and will probably urge that the two of you race to your dog. You need only say, "Take it easy. My dog isn't going to move. He'll still be holding when we get there."

Your friend will not believe it, but slowly walk to your dog. Take your time. When you arrive, your pup will still be pointing, just as predicted. Kick out the big rooster pheasant it's been holding and shoot it. I guarantee your friend will be awestruck. Like most people, he won't understand that once a dog is trained to be staunch it will hold as long as you want.

In training you must incorporate a hand signal with the voice so that the dog stops as quickly to it as to sound. In time, you can get a dog so well trained on "whoa" that it will almost point its trainer.

16. "WHOA"-TRAINING AND BIRDS

Ninety percent of all upland game dogs will hold momentarily on point, but will break without "whoa"-training. The instinct to point should be kept as natural as possible, which is one reason initial training is done without birds. If you start with birds, the bird becomes the center of interest; but if birds are not involved, "whoa" becomes just another command. Before training is considered complete, the dog is expected to respond immediately wherever it is in the field—close in or at full hunting range.

17. VOICE

Your voice is your most important training tool if you learn to use it wisely. Give most commands in a calm voice. When your dog responds correctly, use an "up" voice, raised a little for praise. Add an edge of excitement.

Never shout, scream, or yell. Save your loud voice for corrections, for times when your dog disobeys or screws up, and always let the correction fit the crime. If you give a command, for example, "Rover, heel," and the dog ignores your order, repeat it with an edge of sternness to your voice. Your dog can tell the difference. Give the dog a chance to correct its response. If it ignores you a second time, give the command sharply, like a verbal whip, "ROVER, HEEL!" If you save the loud, sharp voice only for important corrections, nine times out of ten your dog will be so surprised it will knuckle under immediately. On the other hand, if you habitually shout, a correction will have little meaning. Your dog will probably not obey. If a dog continues to ignore an order, you must couple your verbal correction with a tug on the leash.

CHAPTER TWENTY-ONE

First Aid and Safety

The best way to avoid accidents is to be cautious. Play it safe. When hunting, follow the rules of gun safety. Break your gun when walking (don't rely on the safety), and remove the shells when you stop for lunch, travel by vehicle, or finish for the day. At home, keep poisons, poisonous plants, and suspect chemicals out of reach of your pup; and when you and your pup travel in a pickup, use a portable kennel. If you don't, be sure your dog is chained to a centerpost so it cannot reach either side. In some states, California is one, it is now a law that dogs riding in an open truck must be controlled. Never chain or tie your dog with enough length to let the dog jump over a barrier or the side of a truck. The dog will hang itself.

And never leave a dog in an automobile in warm weather. The dog will suffocate even with the windows partially open. On a summer's day, temperatures can hit 140°F inside a vehicle even with the windows "cracked." That's enough to kill the hardiest dog. If you keep your dog in a kennel, remove it from the car or station wagon and place it beneath a tree or similar shady area. If you must keep the dog in a car, buy window screens designed to restrain an animal while providing adequate ventilation. Failing all of this, take the dog with you.

If you keep your dog in a backyard run and are away from home during the day, check your dog each night. If the dog seems happy to see you but nervous and uncertain, something is probably happening during the day that you should check on. Dogs left alone during the day can attract neighborhood kids, and some kids can be vicious. Ruthless kids can frighten a dog by dousing it with a hose, throwing rocks, or making wierd and strange noises.

Even the best-laid plans sometimes go awry; accidents do happen, and it is important to know the ground rules of canine first aid. Below are a handful of basic tips. In every case the suggestions are for field emergencies only. A dog with more than a slight scratch should be given first aid and taken to a vet as quickly as possible.

PROTECTING YOU AND YOUR DOG

If an injured dog is in pain, tie its mouth before moving it or giving first aid. When in pain, the gentlest dog may bite its handler. It is usually easiest to secure the muzzle with a one- or two-inch wide, two-foot length of cloth torn from a shirt. Loop it over the muzzle, top to bottom, with a simple knot at the base. Bring the ends under the ears to the back of the head, and tie them with a square or bow knot. Either can be removed quickly. Never use rope. Its hard surface can injure the flesh. A nylon collar can also be used. The muzzle should be loose so the dog can breathe.

CONTROL BLEEDING

Clean a small cut with fresh water and an antiseptic solution; but if the wound is bleeding profusely, it may signal that a vein or artery has been severed. If the wound is on a leg, consider either pressure from a finger or a tourniquet. You can use a one- or two-inch wide strip of cloth similar to that suggested for the muzzle. It should be twelve inches or more in length. Wrap it around the wound, crossing one end under the other exactly above the wound. Place a small strip of wood—a length of branch is ideal—over the cloth above the wound, and tie the free ends directly above the stick. Twisting the stick should staunch the flow of blood. The tourniquet must be loosened every five minutes and should only be used in an emergency. It is more difficult to control an arterial flow in body areas. Try to find an artery above the wound, at a point at which it surfaces and crosses a bony area. Finger pressure there often helps. Minor cuts should be cleaned with first-aid cream or an antiseptic solution and controlled with a bandage. Do not bandage wounds so tightly that circulation is impaired. If a bandaged leg shows signs of swelling, loosen the bandage immediately.

HEAT PROSTRATION

A dog does not have to be locked in a car to suffer from heat. On a warm afternoon heavy running and warm sun is enough to cause problems. If you suspect your dog is close to passing out from heat, act promptly; and if a dog becomes unconscious, immediately give first aid. Douse its head with water. If at home, use a garden hose. In the field, empty a canteen of water over its head. If ice is available, pack the dog in it, obviously keeping its head above water level. When the animal revives, let it rest.

PORCUPINE QUILLS

Quills are among the more serious of problems because they are barbed like a fishhook, can cause infections, and are painful and difficult to remove. If you are close to a vet, let him do the job. As a professional, he will remove the toughest quills faster, with less pain and scarring. If you are in a remote area, consider the scope of the problem before acting. If there are only a few quills, you may want to remove them, and if they are in sensitive areas such as the buttocks and muzzle, you may need to remove at least a few before moving the dog. Pull only those necessary to the dog's comfort; then take the animal to the vet. If you decide to remove the quills, you should muzzle the dog. With a pair of pliers pull individual quills with quick, powerful jerks. The procedure is extremely painful. You may need to tie the dog to a fencepost or tree to accomplish the task. When completed, clean the wounds with an antiseptic solution.

REMOVING FISHHOOKS

First aid for fishhooks is much like that suggested for quills, though easier. If possible, force the barbed end of the hook upward, through the skin. Remove the barb with pliers and then back the longer end of the hook from the wound in the shortest possible route. Again, clean the wound with antiseptic and bandage if necessary.

DE-SKUNKING AN ANIMAL

The scent of skunk is more annoying than injurious, and no one wants to drive home from a hunt with a dog wearing "eau de skunk." The amount of "first aid" depends on available water and time. A quick rinse helps. If you have boric acid, make a solution of lukewarm water and acid, then rinse the dog. I am not in favor of tomato juice, much touted in folklore. I don't think it works. I wash my dogs with mild soap and water, then rinse with a dilute solution of vanilla extract. It may not eliminate the scent, but the vanilla successfully masks it. Warmth weakens skunk odor, and letting a dog dry in a warm room or in the sun helps.

MOVING AN ANIMAL

If you suspect internal injuries or broken bones, be as gentle as possible when you move the dog. The best procedure is to use a stretcher made from a shirt or jacket. The worst method is to pick up the dog and carry it in your arms. If you have a jacket, gently pull the dog to it. Using the arms and bottom edges as pick-up points, two people can safely carry the animal gently to a vehicle. If broken bones are involved, try to cushion them for the ride to the vet's.

POISON

If a dog has consumed poison but does not yet exhibit signs, make it vomit by forcing an emetic down its throat. Use lots of salt, salt water, a mix of equal parts peroxide and water, or mustard paste. Call the vet and alert him to the problem, and head for his office. If the dog has consumed poison some time before, you should see the signs—weakness, a bloody stool and/or vomitus. In this case do not try to make the dog throw up. If its body is rigid, do not attempt first-aid measures. The effects of some poisons can be made worse with in-the-field first aid. If you know the poison your dog consumed, take a sample with you. It will help the vet. Remember: coffee grounds and chocolate are poisonous to canines and in quantity can be fatal.

GAGGING AND GASPING FOR AIR

If a small bone or other object is stuck in a dog's throat, take immediate, direct action. Open the mouth, place your hand in the throat as far as possible, and try to remove the object. Failing that, try the canine equivalent of the Heimlich maneuver. Grasp the dog around its body below the ribcage. Make both hands into fists, cross them, and squeeze hard several times to force air from the lungs. As with humans, this usually ejects the object through the mouth.

ELECTRIC SHOCK

The problem is more common with small pups who chew than with adult dogs, and is not easily defined. Christmas trees are especially dangerous. On receiving the initial shock, a pup often urinates and the moisture complicates the problem. The moisture improves the ground, and the pup cannot let go. It then receives sufficient current to knock it out. Though unconscious, the animal may not be dead. Turn off power to the cord, removing it from the wall if it is a plug or by throwing the breaker switch. If you can see a bare cord in contact with the animal, remove it with a wooden spoon or rubber gloves. If the pup does not appear to be breathing, give artificial respiration. Keep the animal warm and call your vet.

ARTIFICIAL RESPIRATION

With a small dog, the easiest procedure is to lift the animal by its hind legs, shake it a few times, and then place it on the ground. You may not be able to do this with a larger dog. Immediately place a larger dog on the ground, open the mouth, and pull the tongue forward. Place your hands beneath the rib cage and press upward. Hold the upward stroke for two seconds (count, "one thousand one, one thousand two"), then abruptly release the pressure. Repeat the procedure. Stop two or three times each minute to see if the dog is breathing. Commonly, when an animal begins breathing, it will cough. Artificial respiration is required in electric shock, smoke inhalation, and drowning.

In the case of smoke inhalation, you should also try mouth-to-mouth resuscitation. Breathe into your dog's mouth or nose. Ideally this should be coupled with artificial respiration, one person performing the respiration procedure, the other breathing into the mouth between pressings.

TAKING TEMPERATURES

The only accurate way to take a canine temperature is with a rectal thermometer. It should be inserted in the anus and held there a minute or more. If you have doubts about the technique, ask your vet to demonstrate. A normal temperature is around 101°F. but will vary with the breed and size. Any temperature above 103°F should require immediate action.

CHAPTER TWENTY-TWO

Field Trials

(See Illustrations 82–90.)

The real test of a field dog's training comes when the chips are down, when school is out, when everything is real—in other words, when hunting. And hunting is different from competition. Even the most confirmed competitor will admit that the most enjoyable times are private ones, one-on-one days, just hunter and dog outdoors and always for fun. With pressure removed, these are moments to savor; you, your dog, and elusive birds in a quieter, far simpler world. Most upland game hunters will admit to no greater pleasure.

But there is much to be said for competition. It is not as real as those private times with your dog, but it should neither be damned nor diminished. For upland game dogs competition commonly means field trials, and while most rely on planted birds, some like the National Championships in Grand Junction, Tennessee, use native species. Either way, the action is as close to reality as man can devise. And competition has its own rewards.

Trials—and hundreds are held every year—fill a number of important purposes. Since most are held before hunting season, they let a dog owner work with birds in months when they might not otherwise be available. At the very least, trials offer a glorious excuse to meet other dog owners; on average, they provide a magnificent opportunity to compare your animal with your neighbor's; and at the very best, they give your dog a chance to become a star.

MANY EVENTS

The AKC probably sponsors more high-caliber events than any group, but competition is brewing. New associations are organizing, older groups are growing, and it seems as if everyone wants a piece of the action. The future is undecided. If there is a recognizable trend, it is toward shoot-to-retrieve competitions, and more are being announced every year. Associations such as the National Shoot-to-Retrieve Association (NSTRA) and the American Bird Hunters Association (ABHA) have increased competition schedules and are attracting a mushrooming following.

Procedures and services vary; there is much to choose from and the major associations are in flux. Many are modifying rules and regulations to suit changing attitudes and interests, and it is wise to contact one that interests you for schedules, rules, and regulations. With a schedule you'll be alerted to events close to home, and with the rules you'll be better able to understand what is happening. In most cases schedules are free, while regulations, in booklet form, cost about one dollar.

While there are number of local and regional groups, five associations are currently active over much or all of the nation. For information on local and invitational trials and national championship award programs, contact any of these groups:

American Bird Hunters Association
2505 Gary Lane
Waco, TX 76708
% Ms. Nancy B. Bell, Secretary

American Kennel Club, Inc.
51 Madison Avenue
New York, NY 10010

National Field Trials Champion Association
P.O. Box 38039
Grand Junction, TN 38039
(Information on National Field Trials Championship, The Hobart Ames Open Stake, Amateur Stake competitions, and the National Amateur Invitational.)

National Bird Hunters Association
Dempsy Williams, President
Information from:
Jim Hoy
R.R.1
Pineview, GA 31071

National Shoot-to-Retrieve Association
110 West Main Street
Plainfield, IN 46168
% Mr. Wilbur Shortridge, President

U.S. Complete Shooting Dog Club
P.O. Box 99
Sanford, NC 27330
% Mr. Gerald E. Shaw, President

AKC Events

While basic regulations of the five associations are similar, refinements differ. Most have local affiliates who sponsor sanctioned events on a regular basis and these welcome you as spectator or contestant. Many are advertised and reported in hobby magazines. One of the best sources is *American Field*. Let's consider the AKC first.

AKC-sponsored pointing trials welcome ten breeds—Brittanys, Pointers, German Shorthaired Pointers, German Wirehaired Pointers, English Setters, Gordon Setters, Irish Setters, Vizslas, Weimaraners, and Wirehaired Pointed Griffons—with three types of events: member field trials, licensed field trials, and sanctioned events. Championship points are awarded at member and licensed trials though not at sanctioned events. A sanctioned field trail is "informal." The AKC is a national organization with branches and affiliates in all parts of the nation.

Heats or individual competitions are called "stakes," and a brace, or pair, of animals are run in each. Years ago, Puppy Stakes were called "juniors," a term forgotten by most of us; and today one of the more popular events seems to be the Derby. The structure of AKC activities is simiilar to those of the other four associations, and a brief explanation will give you an idea of what to expect across the board.

Puppy Stakes are for dogs from six to fifteen months of age. Minimum obedience is expected, and blank guns may or may not be used, depending on the decision of officials. Running time ranges from fifteen to thirty minutes. Designed for young dogs with little or no field training, Puppy Stakes provide youngsters with a chance to compete and exhibit a little of the promise their owners pray for. The youngsters make many mistakes, but that's part of the fun.

Derby Stakes generally feature better-trained dogs from six to twenty-four months of age. Points are awarded and guns are used. Performance ratings are considered an indicator of future promise, and those wishing to buy young dogs often attend to see what's offered. Derby Stakes can run from twenty to thirty minutes in length and carry on a tradition begun with the Puppy Stakes. Entrants are unpolished, youthful mistakes are overlooked, and the emphasis is on desire, speed, intensity, and willingness.

Gundog and Limited Gundog Stakes are for fully trained dogs of any age over six months. Entrants are rated on a number of factors including range, the way they check in with their handler, and an ability to find, point, and hold game. Championship points are awarded, and stakes are thirty minutes in length. Obviously, pups rarely stand a chance against well-trained older dogs, but many owners consider the experience well worth the time.

All-Age and Limited All-Age Stakes are for well-trained, experienced dogs six months of age or older. Championship points are awarded, and dogs are expected to demonstrate a number of sophisticated traits only experience and training can deliver, including "independent judgment," or field savvy. A good nose, natural style, and intensity on point are essential. Stakes are thirty minutes in length. Since a brace of dogs always compete, one without game is expected to back automatically when it encounters a stakesmate on point.

These latter categories are designed for polished, trained dogs. Professionals can compete and, as one might expect, performances are as good as one may ever see. Animals entered in prestigious, nationally recognized events, make few, if any, errors.

Amateur All-Age Stakes are similar to those above but are designed exclusively for amateur handlers. The AKC defines an amateur as an unpaid hobbyist, one who "during the period of two years preceding the trial, has not accepted remuneration in any form for the training of a hunting dog or the handling of a dog in a field trial."

These stakes are for the owner who takes pleasure in handling his own dog. Unlike those with professional handlers, the event is a great equalizer. Every handler-owner is a man or woman who earns his or her living outside the canine world. Competition is keen, and many handlers are so good you'd be hard-pressed to tell them from pros.

A number of configurations are allowed for an AKC course, although it must include a backfield and a bird field with good ground cover and sufficient space to permit dogs to hunt naturally. Single, multiple, or continuous courses can be offered, and only one brace, that is, two dogs, can be run at one time on one course. When birds are planted every effort is made to avoid human scent.

Ribbons are generally awarded to four winners: blue for first prize, red for second, yellow for third, white for fourth, and a dark-green ribbon as a special prize.

While a trial's greatest value is an opportunity to see your dog in action, an equally important virtue is the chance for entrants to receive accumulated points eventually totaling enough to achieve a nationally recognized Field Champion rating. A Field Champion (commonly abbreviated FLD. CH.) must win ten points in at least three licensed or member trials with certain restrictions. Amateur Field Champion honors (AM.FLD. CH.) also requires a total of ten points, but with a slightly different composition.

Points depend on the number of dogs entered and range from one for a field of four to seven to five for a field of twenty-five or more. The Club also has a rule that no trial can offer more than one stake providing open championship points, and that no two-day event can offer more than two such stakes unless separate judges and courses are used to run them simultaneously.

Similar events are held for spaniels with a few obvious differences. Dogs are graded on nine factors: control (at all times and under all conditions); ability to scent and use wind; ground coverage (a brisk and well-done pattern); perseverance and courage in face of difficult cover; steadiness to flush, shot, and command; an ability to mark game (and retrieve it); eagerness to accept hand signals; a prompt response and good style; and a tender mouth.

The AKC also sponsors a series of "Hunting Tests" for game dogs. First announced in 1984, the program was initiated to afford an opportunity for "a person to demonstrate a dog's ability to perform in a manner consistent with the demands of actual hunting conditions—and to gauge a dog's natural huntng ability and training." Headed by Robert Bartel, Senior Field Representative, and Ham Rowan, Consultant, the program was devised with the assistance of Professor Robert Van der Wilt of Mankato State University.

Dogs must show a desire to hunt with enthusiasm and intensity, and their performance becomes increasingly polished as they progress through the classifications. A maximum of ten points are given for such elements as hunting desire, boldness and ground coverage, willingness to flush, and softness of mouth; and the test even includes a retrieve over water. A dog can be disqualified for hard mouth, severe gun-shyness, lack of control, blinking, and other factors.

Titles are awarded in three classifications, Junior, Senior, and Master Hunter. A dog is judged in four categories for a Junior rating and five for Senior and Master. Scoring allows a maximum of ten points in each category and a dog must receive at least five points per group to pass. Dogs must be AKC registered.

Entrants can be tested on a single course, with or without birds, or in a bird field only. The bird field must be at least five acres, and any avian species from pigeon to quail can be used. All dogs are foot-handled and only judges and the marshal can be on horseback. Blank guns are used in the Junior event, fired by the handlers. In Senior and Master events, guns are controlled by officials.

NATIONAL BIRD HUNTERS ASSOCIATION

This six-year-old association has 156 affiliate clubs in sixteen states. While the bulk of its membership is currently in the east and midwest, affiliates range as far west as Oregon and Idaho. Designed for foot-handled dogs, its trials are held on large tracts of land—larger than used by some associations—and entrants cover considerable territory. An NBHA event is as much a test of stamina and endurance as anything.

"Our emphasis," says out-going president James Hoy, "is on the complete bird dog—pointing, backing, and retrieving."

The group sanction 250 events a year and offers four classes: Open Shooting Dog, Amateur Shooting Dog, Derby, and Puppy. The NBHA annually honors a national champion, and awards are presented at the association's yearly meeting, generally in July. The 1986 National Bird Hunters Association Champion was Curvin's Cloudy Knight, owned by Jim Curvin of Alabama.

NSTRA

Founded by sportsmen with a common goal, the enjoyment of pointing dogs, NSTRA members are hunters, field-trialers, and dog lovers. The emphasis is on walking or gundogs, and anyone with an interest can join. The current membership fee is $10 a year, which entitles members to compete, sponsor sanctioned local trials, and participate as judge, gun, or field marshal. The country has been divided into regions, and growth has been fantastic. In 1984 NSTRA could barely muster one dozen regions. Today, there are nineteen, and the number is growing. The association offers a Field-Trial Guideline (for a minimal fee) and has completed a video film, *Judging Guidelines*, available for a two-week rental for $15.

"We're moving ahead rapidly," Wilbur Shortridge, association president says, "with increases of more than one hundred new members per month." He adds, "Our concept, conducting competitive field trials under simulated hunting conditions, will not only be the sport of the future, it may be the only method by which our descendants will know hunting."

Sponsored by local breed clubs, NSTRA-sanctioned trials consist of twelve to thirty-two dogs. Entrants are cast off in pairs, each judged on five factors: ground race (0 to 100 points); obedience (0 to 75 points); back (0 to 75 points); retrieve (0 to 100 points); and find (0 to 100 points). Championship certificates are awarded to dogs accumulating eighteen points garnered from NSTRA-approved trials. Nine must be from first-place wins, and double, triple, and additional championship plaques are awarded to dogs achieving still higher status. Points vary with the field. With 12 to 17 dogs, a first-place winner receives one point and other dogs, none. With 18 to 25 entries, first-place receives two points, second one, and those placing lower, none. With 26 to 32 dogs, first place receives three points, second place two, and third place, one. A prestigious Wayne Top Performance Award is given to the dog accumulating the most points in a twelve-month period.

The club holds an annual Champion of Champions Trials and last year hosted the largest event in association history. Held at the Amo Conservation Bird Dog Club in Amo, Indiana, the invitational "Dog of the Year" trials alone hosted ninety-six entrants. Having qualified by placements in regional eliminations, dogs compete for the association's elusive "top point" or "high dog" honor.

Competitors traditionally include some of the best game dogs in the association, and that is saying a lot. Last year more than 17,000 entries were received, up 4,000 over the previous year. The "Dog of the Year" entries nearly doubled.

The top twelve dogs at the National Invitational of the Year Trials in 1986 were:

Dog	Breed	Owner	Points
Quailfinder Joe	Pointer, M	John Varney, OH	960.5
The Thunder Boomer	Pointer, M	Charles Henry, AR	697
Dick's Tomoka Bill	Setter, M	Richard Moore, TN	673
Bradley's Red Feather	Pointer, F	John Protsman, IL	664
Thor's Virginia Thunder	Setter, M	Jim Dorton, VA	620
Natural Ability	Pointer, M	Frank Downs, IA	568
Cindy Little Notion	Pointer, F	Don Rakes, IL	540
High Spark Lucy	Setter, F	Ken Maddox, IN	418
B Field's Choice	Pointer, M	Ken Brassfield, OK	321
Rustoleum's Chip Lee	Pointer, M	Greg Wood, KY	319
Carter's Wisdom	Setter, M	Jim Carter, IN	228
Reid's Gold Roller	Pointer, M	D. Reid/B. Goldston, TN	211

The top four dogs in the NSTRA Dog of the Year Trials in 1986 were:

Dog	Breed	Owner	Points
Dick's Tomoka Bill	Setter, M	Richard N. Moore, TN	1105
Bradley's Red Feather	Pointer, F	John Protsman, IL	936
Quailfinder Joe	Pointer, M	John Varney, OH	827
The Thunder Boomer	Pointer, M	Charles Henry, AR	457

U.S. COMPLETE SHOOTING DOG CLUB

The nation's newest shoot-to-retrieve association began in North Carolina as a group of local hunters with similar interests. Though still concentrated in the southeast, membership has grown from one club to twenty in just three years. Its rules are similar to those of other shoot-to-retrieve groups but have a unique twofold emphasis, first on the abilities of gun or foot-handled dogs themselves, and then on spectator pleasure. USCSDC has found a burgeoning interest in its programs and recently announced plans to go national.

"First we focus on pointing, backing, and retrieving," says R. E. Lee, the association's secretary, "and that's what we mean by 'complete.' Then we consider the spectator."

Unlike other associations, the U.S. Complete Shooting Dog Club attempts to share the excitement. The parent club has even converted a bus to help some of the gallery follow competitors. No other association offers that kind of concern and luxury!

Regulations require member clubs to sponsor at least one sanctioned trials per year, and according to Lee, most gear up for thirty or more. There are four categories—Open Shooting, Amateur Shooting, Open Derby, and Open Puppy. Points that apply toward national championship ratings are awarded for placement in local events, and the group held its first annual championship near Moore, NC. A second annual was held more recently in Marion, SC.

EVENTS WORTH WATCHING

With more than one thousand trials annually, it is obviously impossible to list all of the exciting events worthy of mention, but we'll list a few with apologies for those far more numerous that were omitted.

In Oklahoma the Mid-America Classic is an excellent choice whether you'd like to compete or watch. Held in the fall, a Mid-America Champion emerges from its large field of dogs. In Ohio, the American Pheasant Dog Futurity is superb. Nearing its fifty-fifth running, the event has been held at the Killdeer Plains Wildlife Area near Harpster and Upper Sandusky. Look for it in October.

The Masters Open Quail Championship, held in Albany, Georgia, is commonly a springtime event and comes well recommended. It is held with the first burst of redbuds and has a history of more than twenty years of competition. The winner's purse generally tops $4,000 and the event attracts many of the nation's top dogs. Similarly we can suggest the U.S. Open Pheasant Championships. Held at the Minnesota Horse and Hunt Club, the

Open attracts a large field of classy, stylish dogs. The gigantic Hunter's Banquet is one of the season's popular social events.

The National Walking Shooting Dog Championships attract a large following and large field. Last year more than one hundred dogs competed at Circle W. Farms near Dancyville, TN. Participants must have placed first, second, or third in a recognized NBHA state classic or championship since 1985. Classes include Open Derby, Puppy, an amateur event, and the Shooting Dog classic.

Midwestern dog owners always enjoy the Missouri Open Championships. Popular with setters and pointers, it features an excellent course. The Michigan Open Shooting Dog trials, held at the Iona State Recreation Area, includes a number of nationally known stakes. It is a three-day event. The National Amateur Invitational Championship is another top-drawer trials. Held at the famed Ames Plantation, site of the Grand National Championship, it attracts many of the nation's best-known upland game dogs.

In the west, The Pacific Open Championship is one of the most prestigious. Trials sites vary from year to year. The Washington State All-Age Championships, held near Spokane, are sponsored by the Spokane Field Trial Club. In Hawaii a number of exciting events are held on Mokuleai Ranch on the large island of Oahu. Two worth seeing (and participating in) are the Hawaii Open and the Hawaii Bird Dog Championships. Points awarded in both trials can be used toward national awards.

In California two events—among the many held there that are worth going out of your way to see—are the California Pheasant Championship and the California Valley Quail Championship. Trials are very popular in Canada, and one is hard-pressed to select one as representative, but an event that has long held my interest is the National Amateur Chicken Championships. These are held near Saskatchewan.

RULES FOR COMPETITORS

While regulations vary, there are basic rules competitors should follow. Dogs are expected to be healthy, without communicable diseases. Owners and dogs are shielded from the field while officials plant birds—for obvious sportsmanlike reasons—and handlers should be at the starting line well before judges cast off their brace for possible last-minute instructions. In some events the handler does his or her own shooting, and in others a gunner accompanies the party. Bitches in heat are not allowed to compete.

Be sure to bring all necessary equipment, from guns and shells to water for your dog, and absolutely, bring a portable kennel or other means of controlling your animal off the course. Many competitors prefer a tie-out and some use both. Since trails are two- or three-day events, bring plenty of food, and complete arrangements for sleeping accommodations well in advance. In many areas trials have been held at the same site so often that local motels not only welcome competitors but bend the rules and allow dogs, especially in portable kennels.

RULE FOR SPECTATORS

The way spectators behave is as important to the success of a trials as its quality of competition, and certain rules of etiquette should be observed. Noncompeting dogs are not welcome, and you'd be advised to keep yours at home. Even if a dog is sidelined, it can bark, and one bark at the wrong time may cause a competing dog to turn its head. The dog may then fail to mark a falling bird, and in stiff competition that could spell disaster.

Unlike retriever events, where the action occurs close enough for the gallery to see, trials cover a lot of territory, ten to forty acres or more, and dogs and handlers often disappear from view. Despite this, there is a time for talk and a time for silence. When a dog is close, it is poor form to distract it—even when shouts are meant as encouragement. But when an animal returns after a good job, applause is certainly welcome.

If you've trained your own dog, you know why it's unwise to pet a competing canine, at least without the owner's permission. Generally, vehicles are parked well back from the trials area, and dogs are kenneled or tied beside them. It is okay to walk through the competitor's area to see equipment, to talk to friends, and to check out animals; but if you want to get closer, ask the owner first. Likewise, it is absolutely *verboten* to offer someone else's dog food or snacks. It is distracting and dangerous and can provoke an argument.

Some Important Trials

Alabama Field Trial Club Open All-Age Stake
All America Chicken Championship
American Quail Classic
Border International Chicken Championship
Cajun Open All-Age Classic
California Pheasant Championship
California Valley Quail Championship
Central Arkansas Association Southwestern Championship
Central Carolina FTC OAA
Continental All-Age Championship

Dominion Open Chicken Championship
Duke Cecil All-Age Classic
Florida Open Championship, Suwannee River
Frank Stout Memorial Classic
Georgia Quail Championship
Grand National Grouse Championship
Hawaii Open Championship
Hawaiian Bird Dog Championship
Hobart Ames Open All-Age Stake
International Pheasant Championship
Kentucky Quail Classic
Masters Open Quail Classic
Missouri Open Championship
National Championship
National Free-For-All Championship
New England Open Championship
North American Woodcock Championship
North Carolina Open Championship
Northern States U.S. Chicken Championships
Oklahoma Open Championship
Oklahoma Open All-Age Stake
Pacific Open Championship
Pelican Open All-Age Classic
Quail Championship Invitational
Rend Lake Open All-Age Stake
Saskatchewan Open Chicken Championship
Southern Field Trial Championship
Sunflower State Kansas Open All-Age Classic
Tar Heel Open All-Age Stake
Texas Open Championship
United States Open Championship
West Tennessee Open All-Age Stake

CHAPTER TWENTY-THREE

The Greatest Trials

Each sport has its premier competition, its Super Bowl, its World Series, and of all the varied rivalries in the hallowed calendar of upland game dog action—the trials that separates pups from sires—and dams is America's oldest and most prestigious, the National Field Trial Competition. Held a short drive east of Memphis, Tennessee, near Grand Junction, on the 18,700-acre Ames Plantation, the 15-mile course is the world's finest, a cautious mix of natural cover, scrub brush, briar, creeks, and tall grasses. To the uninitiated it appears as if God created it, but to the informed it represents some of the most carefully controlled acreage on earth. Each bush, each blade of grass, each open space has been carefully calculated to support one thing, upland game birds. Bobwhite quail is king, and from the beginning the course has been home for the most respected of pointing-dog competitions, a rigorous three-hour test of endurance, a tribute to man's passion for the hunt.

Weather, politics, and pestilence notwithstanding, on the third Monday in February a gallery of five hundred or more bird-hunters from across the nation poise astride their horses, tensely waiting for the plantation superintendent to utter words repeated for more than eighty years: "Gentlemen, you may turn them loose." With that, the first brace of dogs thunders into the fields. On horseback, handlers, owners, judges, and the huge, unwieldy gallery follow in dusty pursuit. Only snow or fog so dense the judges cannot see could delay the action.

Bob Crenshaw, former trials judge and an old-line, respected Delta planter, has defined the National as "the World Series of bird-dogging. Only those who have won other carefully selected events can run here," he emphasizes. "That means the dogs you see at Ames are absolutely the world's finest."

"I'd go beyond that," says William F. (Bill) Brown, publisher of *American Field*. "The National Championship is America's number-one sporting event, one of the most grueling tests you'll ever find."

WHO WINS

"Pointing alone will not make a champion," Mr. Ames has often declared. "A winning bird dog must use his brains, nose, and eyes. He must exhibit speed, range, style, courage, character, and stamina. He should always have good manners and be bold, spirited, and snappy."

Not every dog has that winning formula, but the one that does receives the second-largest purse in field-trial competition, perhaps not much by monetary standards, but substantial in the community of trialers. The winner becomes an acknowledged world champion, a canine king or queen. Testifying to that status, his or her photograph appears on the front of *American Field* for fifty-two consecutive issues. The owner receives a silver trophy, a substantial increase in stud fees, and the inalienable right to boast—for one year—that his dog is tops. The handler receives $8,000 and his own full measure of respect. Only the Florida All-Age Open offers a larger purse, $8,260.

SOME HISTORY

The National traces its roots to 1894 when the Tennessee State Sportsman's Association held the nation's first bird dog competition near Grand Junction. Seven years later Boston industrialist Hobart Ames, whose family sold shovels to the Revolutionary Army, was named president of the National Field Trial Championship Association, and with supreme devotion to the cause purchased five neighboring plantations, establishing the nation's first championship trials course. Since 1902 the National has run here, always according to careful, exacting standards established and tested by Hobart himself.

Julia Colony Ames, Hobart's wife, can be credited with making certain her husband's concepts withstand the onslaught of time. In establishing a memorial to her husband when she died in 1950, Mrs. Ames left the property in trust to the University of Tennessee with one important stipulation—that the National Field Trial Champions be held here in perpetuity. For that thoughtful move Mrs. Ames was awarded the prestigious Field Trials Hall of Fame honors posthumously in 1973.

THE DOGS

The fifteen-mile course is keyed for big-running, horse-handling dogs, and a good animal may cover twice the advertised distance in the three hours allotted to it. English Setters took the first dozen Nationals, but in more recent memory all but eleven wins have been monopolized by pointers.

"There's an easy explanation," one spectator said: "a winner has to be a bird-huntin' fool. That's the pointer, a computerized, bird-findin' machine."

"There's a saying in our sport," one husky handler added, "that when a setter dies he goes to heaven, because setters have soul, but when a pointer passes he's just another dead dog. Let me assure you, son, that ain't so. Name another animal that has the sight, the nose, the hearing, and the speed a good pointer must have. Like a man, he has to be rough, tough, and good-looking, and like a woman he needs a heavy dose of style and class. It's not the dog with best bird nose that wins, its the one with the most class."

The man was obviously prejudiced, talking as he was exclusively about pointers. The National is open to any dog who wins any of seventy-eight accepted trials, but competition is practically limited to two breeds, the English Setter and the Pointer. These are horse-handling dogs, and the National is tailor-made for them. Just to finish the grueling trials, a dog must exhibit unbelievable stamina and superior speed a foot-handled dog generally lacks. He (or she) must distinguish between the foot and body scents of birds and is expected to establish a good gait at the start and maintain it for three tiring hours. He (or she) should produce birds in the first, second, and third hours and finish with as much desire as shown at the start.

All of this means that dogs competing here are not only purebred, but inevitably come from a rarified coterie of canines with proven championship backgrounds. The sire and dam have commonly won top trials and many are National champions. Pups are bred for just one thing—to win—and at six months the best begin a grueling training regimen their owners hope will eventually carry them to Ames. They are trained in big-running country, some in the scrub brush of Texas, others in the pine woods of Georgia, a few in other parts of the nation; but everyone winds up for final conditioning in the wheat fields of Canada where acreage is measured in the thousands. As pups they are "roaded," that is, harnessed and run from horseback to build muscle, wind, and endurance. When older, they are run with special weights to toughen them, and after obedience and field training they hit the championship trail with seldom a backward glance.

Of some 1,200 annual trials recognized by *American Field*, just 78 are National qualifiers, a competition trail that snakes from Saskatchewan to Oklahoma to Florida. It covers six calendar months and a full run for the top can cost an owner as much as $10,000 annually, a lot when you consider that in any given year avid competitors may have two dozen dogs in various stages of training and competition.

By any rational yardstick, trials competition such as this can hardly be considered profitable. Neither is it an investment. Unlike horse racing, in which top stallions command stud fees of $100,000 and up, no dog owner goes into trialing for money. Service from a winning pointer rarely brings more than $600, and top pups are generally offered at prices from $350 to $500, despite rumors to the contrary. (Reportedly James Ray was offered $100,000 for his nine-time champion Miller's Chief. He denies it.) When Nationals champions are for sale, which is rare, prices seldom top $15,000.

Gary Lockee, a retired naval captain who has competed at Ames says, "Most field trialers start as hunters, find hunting pales, and eventually want more than birds. They take an interest in dogs, the way they run, their style, class, and elegance. If you were a race-car driver at this point, you'd demand a Ferrari, but for a dedicated bird-dog man all you want is to see great dogs work. Finally, you want the best dog to win, even if it isn't yours."

Ted Baker, a Florida sportsman and entrepreneur who has competed in many events with Chinkapin's Addition explains, "You begin bragging about your dog and someone challenges you. They say, 'Prove it!' That's when you start field trialing."

MAINTAINING AMES

Abundant quail is the secret of success at Ames, and maintaining them is a full-time project. The plantation's 18,700 acres have hundreds of carefully selected "covey headquarters," sections of land featuring a delicate balance of feeder strips, bare ground, light cover, water, and nesting areas. These are home for many quail, and with the help of University of Tennessee biologist Ralph Dimmich and the plantation's "Quail Task Force," Bobwhite populations have been growing. Last year 310 coveys were reported, up nearly 12% over previous counts. These are the birds the dogs hunt.

"We can't stock the National with pen-raised quail," says Richard Harte, Jr., a descendant of founder Hobart Ames and a trustee of the plantation. "That would be cheating. At the Nationals the object is to find quail, not to kill them."

"Kill a bird at Ames," old-timers like to say, "and they'll stop everything to hold a funeral."

In truth there are more than Bobwhites at Ames—populations include a smattering of woodcock, grouse, and other ground birds—but whatever the species, the birds must be judged the nation's luckiest. Populations are disturbed just four times a year—for the running of the Hobart Ames Open and Amateur Stake competitions, the National Amateur Invitational, and the National. Dr. James Anderson, a University of Tennessee agricultural economist, lives on the plantation, supervises research, and is the official host. His assistant is Dr. Rick J. Carlisle.

MORE THAN COMPETITION

The nine days of the National are filled with more than hot sun and rough, hard-fought competition. When a dog is not running, when chores are over, and when the horses are staked, time remains to meet friends not seen between trials. A favorite site is the Peabody Hotel. There competitors funnel into the lobby to drink, swap tips, and tell tall stories. The conversation is interrupted the weekend prior to the trials by lunch at the Memphis Country Club, and the traditional Saturday night chicken barbecue at the La Grange Firehouse. The latter precedes the traditional drawing held on the plantation, at Bryan Hall, to determine the running order. Sunday is packed with brunches, luncheons, and dinners. Mr. and Mrs. S. Richard Leatherman honor owners with a special hour. Mr. Leatherman has competed with such famous dogs as Memphis Blue Max and Miss One Dot, and his wife, Carroll, is well known as the author of *The Old Man and the Dog*, the life story of the legendary Ames winner, Miss One Dot. Peggy and Frank A. McKinnie Weaver recently started a new tradition, a Sunday evening champagne supper. Frank is a director of the association. The couple own Heritage Farms, a plantation in nearby Hickory Valley where they also sponsor their own trials. Their son, Jock, is Vice-President of the First American National Bank in Jackson and is well known at the Nationals.

During the week the rigors of competition are softened by side trips to Dunn's Sporting Goods and an obligatory tour of Wilson Dunn's Field Trial Museum. Then, with the final run in sight, everyone moves to Whippoorwill Farms for Dr. Jack Huffman's famous dinner of fried catfish and moist, tasty hush puppies. Huffman's El Sauz Doll is always a topic of conversation.

CHAPTER TWENTY-FOUR

Electronic Training Aids

Considering the many advances in electronics since World War II, it was inevitable that dog training should benefit; and more than twenty years ago the electronic collar made its debut. It represented a new approach, a unique concept in canine control. The first one I remember was home-made, designed by a couple of professional hunters. One of the first commercial units, designed by Gerald J. Gonda and John Vancza, was introduced in 1968. Benefiting from mini-circuitry and eventually computer design, subsequent generations of collars have had a substantial impact on canine training and conditioning. Today, it is a professional aid more hobbyists should investigate.

The collars have even generated a completely new system of training. The best book on the subject is *Understanding Electronic Dog Training* by Dr. Daniel F. Tortora, a psychologist specializing in canine behavior and training. (The second edition, third printing, is available from Tri-Tronics, Inc. See Chapter 27.) Although the idea has been around more than two decades and several firms produce versions, the collars are still not as widely accepted as they should be. Some trainers use them extensively: others occasionally; some not at all.

At Black Point we recommend and use the electronic collar, though not to the extent suggested by Tortora. I feel it is an important tool, humane and helpful, although not required with every dog. As stated throughout this book, equipment is not as important as the relationship between you and your dog. My emphasis is on one-on-one training, and the electronic collar can fit that concept.

THE VALUE OF A COLLAR

Although more than 500 scientific papers attest to the value of the collar and growing numbers of trainers are discovering its use, it is not a substitute for conventional procedures. It is never used during basic obedience training, seldom on a young dog, and with the exception of severe attitude problems, not before an animal is at least one year old.

Before you use the collar you must take your dog through preliminary training. The dog must be thoroughly grounded, must understand what each command means, and must know the expected response. Once your dog understands, the collar can hasten the learning process and minimize outright disobedience. At Black Point most often it is reserved for "back-sliders," dogs slow in responding to commands they already know. For example, when we accept a dog for training, it is immediately tested on "here," the call to come. If it responds slowly, we retrain it with the collar. Since the dog knows the command and the expected response, the collar becomes a form of correction. Normally we need use it just once or twice.

Remember what I've said about corrections. These come in the form of repetition of commands, a louder, more threatening voice, and finally pressure or restraint on the check line. With an older dog, electronic stimulation can replace these with definite advantages. First, the correction is instantaneous. Low-voltage stimulus is given the moment a dog disobeys or makes an incorrect response. The dog quickly associates it with failure to comply. There is no possibility the dog can misunderstand as it might if a correction were delayed. Second, the dog does not associate its discomfort with the trainer—which preserves the comradeship between you and your dog. Finally, the dog quickly discovers that when it complies, the uncomfortable stimulus is not repeated. Psychologists call this "avoidance" training. It can be a powerful learning tool.

While a collar may seem expensive, it can pay for itself. Realizing the age restrictions, it can be used with all of the training procedures in this book, and most people who try the collar use it throughout the life of their dogs. When a dog understands its power, a collar can help in many ways, even when hunting. It becomes a deterrent. A dog wearing one is less apt to make mistakes.

HOW THE COLLAR WORKS

(See Illustrations 91–94.)

Several firms produce collars, although the only ones I'm familiar with are manufactured by Tri-Tronics. As I describe these, consider that my comments apply equally to other makes and models.

The electronic collar is controlled by radio impulses sent from a hand-held transmitting station. It can be triggered from long distances, a quarter mile or more, and will generate either sound or an electronic current. The current is transmitted to the dog through two electrodes embedded in the collar. Its intensity is controlled by changeable electrodes. Since electronic stimulation is not designed to injure, it is kept purposely low, and not all dogs react to a given intensity in the same way. The reaction depends on temperament. As a rule, the bolder the dog, the more likely it is to disregard minimal stimulation. For extremely bold dogs I often use the maximum intensity.

Tri-Tronics produces three models. There is a basic "correction" version that delivers only electronic stimulation, that is, a low-voltage shock. The dog realizes the stimulation is a correction and soon learns that when it responds properly, there is none. It discovers it can "avoid" the annoyance with a proper performance.

A middle model delivers both a shock and a buzzing sound, which allows you to choose between stimulation coupled with sound and sound alone. The dog quickly associates electrical stimulation with buzzing, allowing you to then successfully use sound alone. That is, the dog will "avoid" the sound (and the possibility of shock) with the same good behavior seen with stimulation. The ability to vary intensity, to choose between sound and stimulation, or to use neither, are all important training techniques.

A third version combines the features of the middle model with a third "safety" tone. The electronic stimulation still represents a major correction, the buzzer is still a light reminder, and the "safety" tone now reassures the dog that everything is fine.

I equate this latter tone with praise, and for this reason prefer the middle model. I feel strongly that praise should come directly from the trainer and believe it is neither as psychologically rewarding nor as satisfying in the form of a disembodied tone.

WHEN TO USE THE ELECTRONIC COLLAR

Although an electronic collar can have many uses, it is not de rigueur for every dog. It is commonly reserved for those bold enough to test their trainer and/or disobey. At Black Point I use the collar first with advanced "here" training, the call for a dog to come. Subsequently it can be helpful teaching "whoa" and steadying a dog to wing. It is especially useful when teaching a fully trained dog not to chase rabbits or to quickly teach one to back or honor a point. Occasionally it can be used when force training, though the process is extremely tricky and should be attempted only by one with an extensive knowledge of training techniques and an ability to understand or "read" a dog.

"HERE" TRAINING

Coming when called is basic to nearly all field training, and a slow dog requires immediate retraining. It needs to discover that when its owner or trainer calls, it must respond instantly. It matters little whether it is sleeping or doing something it likes; when its owner calls it is expected to respond. If you have allowed your animal to become lax, it should be retaught before advanced field training; and if the dog is reluctant, an electronic collar can be of tremendous help. It is better than applying excessive pressure and stress with the check line. A dog should not associate electronic stimulation with its trainer, and the device's "disembodiment" or detachment is an important advantage. You can always tell a dog that has received excessive stress and pressure during advanced "here" training. It comes when called, but on its belly or with its tail between its legs. Trained with electronic stimulation, a dog comes instantly, its tail wagging. It is eager to see its owner.

THE TRAINING SITE

Where you use an electric collar is as important as when. The technique works best in a large, open area. A backyard with a barbecue, a swing, or similar objects is not recommended, nor is a field with such things as parked cars, tractors, and buildings. When a dog receives a shock, it may associate it with the closest object. If there is a swing nearby, it may be frightened of swings for life. A dog may even appear uneasy in a field in which training is given, although there is nothing to which the dog can visibly transfer its feelings. I've had dogs refuse to return to a training field because the collar had been used there. With such power, you should obviously be careful near birds. If a dog believes a bird is responsible for its discomfort, the dog may become a blinker.

Owners often forget this. Not long ago a new customer was trying to get his dog to jump into his truck and then into a new aluminum portable kennel. The dog was wearing an electronic collar and its owner continually commanded the dog to "kennel," pounding on the truck with his hamlike fist, then punching the remote transmitter. As current jolted the dog, it shook its head and drew farther from the truck, fear building in its eyes. The animal was terrified.

Finally, I intervened. "You know why your dog won't obey?" I asked the guy. The man cursed and shook his head angrily. "First, you're overdoing it. Second, you're using the collar too close to the truck and the kennel. The dog thinks one or the other of them is zapping it. It's not about to get closer. If you don't stop, you'll never get the dog in the kennel—or on the truck—again."

Never use the collar in anger. It is not an electronic whip. It is not a device designed to terrorize your dog. Use the collar coolly, objectively, sparingly, and only when a dog disobeys. Conversely, it can also help cool off a hot-headed owner. The ability to react instantly to something his dog has or has not done can calm an intense owner, but sparingly is the key word. Overdo electrical stimulation and you run the risk of hardening the dog. Used too often, an animal can build up a tolerance for current.

Most electronic collars are supplied in a kit with a collar, a hand-held transmitter, and a dummy collar. The latter has the appearance and weight of the real thing, yet is only a shell. It has two recommended uses. It is placed on a dog prior to training to allow the animal to become used to it. After training, some believe it can be worn effectively in place of the real thing. Not realizing the difference, they say, the dog will react as if it were a real collar.

THE FIRST TIME

Begin training by placing the dummy collar on your dog. The electrodes should be positioned against the fur and the collar buckled. As with all collars, it should be loose enough to insert two fingers between it and your dog's neck. Let your dog wear this for two or three days; then replace the fake with the real. If your collar is supplied with changeable electrodes, use a light to middle-range intensity at first. If your dog is timid, use one of less intensity. If the dog seems bold, use a slightly higher rating.

Add a long check line and begin with practice commands. Let the dog range toward the end of the line; then give the command "here." If the dog responds promptly, give lots of praise. If, after repeating the command, the dog disobeys, give a light tug on the line and make the dog come to you. When the dog comes, pet it; then cast the dog off, releasing the check line.

When the dog reaches the point at which it would expect to feel restraint, one of several things can occur. Your dog may stop, expecting to be re-strained. It may look back expectantly, spot the check line and—with a look that can be literally translated "Ah hah!"—take off. Become neither angry nor excited. Give the command "here" in an even tone, or use the whistle; and if your dog does not come, repeat the command once or twice with more authority. If the dog still goes its way, press the button applying electronic stimulation. Do not use the buzzer. On my Tri-Tronic model pressing the stimulator button activates both buzzer and electrical current. The dog hears the buzz and feels the shock at the same time. The concurrent signals, sound and stimulation, are important the first time.

Response to the unexpected shock depends on the animal. Whatever it is, do not repeat the stimulation. Do not buzz. Do not touch the transmitter. See what your dog will do. Most freeze, stopped instantly in their tracks. They turn to look at their owners, probably with a startled look that poses the question, "What happened?" Such a dog is in limbo. It is trying to decide what has occurred and how to respond. If your dog responds this way, be patient. Talk to it. Praise it. Try to coax the dog into returning. "Good boy. That's right. Here, Rover." If the dog comes, give it lots of praise. Be effusive. When using the collar, you must respond with excessive praise. This is one reason I do not like the "safety," or happy, tone. Any correction is stress to your dog. Stress should always be balanced with praise; and since electronic correction involves a lot of stress, the praise should be equally effusive. It is important that your dog be happy—no, that it be eager—to return to you; and to my mind, obvious praise goes farther than a disembodied, impersonal tone.

If a dog is timid, it may panic, leaping and turning as if in intense pain. If this happens, be sympathetic. Coax the dog to return; then replace the electrode with one of less intensity. While the reaction may seem unduly traumatic, a timid dog usually learns its lesson quickly.

A bold dog may shake its head and keep running. If this happens, repeat the command and the electronic stimulation. If all else fails, run down the check line, dump the dog, and bring it back. Replace the electrode with one of greater intensity.

Once you've introduced your dog to the effects of the collar, "heel!" the dog and walk for a few moments to calm it, then cast the dog off. Sometimes the dog will not want to leave your side. It's convinced there is something strange and frightening in the field and feels safer near you. Pet the dog. Talk to it. Build its confidence, then cast the dog off. Most dogs will go, if not on the first try, then with a little coaxing. Let the animal run free for several minutes; then, as it begins to enjoy its freedom, give the command "here." If the dog does not turn, repeat the command and quickly activate the buzzer. The dog should respond by returning; but again, reaction varies. If your dog is either timid or normal, it will have learned from its experience and will respond properly. But if it is bold and defiant, it may continue running. Give it a second or two to correct its actions; then, if it does not come, repeat the command and use the stimulator. Normally, you'll need to do this but once or twice. When the dog learns it cannot escape correction, it should respond as effectively to sound as to electrical stimulation.

AN EXTREME REACTION

The first time a collar is used, most dogs respond in one of the ways above; but occasionally one is so frightened it seeks to hide. If your car or truck is parked in or near the field, the dog may run to it, immediately, hiding beneath the wheels. Do not become angry. The first time the dog does this, it is more frightened than disobedient. Try to coax it into the open. If it is too frightened to move, talk to it; and if you can reach the check line, pull the dog out—gently. No matter how frightened the dog, you must not end the training session on this note. Do that and the dog will have won. You will begin from scratch the next time.

Make the dog come from hiding and carry or walk it to the original place from which it was cast off. Keep the check line attached, and if you're uncertain of your dog, keep the free end in your hand. Let the dog run some distance; then call "here." It is important that the dog responds at least once to the command. If necessary, use the check line for correction and reel the dog to you. When the dog has it right, end the session. As always, give lavish praise. Praise is important. It gives your dog confidence.

If your dog is very frightened, it should be conditioned enough by one stimulation to return quickly the second time—prompted by the buzzing alone. The dog may even run toward the vehicle again. While you must be kind, not angry, you should also be firm. The dog is now defying you. It knows better than to cower beneath the vehicle. You taught the dog that the first time. Coax the dog from cover and make it repeat the command, responding properly. When it does, end the session.

Repeat the training for several days. You should not need electrical stimulation again unless your dog is extremely bold. Sound should be sufficient. The object of repeated training is to condition a dog to respond to sound. Achieve this, and the collar becomes a deterrent of broad value. It can be used with a number of procedures.

Remember our old rule, the one I've discussed so often: once trained, a dog must never be allowed to respond slowly or incorrectly. But remember, too, the best-trained dog will make occasional mistakes. When the dog does, it should be corrected promptly. Then know every dog will occasionally test its handler. The bolder the dog, the more often the test. The dog must not be allowed the upper hand. When a dog tests its trainer and wins, the trainer loses a measure of control.

CHASING RABBITS

An electric collar is an excellent device to stop a dog from chasing rabbits. As mentioned previously, the first time I was aware of the collar was when I was young. Dad headed training at Black Point, and a couple of brothers he knew operated a hunting operation in Arizona. They specialized in expeditions for mountain lion and bear and used hounds in the process. Although the dogs were sent after the advertised game, they would occasionally break to chase deer. The brothers developed a home-made electronic collar, the first I'd heard of, and placed it on their dogs. Each time the dogs were sidetracked by illicit quarry, they were electronically disciplined. In a short time they hated deer. When one crossed their trail, they would do everything possible to avoid it, still retaining full intensity for game the hunters wanted. This is the concept I use to keep upland game dogs from chasing rabbits.

Obviously, you cannot let a bird dog break on its own, and rabbits are a tremendous lure. If "whoa" will not control the animal, you must try something else; and if your dog falls into this category, use an electric collar on your next hunt. It works better than anything I've tried. The first couple of times the dog takes off after rabbits, use electric stimulation immediately, without "whoa," without preliminaries. I suggest this hoping, the dog will associate the sting with the rabbit. If the dog does, it should fear them, and fear is the best of deterrents.

If the dog ignores you, call "whoa" and repeat the electrical stimulation. A dog who will not associate punishment with the rabbit must be made to realize it is being corrected for failing to respond to a command. Normally, two or three stings will give it the proper idea. The dog will either fear rabbits, realize it is being corrected for disobeying a command, or both. The buzzing alone will then keep the dog under control.

HABITUAL BUSTER

In this instance, the collar should be used only after other procedures have failed. If your dog knows the "whoa" command, responds promptly away from birds, but breaks point when you're in the field, you can try the collar; but realize the procedure can be tricky. The dog will either complete training more staunch than ever, or it will go over the edge. Two factors are involved and should be carefully balanced. First, the dog only breaks point when birds are involved—which means you have to use birds in training. Second, it is important that your dog realize it's being disciplined for not obeying "whoa"—which means it must not associate its unpleasant sensations with birds. If that happens, it'll fear them and will refuse to hunt or may become a blinker. Together this underscores the importance of timing: the second at which the stimulation is applied is critical. Current must be given when it does the most good, yet when it cannot be confused with the bird.

Consider the first bird a test, an opportunity to see how your dog reacts. Put the collar on your dog. Choose a good, strong bird, one that can fly well. Have a partner plant it as described in previous chapters. Let the dog flush the bird and chase it. When the bird is some distance away and your dog halfway to it, give the "whoa" command. If the dog fails to respond, apply electrical stimulation.

If the dog stops after stimulation, call it to you. If it continues, run it down. Bring the dog back to the point at which the command was given, give a command to "whoa," and make the dog stay. Kick the grass as previously described, so the dog thinks a second bird is there. If it breaks, repeat "whoa" and follow this immediately with stimulation.

If, on the other hand, your dog returns frightened, tail down, you must still make the dog "whoa," but realize it is timid. The current may be too intense. Use a lighter application.

THE SECOND BIRD

Have your friend plant another bird, and bring your dog to it from an angle. When the dog has the scent, talk to it. Try to coax the dog into holding. If it breaks, and it probably will, use the electronic stimulation sooner, as quickly after the bird breaks as possible.

After one or two applications of current, you should see results. Most dogs will slow their response and will hold longer. Utilize this. Talk to your dog. Try to extend the holding time. Keep the dog staunch as long as you can; then, just before the dog breaks, activate the buzzer. The sound should deter the dog, but be prepared. Watch the dog, not the bird. If the dog still moves, give the "whoa" command on the first step and hit the buzzer on the second; and if the dog tries for a third step, use electronic stimulation. It will take several birds to make it all work. Be patient. Repeat sessions daily or as often as you can, each time making the dog hold longer. Let each bird fly and do not shoot. Your dog must learn that you kill birds only when it points, only when it holds staunchly, only when game is flushed by you.

BACKING

If a dog does not understand backing or honoring a point, the electronic collar can help. Follow the procedures explained in Chapter 18. Using two people and two dogs, bring your dog toward the planted bird after the first dog is on point. When your dog sees its partner on staunch point, give the "whoa" command—no matter how far away. If the dog does not stop, react immediately. If your dog is familiar with the collar, use the buzzer. If not, apply electronic stimulation. Repeat the procedure until your dog automatically honors another's point. You should be able to use sound alone after one or two applications of electricity.

THE DUMMY COLLAR

Most manufacturers insist that once a dog has been trained with an electronic collar, the dummy is as effective a deterrent as the real thing. That has not been my experience. Most of the dogs we've tested seem able to tell some difference. Whether it is a change in weight or, as Dad seems to feel, a change in scent, I don't know. I do know many dogs can, in some way, differentiate.

We've taken students through identical procedures, switching from fake to real and back, installing each collar in the same way. Then we've let them run free. With the real collar, they obey beautifully. We never need the buzzer. The dogs respond promptly to every voice and whistle command. Yet with the dummy attached, they become loose. Many do not mind as well. Some even thumb their noses at us.

CHOOSING A UNIT

A variety of manufacturers produce remote-controlled collars. Whatever the make, a good one should be powered by rechargeable DC batteries. Your kit should include the collar, batteries, battery charger, remote-control transmitter, testing unit, and a dummy collar. A 12-volt field charger is a handy option. It plugs into a vehicle's cigarette lighter. Batteries should be recharged after 40 hours of use.

CHAPTER TWENTY-FIVE

Some Winning Dogs

If you are looking for a pup with championship parents, or if you simply like statistics and records, this chapter is for you. Below are lists of winners, owners, and in some cases handlers, of dogs who have won some of the nation's top events.

FIELD TRIAL HALL OF FAME

Although champion field dogs, owners, and handlers may receive a number of honors during their lifetimes, The Field Trial Hall of Fame is one of the most prestigious. On one side of our list are field dogs honored since the Hall was initiated in 1954. On the other side, are top sporting figures who have been named to the roster. Appropriately, the first name is that of the founder of the National Championship Trials, former president of the NTFC, Mr. Hobart Ames. His memory has been honored in many other ways as well, by the plantation on which the sport's top race is annually held and by two important stakes also held there. Many of those listed are breeders and trainers who are still active. They can be considered as sources of fine, quality pups, helpful information, and guidance.

New honorees included George D. Moreland and Frank Arant, Jr. Mr. Moreland, of Leesburg, Georgia, is squire of 6,200-acre Coney Lake Plantation, the site of numerous field trials. He has been instrumental in the success of many championship dogs including Judy Warhoop, Medallion, and Paladin's Royal Flush.

Mr. Arant is a professional handler from South Carolina. He became a professional, full-time handler after World War II and won his first field trials in 1945. His facility, Congaree Kennels, is world famous. Mr. Arant has trained and handled numerous winners—Miss Mary Doone, Rocky Creek Ben, Rambling Rebel, and Homerun Bob, among others.

Nineteen eighty-six inductees included two interesting pointers, one male, one female. Allure, a white-and-orange female owned by Jimmy Hinton, Safford, Alabama, was whelped February 28, 1974, and died September 8, 1985. She was by Ormand Smart Alec, another Hall of Fame inductee, and Risqué. Allure follows her kennelmate, Wrapup (elected in 1985), onto the honor roll.

Guard Rail, a white-and-liver pointer male, was owned by Eugene Casale, Glastonbury, CT. Rail was whelped January 2, 1976, and was killed in a highway accident in 1984. The dog was by Smart and Nell's Rambling On. In his brief lifetime, Guard Rail recorded more than 42 placements, including 21 firsts and a number of championship titles.

Field Trial Hall of Fame Inductees

Year Elected	Dogs
1956	Air Pilot's Sam, Pointer
1959	Alford's John, Pointer
1986	Allure, Pointer
1964	Antonio, Setter
1977	A Rambling Rebel, Pointer
1957	Ariel, Pointer
1972	Askew's Carolina Lady, Irish Setter
1960	Becky Broom Hill, Pointer
1983	Buckboard, Pointer
1979	Buddwing, Irish Setter

Year Elected	Dogs
1977	Candy Kid, Setter
1983	Clancy O'Ryan, Irish Setter
1962	Comanche Frank, Pointer
1967	Commander's Hightone Beau, Setter
1955	Count Gladstone IV, Setter
1959	Count Nobel, Setter
1960	Count Whitestone, Setter
1980	County Clare's Country Lass, Irish Setter
1959	Doctor Blue Willing, Pointer
1958	Eugene M, Setter
1963	Eugene's Ghost, Setter
1963	Fast Delivery, Pointer
1970	Feagin's Mohawk Pal, Setter
1980	Ferris' Jake, Pointer
1954	Fishel's Frank, Pointer
1978	Flaming Star, Setter
1979	Flush's Country Squire, Pointer
1955	Geneva, Setter
1961	Gladstone, Setter
1969	Glencrest Doctor, Setter
1981	Grouse Ridge Will, Setter
1986	Guard Rail, Pointer

Year Elected	Dogs
1970	Gunsmoke, Pointer
1963	Hard Cash, Pointer
1968	Home Again Mike,
1981	Ike Jack Kendrick, Irish Setter
1984	Jerry's Runaway Bandit, Pointer
1964	Jingo, Pointer
1982	Joe Jr., Irish Setter
1954	John Proctor, Pointer
1980	La Besita, Setter
1963	Lady Ferris, Pointer
1965	Lady's Count Gladstone, Setter
1960	Lester's Enjoy's Wahoo, Pointer
1983	Little Diamond, Pointer
1974	Lone Survivor, Pointer
1966	Lullaby, Pointer
1954	Luminary, Pointer
1961	Manitoba Rap, Pointer
1954	Mary Montrose, Pointer
1981	Miller's Miss Knight, Pointer
1983	Milligan's Dan, Pointer
1961	Mississippi Zev, Setter
1962	Mohawk II, Setter
1976	Mr. Thor, Setter
1954	Muscle Shoal's Jake, Pointer
1976	Oklahoma Flush, Pointer
1979	Ormand Smart Alec, Pointer

Year Elected	Dogs
1984	Page's Shuriridge Liz, Gordon Setter
1959	Paladin's Royal Flush, Pointer
1965	Paladin's Royal Heir, Pointer
1965	Palamonium, Pointer
1972	Rambling Rebel Dan, Pointer
1973	Red Water Rex, Pointer
1975	Riggins White Knight, Pointer
1960	Rip Rap, Pointer
1969	Safari, Pointer
1964	Satilla Wahoo Pete, Pointer
1981	Saturday Night Ed, Irish Setter
1962	Seaview Rex, Pointer
1971	Shore's Brownie Doone, Pointer
1957	Sioux, Setter
1955	Smokepole, Pointer
1955	Sport's Peerless, Setter
1962	Sport's Peerless Pride, Setter
1985	Springset Cascade Thunder, Gordon Setter
1964	Spunky Creek Boy, Pointer
1982	Texas Fight, Pointer
1973	The Arkansas Ranger, Pointer
1967	The Haberdasher, Pointer

Year Elected	Dogs
1982	The Kansas Wind, Pointer
1957	The Texas Ranger, Pointer
1980	The Texas Squire, Pointer
1974	Tiny Wahoo, Pointer
1985	Tomoka, Setter
1971	Turnto, Setter
1958	Tyson, Pointer
1984	Vali Hi Country, Irish Setter
1965	Village Boy, Pointer
1961	Warhoop Jake, Pointer
1966	Wayriel Allegheny Sport, Pointer
1984	White Knight's Button, Pointer
1975	Wonsover, Setter
1985	Wrapup, Pointer

Year Elected	People
1954	Hobart Ames
1973	Julia C. Ames
1986	Frank Arant, Jr.
1968	Fred C. Ash
1956	James M. Avent
1965	Charles H. Babcock
1983	Henry J. Banks, Sr.
1976	Henry Berol
1965	Henry L. Betten
1959	Jake Bishop
1974	Lebbeus F. Bissel
1981	A. Bracey Bobbitt
1963	Louis M. Bobbitt
1983	J. D. Boss
1982	William F. Brown

Year Elected	People
1981	W. R. Brown
1963	Dr. William A. Bruette
1963	Nash Buckingham
1964	C. E. Buckle
1961	Herbert H. Cahoon
1965	George M. Crangle
1971	Arthur S. Curtis
1964	Henry P. Davis
1961	Edward Dexter
1954	Carl E. Duffield
1980	W. A. Dumas
1979	D. Hoyle Eaton
1982	Ed Mack Farrior
1956	Edward Farrior
1977	Verle Farrow
1962	U. R. Fishel
1979	Pete H. Frierson
1978	John Rex Gates
1960	John S. Gates
1969	Rowan A. Greer
1973	George L. Harden, Jr.
1972	Jack P. Harper
1958	Chesley H. Harris
1977	Virgil P. Hawse
1985	A. H. Hembree
1975	Jimmy Hinton
1960	Raymond Hoagland
1954	Albert F. Hochwalt
1970	H. N. Holmes
1955	Dr. T. Benton King
1961	Harry D. Kirkover
1966	Guy H. Lewis, Jr.
1968	Sam R. Light
1965	Mrs. G. M. Livingston
1961	J. Horace Lytle
1967	Lewis B. Maytag
1967	Bethea McCall
1985	Dr. W. H. McCall
1960	Col. Arthur Merriman
1986	George D. Moreland. Jr.

Year Elected	People
1985	Cylde Morton
1980	Dr. A. H. Nitchman
1966	Dr. George Oehler
1975	Mary C. Oliver
1976	John. S. O'Neall, Sr.
1984	John S. O'Neall, Jr.
1962	Claudia L. Phelps
1954	Cecil S. Proctor
1984	W. F. Rayl
1964	Frank Reily
1960	David E. Rose
1959	Dr. Nicholas Rowe
1954	A. G. C. Sage
1964	Michael Seminatore
1957	Reuben H. Scott
1957	E. M. Shelley
1980	Dr. T. W. Shore
1978	Elwin G. Smith
1978	Herman F. Smith
1976	Luther Smith
1962	Ray Smith
1967	Edward Soph
1959	W. W. Titus
1983	Gerald Tracy
1969	Paul S. Walker
1963	Stewart J. Walpole
1974	Robert G. Wehle
1959	W. Lee White
1972	Walter H. Wimmer
1962	Frank M. Young
1980	William Ziegler, Jr.

BRITTANY

A small dog, 45 pounds or under, with looks someplace between a small setter and a larger cocker, the Brittany is extremely popular. It is ideal for condo and apartment living, makes a super hunter and an ideal gundog for anyone who prefers a small-ranging dog. It works like a pointer, though with less range, and has an exceptional nose.

The Brittany Club of America maintains a lengthy list of dogs that have earned Field Champion, Amateur Champion, and Dual Dog Championship ratings. With eighty-eight clubs nationally, the list is obviously a long one. Information on champions is available from Ms. Velma Tiedeman, Executive Secretary, American Brittany Club, 2036 N. 48th Ave., Omaha, NE 68104.

ENGLISH SETTER FUND AWARDS

The John. S. O'Neall, Sr., English Setter Fund is world famous for its recognition of the breed and is now in the process of assembling a permanent trust fund for a special Elwin G. Smith Setter Shooting Award. Last year the fund announced four awards:

Ray's Daily Express, a white setter with black ticks, owned by Arthur E. Ray of Tuscumbia, AL, and handled by Randy Downs of Rienzi, MS. The dog was whelped March 9, 1983, and was sired by Ch. Royal Flag out of Blue's Dot. It carries the bloodlines of Mr. Thor, Toronado, and Hickory Pride, as well as strains of Hightone and Commander from Carl Duffield. Express has won handily in Canada as well as the All-America Open Derby.

The dog joins five other setters—Ch. Tekoa Mountain Knikki, Wiregrass Thor's Pabst, Ch. Mr. Motion, Ch. The Sportsman Briar, and Ch. Andy's Safari Sami—in sharing the award.

Pardon My Dust, a white-and-orange setter whelped January 2, 1984, was named winner of the Herman F. Smith Setter Derby Awards. Sired by Just A Swinging out of Fury, his background includes crosses of Thor's Pacesetter and Flaming Star among others.

Brawny Lad was named winner of the Third Annual Elwin G. Smith Setter Shooting Dog Awards. A white dog with black ticking, the eight-year-old dog is a seasoned campaigner and was also winner of the National Open Pheasant Shooting Dog Championships. Brawny Lad is owned by Elwin and Inez Smith of Wexford, PA, and is handled by Harold Ray of Waynesboro, GA.

The prestigious Bill Conlin Shooting Dog Derby Award was presented to a young setter, Grandeur, also owned by Elwin and Inez Smith. The dog was bred by Stanley White at Grandeur Stables and sired by the late Ch. Branigan ex (bred with) Mac's Kelly Patrick. Whelped January 5, 1984, Grandeur is handled by Harold Ray of Waynesboro, GA.

GERMAN SHORTHAIRED POINTER CHAMPIONSHIP

For thirty-five years, national championships have been held across America, each providing the year's top German Shorthair. A recent competition, at Branched Oaks, Nebraska, had sixty-two entries. An all-age event, the competition is easily the top-drawing trials for the breed. The 1985 champion was Uodibars Koonas (FC Dixielands Rusty X Uodibars Dirty Gerty) owned by John Rabidou and handled by Lee Sienkowski, Jr. Runner-up was Thrashers Ammertal Zack (NFC/FC Ammertals Boxz Ranger X Mocha Delight) owned by Robert Dressler and handled by Keith Gulledge. Third place went to Dixielands Mocha Delight (Dixielands Rusty X Mocha Delight) owned by Michael LaRose and handled by Ed Husser. Fourth spot went to Checkmates Challenger (FC Checkmates Dandy Dude X Hurches Choice of Navajo) owned by John Voglein and handled by Lee Sienkowski, Jr.

NORDEN TOP SHOOTING DOG AWARD

Introduced in the early 1980s and presented in cooperation with Norden Laboratories, winners of these trials are selected annually on the basis of points earned during regular competition. Point trials are now held in twenty-eight states and two foreign countries, and in an average year, 1,600 to 2,000 entries are involved. Each year's winner has earned more points than the previous winner. In 1985–86 there were fifteen trials at which 500 or more points could be earned. These were held in fourteen states. The winning owner receives a silver cup, an original oil painting of his dog, a special plaque, and a memorial jacket. The handler receives $1,000 and a memorial jacket.

In the 85–86 season, eighty-seven dogs accumulated points, a 30% increase over the previous season. The 1985–86 winner had a total of six placements in points trials. The 1985–86 winner was Mickette, a pointer owned by Robert Mickolyzck of Milford, CT.

Year	Dog	Owner
1983	Rocky River Buck, Pointer, Male	Irv Mohnkern State College, PA H. Gerald Tracy, Broadbeck, PA
1984	Barnum, Setter, Male	Elwin G. Smith Wexford, PA H. Harold Ray, Wexford, PA
1985	Warhoop Express Liz, Pointer, Female	Lester C. Shephard Conroe, TX H. Gordon Hazlewood Navosta, TX

Year	Dog	Owner
1985–86	Mickette	Robert Mickolyzck, Milford, CT H. Bruce Jacobs, Middletown, CT

German Shorthaired Pointers
National Field Trial Champions,
German Shorthaired Pointer Club of America
Winners of Annual National Trials

Year	Dog	Owner
1953	Dandy Jim Von Feldstrom	Dr. Clark Lemley, Detroit, MI
1954	Wendenheim's Fritz	Frank Nuzzo Chicago, IL
1955	Gunmaster's Jenta	James A. Karns Akron, OH
1956	Traude Von Der Wengenstadt	Oliver M. Rousseau San Francisco, CA
1957	Bobo Grabenbruch Beckum	Dr. William J. Schimmel Atwater, CA
1958	Dixon's Sheila	Russel Dixon New Haven, MI
1959	Oloff Von Der Schleppenberg	Roy J. Thompson Ingleside, IL
1960	Duke Von Strauss III	Steve Molnar Cudahy, WI
1961	Von Saalfield's Kash	Walter Seagraves Saratoga, CA
1962	Moesgaard's Dandy	Dr. & Mrs. Kline Orlando, FL
1963	Moesgaard Angel	Donald S. Praeger Alamo, CA
1964	Shockley's Pride	Luther Shockley Crete, IL
1965	Onna V. Bess	R. G. Froehlich Bakersfield, CA
1966	Fieldacres Bonanza	Harold & Jean Dowler Union City, PA

Year	Dog	Owner
1967	Rip Traf Von Bess	Gene & Erica Harden Salinas, CA
1968	Halberg's Seagrave Chayne	Don Miner Saratoga, CA
1969	Blick Von Shinback	Brad Calkins Denver, CO
1971	Patricia Von Frulord	Gladys & Fred Laird Seattle, WA
1972	Wyatt's Gip Von Shinback	Mickey & Warren Palmer Sherman Oaks, CA
1973	Patricia Von Frulord	Gladys & Fred Laird Seattle, WA
1974	Cede Mein Georgie Girl	R. A. Flynn & A. P. Troutman Mentor, OH
1975	Mark C's One Spot	Ronald Rainey Caldwell, ID
1976	Frulord's Tim	Gladys & Fred Laird Seattle, WA
1977	Jocko Von Stolzhafen	Dr. J. S. Brown Lewiston, PA
1979	Dual CH. Lika Buckskin	Garv & Harriet Short
1980	Ammertals Boss Ranger	Gary Nehring
1981	Checkmate's White Smoke	Steve Lyons
1982	Erlicher Abe	Linda Cross
1983	Dual. CH. Checkmate's Challenger	John W. Voglein
1984	Gretchen's Pride	Bill Bussy & Donna Kurtz
1985	Windswepts Little Big Man	Frank Alexander

NSTRA—WAYNE'S PET FOOD TOP PERFORMANCE WINNERS

Sponsored by Wayne's Pet Foods and presented by the National Shoot-To-Retrieve Field Trial Association, winners are selected on the basis of points earned during regular trials competition. Points are accumulated annually from July 1st through June 30th. The first-place winner at a trials receives three points, the second-place winner two and third one. The dog with the highest point standing wins a special plaque and year-long honors. The award was begun in 1981.

Year	Dog	Owner
1981–82	Rustoleum's Flush, Pointer, M Sire: Flush's Hoosier Pal Dam: Miss Freckles Rex Seven-time NSTRA Champion Active in NSTRA competitions	John G. Smith, Sr. Economy, IN
1982–83	Rustoleum's Flush (See above)	John G. Smith, Sr. Economy, IN
1983–84	Carson Creed Jodi, Pointer, F Sire: Malone's Paladine Joe Dam: Tall Oak's Druggist Four-time NSTRA Champion Not active	Mike Wrenn Greenville, SC
1984–85	Barb's Dixie Bell, Setter, F Sire: Cashmaster's Tornado Dam: Carter's Chippy Active in NSTRA competition	Terry Neher, Danville, IN
1985–86	He's Just Right, Pointer, M Sire: Wahoo's Trouble Doc Dam: Good News Sally Active in NSTRA competition	L. Dale Loveall Sturgeon, MO

PURINA AWARD—THE TOP FIELD-TRIAL BIRD DOG

Ralston Purina established its Top Field Bird Dog Award in 1963 to honor the nation's best field-trial bird dogs. The company sponsors the program, provides awards, and hosts an annual dinner at which the award is presented. The winning dog is selected by an awards committee composed of six respected and prominent bird-dog experts: Mr. S. R. Cline, Dr. D. E. Hawthorne, Mr. Joseph H. Hurdle, Dr. William H. McCall, Mr. George M. Rogers, and Mr. William West.

The winner is chosen from competitors in forty-five trials competitions, ranging from the Saskatchewan Open Chicken Championship in Canada to the Cajun Open All-Age Classic in the south. In the west, points can be accumulated at the California Pheasant Championship, the Pacific Coast

Open Championship, and the Hawaii Bird Dog Championship, among other events. In the east the list includes the Hobart Ames Open All-Age Stakes and the Tar Heel Open All-Age Stakes. In many cases the Purina selection has been the winner of the National Championship at Grand Junction. This was the case with the 1984–85 selection, Fleetwood Hank.

Scoring is based on the number of dogs drawn and the final placement in each trial. The winning dog receives ten points for each dog drawn; second receives five points for each dog drawn; and third receives one point for each dog drawn. Bonus points are awarded to the winner of five events: National Championship (850), National Free-For-All Championship (500), Continental Championship (250), Southern Championship (250), and Quail Championship Invitational (130).

The award is commonly presented to big-running dogs, generally either an English Setter or a pointer, and well-known kennels and handlers normally receive the acknowledgment. In 1984, for example, 74% of all wins were recorded by just ten handlers. (D. Hoyle Eaton six wins; Billy Morton, three; John Rex Gates, Bud Daugherty, Collier Smith, and Robin Gates, each two.)

The 1984–85 award must have been particularly satisfying to Fleetwood Hank's handler. Twenty-three years ago Mr. Gates's father was the first handler to win the Purina Award for War Storm. Gates won his first open championship at the age of seventeen and has since gone on to win thirty-five others. Honea and Gates went on to repeat again in 1985–86 with 2,735 points.

Annual Purina Awards

Year	Dog	Owner/Handler
1963–64	War Storm	Owner: B. McCall Handler: John S. Gates
1964–65	Red Water Rex	Owner: W. T. Pruitt & E. B. Alexander, Jr. Handler: D. Hoyle Eaton
1965–66	Safari	Owner: S. H. Vredenburgh Handler: John Rex Gates
1966–67	Riggins White Knight	Owner: R. W. Riggins Handler: D. Hoyle Eaton
1967–68	Riggins White Knight	Owner: Dr. N. E. Palumbo Handler: D. Hoyle Eaton
1968–69	Red Water Rex	Owner: W. T. Pruitt & E. B. Alexander, Jr. Handler: D. Hoyle Eaton

Year	Dog	Owner/Handler
1969–70	Johnny Crockett	Owner: H. P. Sheely Handler: W. C. Kirk
1970–71	Wrapup	Owner: J. T. Payne & Jimmy Hinton Handler: Billy Morton
1971–72	The Texas Squire	Owner: Edwin Brown Handler: John Rex Gates
1972–73	Miller's Miss Knight	Owner: Roger H. Hays Handler: M. Faye Throneberry
1973–74	Crossmatch	Owner: Dr. M. E. Gordon Handler: Bud Daugherty
1974–75	White Knight's Button	Owner: Jack Fiveash Handler: Collier Smith
1975–76	Miller's White Cloud	Owner: W. S. McIlhenny Handler: D. Hoyle Eaton
1976–77	Buckboard	Owner: Dr. D. E. Hawthorne Handler: Bud Daugherty
1977–78	Rex's Cherokee Jake	Owner: Jimmy Hinton Handler: Billy Morton
1978–79	Allure	Owner: Jimmy Hinton Handler: Billy Morton
1979–80	Blackbelt	Owner: Dr. W. O. Pardue Handler: Freddie Epp
1980–81	Allure	Owner: Jimmy Hinton Handler: Billy Morton
1981–82	Heritage's Premonition	Owner: Jim & Judy Cohen Handler: Freddie Rayl
1982–83	Whippoorwill's Rebel	Owner: S. R. Cline Handler: Tommy Davis
1983–84	Native Tango	Owner: J. D. Allen & Dr. David Kuykendall Handler: Collier Smith
1984–85	Flatwood Hank	Owner: Jimmy Honea Handler: Robin Gates
1985–86	Flatwood Hank	Owner: Jimmy Honea Handler: Robin Gates

Glossary

Albino: A dog born without pigmentation.

American Bird Hunting Association: A shoot-to-retrieve organization designed for the upland game hunter. Also: ABHA.

American Kennel Club: The premier U.S. dog club. It is noted for its purebred registration certification as well as for educational efforts and a variety of bench and field events. Also: AKC.

Apple-headed: A canine with a noticeably domed skull.

Back-casting: Refers to the action of a dog in the field. Seeking birds behind a hunter. The opposite of working ahead.

Backing: Honoring another dog's point.

Back pocket: A locution. A dog so well trained it is thoroughly trustworthy is said to be "in my back pocket."

Balanced: A symmetrically proportioned dog.

Bandy: A bow-legged dog.

Bark limiter: An electronic collar that automatically punishes or corrects a barking dog. Used to break animals of that habit.

Belton: Intermingled white and colored hairs; common on the English Setter.

Bench show: A competition event, so named because each dog is provided with a bench. Field trials competitions do not use benches.

Biddable: A compliant dog. One who obeys without problem.

Bird crazy: A dog with too much desire.

Birdiness: An indication of a dog's desire to hunt. A dog that is not very birdy has little intensity or desire.

Bird release: A mechanical device that holds a bird humanely, releasing it at the trainer's discretion. There are two versions, one activated manually and another by electronic control. Also: bird-releaser. See also *Popper, Release.*

Bitch: A female dog.

Bite: The relative position of the upper and lower teeth with the mouth closed.

Blaze: A noticeable white marking on the head of a dog with an otherwise colored head.

Blinker: A dog that fears birds. One that abandons a bird it has found. In competition such a dog can be disqualified.

Bloodline: A synonym for a pedigree; generations of breeding to one canine family.

Blue: Reference to a special color of hair, normally gray or blue-gray. Not common to upland game dogs.

Bobtail: A short docked tail. Also a nickname for the Old English sheepdog.

Bold: An outgoing dog, one sure of itself. The opposite of timid.

Bonding: Socialization. A procedure designed to create a sound relationship between dog and humans.

Brace: A field-trials term. A pair of dogs competing in the same heat.

Breed: The variety or type of dog. The term applies only to purebred animals.

Brisket: That portion of a dog's body between the chest and forelegs.

Broken color: A solid color broken by another, generally white though not always.

Burr: First, an irregular formation inside the ear; second; one of a variety of coarse weeds that can become attached to the fur. Example, cockleburr, a prickly weed of the genus *Xanthium*.

Buster: A dog with an exaggerated interest in birds, but refusing to point.

Buster-blinker: A dog combining the attributes of blinker and buster. One not totally afraid of birds. A manmade fault, caused by too much pressure at the wrong time and perhaps too little at the proper moment.

Canine hepatitis: A viral disease that attacks the gastrointestinal tract, the liver, and occasionally the kidneys.

Canker: An external ear infection.

Cast: To send a dog away from its handler, generally on a hunt or retrieve. Also: cast off.

Cat foot: Compact, short, rounded feet, i.e., like those of cat.

Check line: A leash, generally one longer than twelve feet and commonly home-made.

Coccidia: An intestinal disease caused by microscopic parasites.

Collar: First, the markings around the dog's neck, commonly, white; second, a devise worn around the dog's neck to which check line and leads are attached, normally of nylon or leather.

Colors: The predominate hair coloring of a dog. In addition to single colors, such as brown, black, and white, there are specific combinations and mixes such as liver and roan.

Conformation: The manner in which the parts of the body, considered as a whole, conform to accepted standards.

Coronavirus: A relatively new virus, it is also known as canine viral enteritis. The condition can be treated.

Correction: A reprimand. Compelling a dog to properly repeat an incorrectly performed command.

Cow-hocked: A portion of the rear legs that turn inward.

Creep: To move slowly toward game already pointed, though commanded to stop.

Cropped ears: Ears trimmed to stand erect. The practice is illegal in some countries. When used, it is done only on puppies. Not common among upland game dogs.

Cross breed: Same as cross-bred. See *Mixed breed.* Not purebred.

Cynology: The study of dogs.

Cyptorchid: An adult male in which one or both testicles have not dropped.

Dam: A bitch, the female parent.

Dappled: Mixed or mottled markings of various colors.

Delayed chase: A late response to a wild flush. May occur minutes after a bird breaks. May also be seen as movement toward a site previously known to have scent.

Desire: A measure of a dog's interest in finding and pointing game, especially birds.

Dew claws: A rudimentary claw commonly found on the lower inside of the forelegs. Sometimes found on the rear as well. They are regarded as unnecessary and are often removed.

Dewlap: A pendulous fold of loose skin found beneath the throat.

Dickey bird: Any of a number of species of field birds.

Dished: A dish-shaped, concave head line common on pointers.

Distemper: A serious, often fatal disease that first attacks body tissues and then the brain.

Distemper teeth: Discolored, pitted teeth caused by distemper.

Dock: First, removal of a portion of the tail to shorten and keep it from damage. This is not done with every breed. Second; a nickname for a tail.

Dome: A convex area of the skull.

Dominant: i.e., gene or trait. A marked parental characteristic transmitted to a descendant.

Down-faced: The nasal bone that slopes to the nostrils.

Drop: To lie flat, a command given only to flushing dogs.

Dump: A severe correction. Up-ending a dog, generally through the use of a check line. Also: dumped.

Dysplasia: A debilitating disease of the hip bone and socket. Also: hip dysplasia.

Ectropion: An outward rolling of the eyelid.

Elbow: The area above the forearm at the foreleg.

Entropion: An inward rolling of the eyelid. It is correctable.

Fancier: A person especially interested in dogs.

Feather: A fringe of longer hair, especially on the legs, tail, and ears. Found only on certain breeds. Also: feathers.

Fiddle legs: Forelegs that bow out at the elbows and turn in at the pasterns. Also: fiddle feet.

Field: An area in which an upland game dog hunts. Also a specific section of land used for trials competition.

Field trials: A competition for sporting dogs. May be limited to retrievers or upland game dogs.

Flagging: An undesirable tail movement. The tail is not erect on point. Shows reduced intensity.

Flash point: A quick, instinctive point commonly given by an untrained pup.

Flea: A parasite that causes itching and other allergenic reactions.

Flecked: A coat neither spotted nor roan but lightly ticked with another color.

Fluke: An internal parasite spread through the consumption of raw fish.

Flush: First, the action of a bird breaking from hiding into the air; second, to force a hiding bird to fly.

Flusher: A dog bred to force game birds to fly or to capture one before it is airborne.

Foot-handling: A game dog bred for the hunter who walks. Generally a pointing dog that does not range as far as those bred for horse-handling.

Foreface: That portion of the face between the nose and eyes.

Force training: Mandatory retriever training generally given a dog with little or no retrieving instinct. Also: force-trained, force breaking, force-broken.

Foundation Stock: A small number of purebreds from which a breed can be propagated and developed.

Foxy: A dog with a head or expression that is sharp, alert, and pointed like a fox.

Free-floating: A dog running with its check line attached to the collar but not held by the trainer, i.e., with the check line dragging behind the dog.

Gaily: A happy tail that waves as the dog works a field. See also *Merry tail.*

Gait: The way a dog walks or runs.

Glaucoma: An eye disease caused by increased pressure.

Grizzle: A metallic or blue-gray color, also a mix of black and white hairs.

Ground race: A measure of the way a dog hunts. Includes its general style, style of working, and intensity. Used in grading field trials. Also: ground work.

Gundog: One bred for the walking hunter. See *Foot-handling.*

Hack: First, controlling a dog; second, an owner who nags or controls his dog excessively. Possibly from golf.

Handler: First, one who handles dogs at field trials and dog shows. A professional who may not be the owner. Second, sometimes a synonym for an amateur owner-trainer.

Harlequin: A dog predominantly white but with irregular blue or black markings.

Hard mouth: A dog that abuses, severely bites, or marks a bird during retrieve.

Haunch: The rump or buttock.

Heat: In the breeding cycle, i.e., ready for breeding. The oestrum or season. Also: in heat. Also: one round of competition for a brace of dogs. Dogs may or may not have more than one chance to compete—i.e. more than one heat—in an event.

Heartworm: An increasingly common parasite that affects the heart. Medication can prevent the problem.

Heel: A command that requires that a dog walk close to its handler.

Height: Measurement of a dog from the ground upward to the withers.

Hock: A joint found between the pastern and the upper part of the hindlegs.

Hi-on: A British term used to cast off or urge a dog on.

Honoring a point: Stopping when another dog has pointed game, so as to avoid pressuring or flushing it. The same as backing.

Hookworm: A small internal parasite that anchors in the intestines.

Horse-handling: A game dog so wide-ranging and far-running that the handler controls it from horseback.

House-breaking: First, training a dog to relieve itself outside; second; basic obedience training required for dog and owner to live successfully together.

Human bonding: A process partly conscious, partly unconscious by which a dog is conditioned to accept and seek human companionship. A synonym is socialization. It is commonly begun before a pup leaves the litter and commonly no later than the eighth or ninth week.

Hup: The command given flushing dogs to make them immediately stop and sit. "Whoa" is the counterpart for pointing dogs.

In-breeding: Breeding from closely related bloodlines.

Intensity: Considered instinctual, it is a noticeable desire to point and hold staunch on that point. Every muscle is locked as the dog points the game it has found.

Keel: The sternum.

Kennel: First, commonly a dog's outdoor accommodations; second, a professional or amateur breeding or housing establishment; third, the command that requires a dog to enter its kennel, portable kennel, or similar enclosure.

Kennel cough: One of several diseases that affect the respiratory system.

Leggy: A dog too high or with too much leg.

Leptospirosis: A virus that attacks the kidney and liver.

Level bite: Teeth that meet evenly.

Lice: An external parasite.

Liam: A British term for leash.

Line cast: A dog that works a field in straight lines, yo-yolike, from one side to the other.

Lippy: Pendulous lips that fail to meet.

Litter: A family of pups, those born of one whelping.

Liver: A color of coat, a deep reddish brown.

Loin: That segment of a dog along its vertical column from the ribs to the hindquarters.

Mask: Hair of a darker color on the face.

Merry tail: An active, erect tail. The sign of a bold, happy dog, one eager to find birds.

Mites: An external parasite that causes skin problems.

Mixed Breed: A dog with a lineage composed of more than one breed. Not purebred.

Mongrel: A dog of mixed breed.

Molting: The seasonal sloughing of the coat.

Muzzle: That portion of the head from the eyes to the nose.

National Bird Hunters Association: A national organization of bird hunters, both water fowl and upland species. Also: NBHA.

National Shoot-to-Retrieve Association: An association of those interested in upland game and dogs. Sponsors, among other events, of field trials. Also: NSTRA.

Neutered: A sterilized male dog.

Nonslip: A well-trained retriever or spaniel capable of working without a lead.

Nose: That quality in a dog that allows it to scent game. The more certain its ability, the better its nose.

Occiput: The rear point on the skull.

Overshot jaw: A condition in which the upper teeth project beyond the lower ones.

Pack: Hounds used for hunting.

Paddlefoot: Feet that toe out.

Pads: The soles of a dog's feet.

Papers: Referring to certification of a dog's ancestry. Limited to purebred animals. Also: papered.

Particolors: Two separate, clear colors.

Parvovirus: A relatively new disease that affects the gastrointestinal tract. Puppies are especially vulnerable.

Pastern: That portion of the leg below the knee or hock. The lowest portion.

Pedigree: A system of notating canine ancestry.

Pied: Patches of white and one other color unequally divided.

Pig jaw: An overshot jaw.

Pigment: Coloration on the nose, lips and rim of the eye.

Plait: A manner of locomotion in which the legs cross. May be observed walking or running.

Plume: The long hair on a tail.

Pointer: More than a breed, the term refers to any game dog that indicates the position of a bird with its nose and body rigidly oriented to the game.

Point: The act of indicating game.

Popper: Another name for a bird release.

Portable kennel: A small, light-weight unit, commonly made of aluminum or plastic, used to transport dogs.

Potter: also pottering and potterer. A lackadaisical dog. One with little interest or intensity. A dog not working a desirable ground race.

Prepotent: That which is influential in breeding; of exceptional power.

Pressure: Another word for stress associated with training, correction, and handling. Among professional trainers it is also a synonym for a training session.

Proud: A head or tail held high.

Puppy: Any dog less than one year of age.

Pussyfoot: After pointing, to creep forward toward game one step at a time.

Purebred: A dog with ancestors of the same breed.

Quarantine: First, isolation of any dog, generally to prevent the spread of infectious disease; second, the isolation of a dog prior to entry to the U.S. for similar reasons.

Quarter: Commonly used with flushing dogs. Systematically working a field to a consistent pattern. The opposite of working to objectives. Also: quartering.

Rabies: A virulent disease that comes in two forms and is considered incurable.

Racy: A dog slight of build but long of leg.

Range: The distance from a hunter at which a dog habitually works.

Recessive: In reference to heredity it is the opposite of dominant, i.e., a factor that may not show in offspring.

Recognition: The acceptance of a breed by a national registry such as the AKC.

Registration: The names and pedigrees registered by a national organization such as the AKC.

Release: Still another term for a manual or electronic bird release. The common locution is popper. Also: releaser.

Relocation: Abandoning a fruitless point to seek game.

Retinal atrophy: A disease of the eye.

Retrieve: Chasing down, picking up, and returning with a downed bird.

Retriever: A dog bred and trained to retrieve.

Ring: A term best known to owners of bench show dogs. An area where dogs are presented for judging. Not common in trials.

Roach back: A back that rises above the loin and curves to the tail.

Roan: A combination of hairs white and any other color.

Roman nose: A high-bridged, slightly convex nose.

Ruby: A reddish color seen most frequently in the King Charles Spaniel.

Ruff: The coarser hair around the neck.

Runner: First, a dog participating in trials competition; second, a bird wounded, generally in the wing. It is unable to fly but is still able to run.

Sable: The mingling of black hairs with those of a lighter color.

Saddle: Saddle-shaped black markings sometimes found on the back.

Scent: The unmistakable odor left by an animal. For upland game dogs it commonly indicates birds.

Scissor bite: A condition in which the upper teeth barely overlap the lower.

Season: Oestrum. The time at which a bitch is ready to breed. See also *Heat.*

Self-colored: Of one color.

Self-taught: lesson. Training designed to let a dog teach itself. Also, a dog's ability to learn and understand on its own. Also: self-taught.

Septum: The nose bone between the nostrils.

Service: Canine copulation.

Setter: A pointing breed.

Short-coupled: A body in which the distance between the ribs and hips is shortened.

Shoulders: The top portion of the forlegs joining the body. The scapula.

Sire: The male canine parent.

Sit: A command that requires a dog to sit on its haunches. It is never used with pointers, only with flushing dogs.

Soft mouth: A game dog that retrieves with minimal damage to the game. The meaning is the opposite of hard mouth.

Solid: The same as self-color. A dog with hair of one, consistent color.

Spaniel: A medium-sized game dog. Some point game, some flush. All are good retrievers.

Spayed: A surgically sterilized bitch.

Socialization: The same as human bonding. Conditioning an animal to accept human companionship.

Soft: A timid dog.

Spot: A touch of colored hair surrounded by a white blaze. It is found on the top of the head and commonly on spaniels.

Standard: The specification of a breed as accepted by national and/or international authority. That by which dogs are judged for conformation.

Stay: A command that requires a dog to remain motionless at the point at which the command is given. For field dogs it is the precursor of "whoa."

Steady: A dog that is staunch.

Steady to wing: A dog trained to hold staunchly though game breaks and flushes.

Steady to shot: A dog trained to hold staunchly after game is shot.

Staunch: Holding firm on point, especially for a length of time.

Sternum: The breastbone.

Stop: A step between the nose and skull.

Stripping: An intentional thinning of the coat. Done only on certain breeds and with a special comb.

Stud: A male dog used for breeding.

Studbook: A registry or record of breeding.

Tapeworm: Long, pinkish, parasitic worm that attach itself to the inside of the intestinal tract.

Thumbmarks: Black marks found near or on the pastern.

Thrifty: A dog that puts on good weight for the food provided. Also: thriftiness.

Throaty: Excessive loose skin found on the throat.

Tick: An external parasite. Some spread a virulent fever.

Ticking: Small areas of black or color on a coat basically white.

Topknot: Long hair occasionally found atop the head.

Tricolor: Descriptive of those breeds that allow three colors in the coat.

Trials: Commonly field-trials competition.

Type: Related to standards. The basic characteristics that distinguish a breed.

United Kennel Club: A national registry similar in scope and service to the American Kennel club, though neither as large nor as powerful.

Undercoat: The softer, woollike hair below the surface on breeds with double coats.

Undershot jaw: A condition in which the lower jaw protrudes beyon the upper one.

Varminty: A bright, keen, piercing expression.

Venery: Hunting and related fields.

Vent: The anal opening.

Weaving: The crossing of feet, front or rear, when walking or running.

Wheaten: Fawn- or yellow-colored hair.

Whelping: Birthing a litter.

Whip tail: A tail carried straight and stiffly pointed.

Whipworm: A small, round, tapered worm found in the colon and cecus.

Whoa: The command that stops a pointer instantly.

Whoa bench: A bench used by some trainers in the early stages of teaching "whoa."

Whoa point: A learned response to point as opposed to one generated by instinct. Since it is man-taught, it commonly lacks intensity and is not considered as stylish as a natural point.

Whoa post: Another device used by some trainers when teaching "whoa."

Windshield wiper: A dog that works a field in an inconsistent, sweeping pattern.

Wirehair: Distinguished from a breed with the same name, it is any dog with crisp, harsh, wiry hair. Also: wire-haired.

Wrinkle: Loose folds of skin on the sides of the forehead or face.

Product and Information Sources

Long-time hunters are familiar with specialized sources for a variety of products and services, from pedigree registrations and electronic training devices to mail order houses with a variety of products. But for readers new to the sport, we list below suppliers for many items used in training and upland game hunting. Most suppliers on our list sell at retail, but in some cases wholesalers and manufacturers have been included because they are the only national informational source for specific products. If these firms will not sell direct, a letter to them should bring the address of a local source. Every effort has been made to make the list accurate, but we cannot be responsible for changes due to moves or the closing of business.

NATIONAL KENNEL CLUBS

The American Kennel Club Inc.
51 Madison Avenue
New York, NY 10010

Purebred canine registry; sponsors field trials and other events. Offers a number of informational publications.

The United Kennel Club
100 E. Kilgore Road
Kalamazoo, MI 49001

Purebred canine registry; offers a number of monthly and other publications.

Tattoo-A-Pet,
1625 Emmons Avenue
Brooklyn, NY 11235

World's largest tattoo identification registry. Contact: Ms. Judy Moscove.

BREED CLUBS

(National Club Offices)
Brittanys:
American Brittany Club
% Velma Tiedman.
2036 N. 48th Avenue
Omaha, NE 68104

Cocker Spaniels:
American Spaniel Club
% Mrs. Margaret Ciezkowski
12 Wood Lane S.
Woodmere, NY 11598

English Setters:
English Setter Association of America
% David S. Ronjak
11469 Aquilla Road
Chardon, OH 44024

English Springer Spaniels:
English Springer Spaniel Field Trial Association
% Ms. Alice Berd,
67 Old Stafford Road
Tolland, CT 06084

German Shorthaired Pointer:
German Shorthaired Pointer Club of America
% Geraldine A. Irwin
1101 W. Quincy
Englewood, CO 80110

German Wirehaired Pointers:
German Wirehaired Pointer Club of America
% Judy Cheshire
46 Southridge Drive
Glen Cove, NY 11542

Gordon Setters:
Gordon Setter Club of America
% Jane Matteson,
632 W. El Morado Court
Ontario, CA 91762

Irish Setters:
Irish Setter Club of America
% Joyce Mumford
Rte. 1, Hwy. 62
Charlestown, IN 47111

Pointers:
American Pointer Club
% Susan Savage
278 Ridgebury Road
Ridgefield, CT 06877

Vizsla:
Vizsla Club of America
% Linda Bush
R.R. 1
Poplar Grove, IL 61065

Weimaraners:
National Weimaraner Club of America
% Judy Edwards
25035 Rainbow Drive
Cleveland, OH 44138

Welsh Springer Spaniel:
Welsh Springer Spaniel Club of America
% Charles E. Trefzger
3854 Williams Road
Lewisville, NC 27023

RELATED ASSOCIATIONS

The Amateur. Field Trial Clubs of America
Ms. Leslie Anderson, Secretary
Rte. 3, 2302 Byhalia Road
Hernando, MS 38632

American Bird Hunters Association
Lindel Fair, President
Nancy B. Bell, Secretary
2505 Gary Lane
Waco, TX 76708

Amateur Field Trials Club
Ms. Leslie Anderson, Secretary
Rte. 3, 2302 Byhalia Road
Hernando, MS 38632

National Bird Hunters Association
Jim Hoy, President
R.R. 1
Pineview, GA 31071

National Field Trials Champion Association
P.O. Box 38039
Grand Junction, TN 38039

National Shoot-to-Retrieve Association
110 W. Main Street
Plainfield, IN 46168
Sponsors a number of popular trials events. Offers a variety of informational items.

North American Versatile Hunting Dog Association
1700 N. Skyline Drive
Burnsville, MN 55337
Supplies information and related services.

U.S. Complete Shooting Dog Club
Mr. Gerald Shaw, President
P.O. Box 99
Sanford, NC 27330

MAIL-ORDER SUPPLIES

Cabela's
312 701 Street
Sidney, NE 69160
Hunting and sportsman's supplies. Offers a free catalogue.

Creative Sports Supplies
P.O. Box 765
Attalla, AL 35954
Dog, hunting, and related supplies.

Dogs Unlimited
P.O. Box 1864
263 Delano Avenue
Chillicothe, OH 45601
Hunting and dog supplies. Offers a free catalogue.

Dunn's, Inc.
Hwy. 57E
P.O. Box 449
Grand Junction, TX 38039
Hunting and dog supplies. Offers a free catalogue.

Sporting Dog Specialties
P.O. Box 68
15 Turner Drive
Spencerport, NY 14559
Hunting and dog supplies. Offers a free catalogue.

MISCELLANEOUS SUPPLIES

Bush Products
1520 Cavitt Street
Bryan, TX 77801
Aluminum dog and horse trailers.

Doscocil, Inc.
P.O. Box 1246
Arlington, TX 76010
Transportable plastic dog carriers. Wholesale: product and source information only.

E-Z Bird Dog Training Equipment Co.
P.O. Box 333
Morganfield, KY 42437
Bird releases and traps. Available in three models: a plain release with no catapult, spring-loaded; a manual model with a six-foot release; a remove version with a 50-foot pushbutton release or a universal radio release.

Five Points Products
P.O. Box 164
Kenton, OH 43326
Thermo Bowl electric water heater.

Dave Hill
R.R. 3, Emerson Road
Beloit, WI
Dog trailer.

Invisible Fence Co. of Minnesota
1102 E. Highway 13
Burnsville, MN 55337
Electric fencing.

Jones Trailer Co.
P.O. Box 242
Woodson, TX 76091
Stainless-steel dog trailer.

Mason Co.
P.O. Box 365
Leesburg, OH 45135
Prefabricated fenced runs and kennels.

McKee Industries
P.O. Box 9011
L.A. Airport Station
Los Angeles, CA 90009
Transportable kennels; game-bird transporters.

Migatz & Migatz, Inc.
20533 Boca Chica Drive
Malibu, CA 90265
Pinch and other chain collars; an imported electronic collar. Wholesale: product and source information only.

Nelson Mfg. Co.
3049 12th S. W.
Cedar Rapids, IA 52406
Heated dog waterer.

Oldtimers
1560 Greenwood Circle
Piedmont, OK 73078
Transportable fiberglass dog kennels.

Powell Enterprises
P.O. Box 361,
Buda, TX 78610
Electronic kennel silencer

Rose Metal Products, Inc.
P.O. Box 3238
Springfield, MO 65808
Port-A-Dog cages: two-, three- and four-compartment cages for pickup trucks.

Sensitronix
P.O. Box 920880
Houston, TX 77292
Electronic training collar.

Tracker Electronic
24350 Falcon Avenue
Forest Lake, MN 55025
Electronic tracking equipment.

Tri-Tronics,
7060 E. 21st Street
P.O. Box 17660
Tucson, AZ 85731
Electronic devices: bark-limiter, electronic training collar, and electronic bird releases.

Wag Ag
P.O. Box 332
Rosalia, WA 99170
Electronic bird release.

Whitey's Halter Co.
2501 Middle Country Road
Centereach, NY 11720
Transportable plastic dog carriers; wholesale, product, and source information only.

PUBLICATIONS

American Field Publishing Co.
222 W. Adams Street
Chicago, IL 60606
American Field is a premier monthly publication devoted to reports of field trials and dogs. It carries news reports plus excellent breeding and stud information.

Maxine Collins
R.R. 3
8542 Elm
Newyago, MI 49337
German Shorthair Pointer Yearbook.

German Shorthair Pointer News
P.O. Box 850
St. Paris, OH 43072

Maclean Hunter Publishing Co.
300 West Adams Street
Chicago, IL 60606
World's largest all-breed magazine. Not specifically for upland game dogs.

Quail Unlimited
P.O. Box 10041
Augusta, GA 30903
Conservation efforts, monthly publication.

Stover Publications
P.O. Box 35098
Des Moines, IA 50315
Wing & Shot magazine; *Gun Dog* magazine.

Understanding Electronic Dog Training
By Daniel F. Tortora
2nd Edition, third printing
From: Tri-Tronic, Inc.
P.O. Box 17660
7070 East 21st Street
Tucson, AZ 8571
Training with an electronic collar.